Electronic Tigers of Southeast Asia

Electronic Tigers of Southeast Asia

The Politics of Media, Technology, and National Development

Drew McDaniel

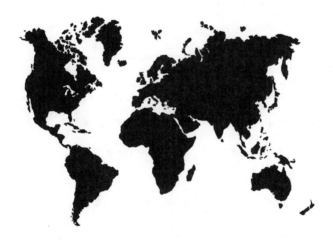

International Topics in Media

Iowa State University Press
A Blackwell Science Company

DREW McDANIEL is a professor in the School of Telecommunications, Ohio University at Athens. He is a widely known expert on international communication, specializing in the media of Southeast Asia.

© 2002 Iowa State University Press
A Blackwell Science Company
All rights reserved

Iowa State University Press
2121 South State Avenue, Ames, Iowa 50014

Orders:	1-800-862-6657
Office:	1-515-292-0140
Fax:	1-515-292-3348
Web site:	www.isupress.com

∞ Printed on acid-free paper in the United States of America

First edition, 2002

Library of Congress Cataloging-in-Publication Data

McDaniel, Drew
  Electronic tigers of Southeast Asia : the politics of media, technology, and national development / Drew McDaniel—1st ed.
  p. cm.
Includes bibliographical references (p.   ) and index.
  ISBN 0-8138-1907-5
  1. Mass media policy—Asia, Southeastern. 2. Mass media and technology—Asia, Southeastern. 3. Mass media—Asia, Southeastern—Audiences. 4. Mass media—Censorship—Asia, Southeastern. I. Title.
  P95.82.A78 M37 2001
  302.23'0959—dc21   2001004130

The last digit is the print number: 9 8 7 6 5 4 3 2 1

Contents

Foreword

As coeditors, we are pleased to introduce the first book in the Iowa State University Press new international communication series—Professor Drew McDaniel's *Electronic Tigers of Southeast Asia: The Politics of Media, Technology, and National Development.*

Since the mid-1980s, the Straubhaar/Boyd international research collaboration has resulted in one book and many convention papers, book chapters, and refereed publications, all dealing with international communication. In looking for international publication opportunities, we especially liked the commitment that Iowa State University Press has had to journalism and communication in general, and specifically the international aspects of these two important areas. One of us, Doug Boyd, has published two books with Iowa State University Press: the 1993 and 1999 editions of *Broadcasting in the Arab World: A Survey of the Electronic Media in the Middle East.* We look forward to a long-term relationship with ISU Press as we seek to feature high-quality manuscript submissions that will lead to more publications such as this one. In our opinion, Dr. McDaniel's book exemplifies the type of scholarship we will be featuring.

Professor McDaniel of Ohio University is a widely known expert on international communication, specifically the media of Southeast Asia. As you will learn from his work, prior to 1980 the media in this region served primarily as allies of politicians in power. Both the electronic and print media fostered "developmental" roles that encouraged citizens to accept and follow the lead of those in power. Unfortunately, this resulted in perpetuating the power of the government of the day. As the countries in Southeast Asia became more prosperous, they both manufactured and purchased communication-oriented consumer products. The "new media," starting with the video tape recorder, ultimately allowed the consumer, rather than the government, to gain control of what was seen and heard. Individual media choices in Southeast Asia increased dramatically with the advent of home satellite receiving during the 1990s. As a means of countering this occasionally unwelcome competition for local television, there was some restructuring on a national level, as well as the allocation of some private radio and television stations. Then the Internet arrived. Some officials saw this as a boon to economic development, but enthusiasm was soon tempered by the realization that the Internet provided a channel for views not always supported by the government in power.

In short, you will find what follows to be an engaging analysis of the media development in Southeast Asia that has helped change the governments' traditional media hold and thus provided alternative entertainment and news to ordinary citizens.

Joseph D. Straubhaar is the Amon G. Carter, Sr., Centennial Professor of Communication at the University of Texas at Austin.

Douglas A. Boyd is Professor, Department of Communication and School of Journalism and Mass Communication, College of Communications and Information Studies, and Director, Office of International Affairs, University of Kentucky.

Electronic Tigers of Southeast Asia

Chapter One

Culture, Economics, and Information Policy in Southeast Asia

As the final years of the twentieth century slipped away, a political transfor- 3
mation was gaining momentum—a significant shift yet one subtle enough
that its presence might be missed. This trend could be seen in the small movements of individual actors and political figures and in the minor tilts of power,
which often are the only signals of an era's passing. In the overused current par-
lance, a paradigm shift was taking place. It involved a connection between
public participation in governance and changing technology. Put simply,
changes in the way that information is packaged, disseminated, and accessed
by the public have altered the practice of politics in many parts of the world.
These changes have stolen from the economic, political, and social elites some
of their power to influence public opinion and thereby to control decision
making. The degree to which this political metamorphosis can be observed in
individual countries varies greatly. This text concerns itself with Southeast
Asia, where the twin pressures of political change and reform of information
policies have produced especially conspicuous and provocative results. In the
following pages I will attempt to show how the forces working in the political
arena have been deflected by changes in the technology of information and entertainment media.

Southeast Asia is not one place but many; it is a collection of historically,
politically, culturally, and economically diverse nations that nevertheless share
certain fundamentally important qualities. A look at a map helps to explain
why this region is different than other parts of the world. Southeast Asia is
squeezed between mainland Asia to the north and Australia to the south. The

Malay-Indonesian archipelago forms a narrow passage between the Indian and Pacific Oceans. As interregional movement occurred, travelers between East and West had to pass through the Southeast Asian region. Because sea traffic funneled through the narrow Strait of Melaka, areas of modern-day Malaysia and Indonesia enjoyed centuries of contact with the outside world. Over time, acquaintance with this stream of humanity introduced into Southeast Asian societies an adaptability and a tolerance of foreign cultures. Asian peoples living along these trade routes were still comfortable with their own values, yet open to and curious about others.

These cultural conditions may have given nations of Southeast Asia special advantages in the economic globalization that occurred during the late twentieth century. Whether or not this was the case, certain Southeast Asian countries did join the select group known as the "Asian Tigers"—nations whose burgeoning trade and aggressive economies made them as ferocious as tigers. These countries set a standard for the entire developing world and moved them beyond the status of developing economies to one of "newly industrializing economies" (NIE). Most often referred to as tigers were East Asia's Korea, Hong Kong, and Taiwan, but also mentioned were Singapore, Malaysia, and Thailand. The tiger economies could also be considered to encompass countries not in the exclusive NIE club. The extended group included Vietnam, which although one of the world's poorest nations, experienced the highest gross domestic product (GDP) growth of any country in the world for a time in the 1990s, and Indonesia, which as the world's fourth most populous country enjoyed a flourishing export trade in the first half of the 1990s.

So, as the end of the twentieth century drew to a close, the countries of Southeast Asia had become successful economic and political models for developing regions around the world. Peaceful and prosperous, they seemed poised to become developed nations early in the twenty-first century. Nations of Southeast Asia were characterized by stable governments and at least steady—but sometimes spectacular—economic growth. A major reason for the region's trade growth was its participation in the electronic revolution of the twentieth century. Innovations in the field of electronics created huge worldwide demand for consumer goods built from components manufactured in Southeast Asia. Basic components included computer chips, integrated circuits, transistors, and similar items. Video recorders, televisions, pocket compact disc players, cassette tape recorders, electronic games, radios, and so on, were manufactured in factories scattered across the region. There were also appliances such as rice cookers, electric fans, air conditioners, and a host of electrical accessories for automobiles. All these experienced a booming demand that peaked in the 1980s and 1990s. Exports of manufactured products helped fuel a dramatic increase in wealth that trickled through all levels of Southeast Asian societies. During this time Malaysia became the world's largest producer of integrated circuits and air conditioners and a leading producer of many

other types of finished products. Similar results were produced in Thailand,
Singapore, Indonesia, and—to a lesser extent—in the Philippines.

The achievements of economies in Southeast Asia produced an optimism bordering on euphoria. Ambitious projects blossomed practically everywhere. In Malaysia, the world's tallest building, the Twin Towers skyscraper, was built on Ampang Road, not far from the heart of the capital city. In Indonesia, a huge plan for modernization of the telephone system was put out to bid. In Thailand, giant plans for development of an information infrastructure were drawn up. A frenzy of building swept across Southeast Asia in the mid-1990s, so that major cities' skylines became crowded with construction cranes and the skeletons of half-constructed high-rise buildings. Even the Philippines had begun to show signs of a commercial revival after decades of economic mismanagement. There seemed to be no end to the possibilities of national development.

A SKETCH OF SOUTHEAST ASIA

The Southeast Asia region consists of ten countries: Philippines, Indonesia, Brunei, Singapore, Malaysia, Thailand, Cambodia, Laos, Vietnam, and Myanmar (formerly Burma). This region is united not only by geography but by regional trade and business cooperation and by the multifaceted Association of Southeast Asian Nations (ASEAN). Originally formed as a cultural, trade, and social organization largely as a response to Communist insurgencies in Indochina and Malaysia, ASEAN has grown from a membership of only five countries to include all Southeast Asian nations. The organization also has begun to take on a more general personality than it had in its formative years, an orientation that embraces the ideologies even of Myanmar and Cambodia, two nations that have engendered worldwide disapproval.

The region's cultural makeup might seem bafflingly complex to the outsider. Dozens of languages are spoken, and written forms are recorded in more than a half-dozen distinct scripts. But at least one local language, Malay, enjoys wide currency. It is the national language of Brunei, Malaysia, Indonesia, and Singapore and is also spoken by people living in enclaves of Myanmar, Thailand, Vietnam, and the Philippines. In colonial times French was an important link language, but today English is the dominant language of international communication, partly because of British and American colonization of half the countries in the region. In major cities of the region, especially in Singapore, Philippines, and Malaysia, English is the common language of commerce and enterprise. Chinese languages survive throughout the region where numbers of native speakers are sufficient and where Chinese culture is not suppressed.

Southeast Asia's colonial heritage from the sixteenth through the twentieth centuries presents an intricate pattern. Myanmar, Singapore, Malaysia, and

Brunei were British colonies. In Indochina, the French ruled areas that are now Laos, Cambodia, and Vietnam. The United States colonized the Philippines, and the Netherlands held most of contemporary Indonesia as the Dutch East Indies. Only Thailand escaped colonial rule. Among the colonized countries, administrative structures were varied. For example, Malaya was a British administrative territory located on the southern portion of the Malay peninsula, south of Thailand. Malaya of the 1930s was made up of three separate territories: The colony of the Straits Settlements had its capital in Singapore and was made up of three small trading and shipping enclaves of the Malayan Peninsula. Britain was also responsible for the Federated Malay States (FMS) and the Unfederated Malay States (UMS). The UMS comprised the northern states of modern Malaysia, plus the southern state of Johore. The Federated Malay States (FMS) constituted the remaining Malaysian states. Kuala Lumpur was the capital of the FMS and UMS. Even though the FMS and the UMS were not technically colonies, Great Britain's Colonial Office provided general governance and advised the Sultans, who were nominal rulers of their individual states. Such complicated administrative arrangements meant that today one can find few common threads binding this group of ten nations with their colonial past.

The ethnic mix of Southeast Asia seems equally bewildering. Indonesia, for instance, has more than a dozen of identifiably distinct ethnic groups, including the Javanese, Sundanese, Balinese, Malay, Madurese, Acehnese, Minangkabau, Batak, and so on. Malaysia's population is divided into three main ethnic groups: Malays are somewhat more than half of the population, Chinese come to a bit less than one-third, and Indians (most of whom are Tamil) constitute approximately 10 percent of the rest. Each country has one or more groupings of aboriginal people known by various names, such as *Orang Asli* in Malaysia, Singapore, and Brunei.

The Chinese represent a special situation in Southeast Asia. They began immigrating to Southeast Asia in prehistory times, but an especially large influx occurred at the end of the nineteenth century because of political and social disruptions in China and British colonial policies that favored imported labor. Today numbers of Chinese vary greatly from country to country. Chinese now are a majority only in Singapore, where their numbers amount to about three-quarters of the population. Although Chinese have found a place in all sectors of the economy, more than a small proportion have had success in commerce. In certain countries, Chinese own a large share of the wealth. Although comprising only a small percent of the Indonesian population, the Chinese share of national wealth is estimated to be as high as 70 percent. Such a disproportionate allocation of wealth presents obvious social and political problems, and several nations have formulated laws to check the imbalance. Chinese speak one or more of several dialects, commonly Cantonese, Hokkien, or one of the dialects spoken in the Southern region of China from which most immigrants originated. Mandarin is also widely used to communicate among people speaking different dialects, and it is the language of formal education among Chinese.

ECONOMICS AND INFORMATION POLICY

Because their wealth expanded with such remarkable speed, countries of Southeast Asia became targets of envy and emulation within the developing world. Analysts sought to determine which factors led to their success, but consistent findings were hard to identify. For instance, Hewison (1989) concluded that neither modernization nor dependency theories were good explanations for the economics of Thailand. He found a strong tilt toward business interests in policy making, which was evident in "less than kind" treatment of organized labor and in favoring capital over social interests. Another explanation held that values inherent in Asian societies gave them economic advantages. Singapore Senior Minister and Prime Minister Lee Kuan Yew once claimed that Confucianism in his country was the secret of its financial success.

Generally, the development prescription that political leaders offered, not excluding even Socialist governments in Vietnam, Cambodia, and Laos, was a neo-liberalized, market-oriented economy. This approach became a guiding principle in several countries, notably Malaysia and Singapore. When Datuk Seri Dr. Mahathir Mohamad was elected to office in 1981, he immediately put in motion a set of initiatives to follow the liberalization path and to stimulate a national economy heavily invested in state enterprises. The first step was privatization of state-owned businesses, the majority of which were considered to be under-performing. At the same time, the government borrowed a concept from Japan and implemented a "Malaysia Incorporated" strategy. As Mahathir explained it,

> The Malaysia Incorporated concept ... requires that the private and public sectors see themselves as sharing the same fate and destiny as partners, shareholders and workers within the same "corporation," which in this case is the Nation. The "corporation" will only prosper if its commercial and economic arm, that is, the private sector does its best to promote such things as production, marketing and sales, while optimising the returns on investment (Mahathir, 1984, pp. 1–2).

The principles of the Malaysia Incorporated were promoted via media and personal contacts between government and corporate officials. Most people applauded the ambition of the concept, but a few thought that the plan considered so successful in Japan might have a different result in Malaysia. As Lee (1988, p. 37) pointed out, the concept was based on "loyalty to the company for which the Japanese are famous. ... If Malaysia were to adopt successfully the 'Malaysia Incorporated' concept we must first learn to work towards the collective good and be less individualistic."

Over time, observers began to express doubts about the costs and benefits of some of government initiatives. The Bakun Dam project in Malaysia drew fire from critics because of its gigantic scale, projected to cost RM13.6 billion (USD $3.6 billion) and because of environmental concerns about its planned destruction of seventy thousand hectares of tropical rainforest. In Indonesia the chief concern was concentration of wealth in the hands of associates and family members of President Suharto. Giant conglomerates with ever-expanding holdings gained enormous advantages because of their connection to political leaders. For instance, Suharto's second son, Bambang Trihatmodjo, controlled Bimantara Corporation in 1994 when it won—without any fee—a license to provide international telephone services, a privilege shared only with PT Indosat (Sender, 1996). Issues similar to these raised misgivings about economic policies in other countries of Southeast Asia, too, but critics were hardly noticed in the exhilaration over growing wealth.

Suddenly, in mid-1997, this period of wonderful prosperity and stability came to an end. The start of a downward slide began with abrupt devaluation of the Thai Bhat in July after weeks of procrastination and denial. The valuation of currency in most Asian countries began to slide, some more precipitously than others. Within a matter of months, Indonesia's Rupiah fell from an exchange rate of less than 3,000 to USD $1 to more than 14,000Rp to USD $1. In Malaysia, the Ringgit began a decline from its valuation at about RM2.50 to USD $1 to more than RM4.60 to USD $1. Even after devaluation, the Thai Bhat lost a further half of its value against the US dollar, and the Philippine peso suffered similarly. Singapore escaped with minimum pain, however, dropping in value only by about 20 percent. The decline in currency values reflected a loss of confidence in the economies of the region, a condition that their leaders strenuously argued had no rational basis.

Dismissed at first by government officials as an insignificant temporary glitch and jokingly referred to as the "Asian flu," it soon became apparent that the situation was truly serious. The results were, in fact, devastating. In calendar year 1998, Indonesia's economy shrank by about 17 percent. In Malaysia, there was negative growth also, although at a more modest −8.6 percent rate (Indicators 1998, 1998). In Thailand and Indonesia, banks had to undergo massive restructuring to accommodate large portfolios of nonperforming loans. The impact on ordinary citizens was extremely painful, especially in Indonesia where the situation became so severe in 1998 that food shortages in basic commodities occurred in rural areas. Local farmers forced their way onto the Suharto cattle ranch in West Java where they tried to reclaim land for small rice and vegetable plots. Hundreds of miles away in Kalimantan and Sumatra, mobs broke into and looted shopping centers. Inflation shot up to levels close to hyperinflation; in Indonesia it topped 60 percent in 1998, following years of a sustained rate of less than 10 percent. In September, the food ministry acknowledged that about 70 million Indonesians were suffering severe food shortages, not because staples were unavailable, but because they were unaffordable (Tesoro, 1998). Southeast Asian countries showing growth in 1998 were Myanmar, Brunei, and the socialist countries of Indochina. Vietnam's GDP expanded that year at an impressive rate of 8.8 percent, and Laos was not far behind at 7.2 percent.

Although recovery seemed to have begun by the end of 1998, the financial downturn still depressed significant sectors of the economy in Asia. In Malaysia, foreign investment fell by more than 12 percent in 1998 from the preceding year. Indonesia seemed to fare worse than other countries, in large measure because Suharto resisted pressures from the International Monetary Fund (IMF) for wholesale revisions in economic policy. The public perceived the president's reluctance to accept these changes as an attempt to preserve his family's large holdings in corporate conglomerates. This, plus the growing desperation of the masses of people living on the margins of dwindling resources, produced a social and economic meltdown. Waves of rioting escalated out of control in May, after soldiers shot and killed four students at a campus protest in Jakarta. It became a time to exact revenge; violence broke out in many places, often directed against Christians and ethnic Chinese minorities. Well-known Chinese entrepreneur Liem Sioe Liong, reputedly Indonesia's richest man, had his Jakarta mansion sacked and burned by mobs. Finally, on May 21, 1998, Suharto stepped down as president of Indonesia and handed the reins to an interim government headed by B. J. Habibie, a close associate of the former president. Across Asia, other national leaders paid the price for the economic crisis; Thai Prime Minister Cavalit Yongchaiyudh was forced from office, and Japanese and Korean heads of state lost credibility, political strength, and eventually their jobs.

The exact cause of the economic turbulence remains a matter of disagreement. Malaysia's Prime Minister Mahathir placed the blame on currency traders—and more specifically on well-known arbitrager George Soros. This, as Mahathir saw it, fit within the general framework of Western institutions' assault on Eastern nations and their economies. About this he said, "All these [Asian] countries have spent 40 years trying to build up their economies and a moron like Soros comes along." To which Soros replied, "Dr. Mahathir is a menace to his own country" (cited in Saludo and Assif, 1998). The International Monetary Fund analysis was less simplistic. According to Stanley Fischer, IMF's first deputy managing director, a complicated set of factors were at work.

> The build-up of structural problems in the financial and corporate sectors, and, to varying degrees, inadequate macroeconomic policies caused the crisis in East Asia. Movements in the yen-dollar rate and large-scale—particularly short-term—capital—inflows, funded at low rates from the major capital markets, were contributors. Contagion effects helped the crisis spread (Fischer, 1998).

Such explanations were neither satisfying nor helpful for Southeast Asians, many of whom saw the value of their lifetime savings dwindle to practically nothing.

Residents of Southeast Asia wanted answers to questions about the economy and the changing perception of their own financial stability, but they wanted answers they could understand, not the arcane expositions of economists. They needed explanations to plan their own lives. To get this needed information, the only sources most had were the mass media, but many residents were unsure about the reliability of media. A small e-mail survey that Rozhan conducted in 1998 at the Universiti Kebangsaan examined the political opinions of technologically sophisticated Malaysians. He found deep dissatisfaction with national economic policy and with the media's role in providing information on the economy. When asked to rate the seriousness of a number of issues on a scale of 0 to 5, where 5 represented a serious problem and 0 represented no problem, respondents' mean ratings of "extravagant spending on unimportant projects," "corruption," and "nepotism" were each greater than 4.0. When asked whether they agreed that "the country's media [had] done a good job in educating Malaysians on the economic crisis," only 8.3 percent agreed, 40 percent answered "only some of them," and 51.7 percent disagreed (cited in Suh, 1998). Early optimistic predictions about a quick end to financial problems reported by most media outlets no doubt undercut public confidence in them, but there were other reasons for skepticism.

MEDIA IN SOUTHEAST ASIA

In Southeast Asia before 1980, media served as allies of incumbent political leaders, providing audiences with information and entertainment tailored to match the goals of government authorities. Newspapers, radio, television, and movies assumed "developmental" roles, encouraging citizens to accept and follow the lead of official planning. Whether the country was Vietnam led by Party Congresses or Philippines led by Ferdinand Marcos and his associates, the method was similar. All types of content, even news reporting, tended to promote the economic, political, and social objectives of government policies. This practice also had the effect of cementing the power of political figures. In every country but the Philippines, the main broadcasting organization was operated either directly or indirectly by the government. In part, this situation had simply been carried forward from colonial days when authorities distrusted local control and feared that uncensored radio programs might be employed to promote independence. Centralized control suited the rather authoritarian regimes that emerged in Southeast Asia after independence. Based on the ability of a single strong personality to control politics, figures such as Ferdinand Marcos, Ho Chi Minh, Lee Kuan Yew, Sukarno, Ne Win, and Pol Pot rose to prominence. Arguments can be made about these individuals' contributions to their nations, but this is not the point here. Rather, it is that powerful, concentrated government authority fit harmoniously with the highly focused and tightly managed media that characterized Southeast Asia in the post-independence period.

National information policies were formulated with the assumption that official control of media just outlined would be maintained. Across Southeast Asia, not only was broadcasting generally government operated, newspapers tended to be owned by groups aligned with political leadership or were held in check by strict regulations. As a rule, media were stringently censored. Tight controls kept media from straying far from official positions on controversial issues or from advancing—or even articulating in many cases—the viewpoints of opposition political parties or figures. Complaints about these policies came from many sources, especially opposition political leadership and Western critics. Government authorities countered these objections with several arguments: that their policies reflected "Asian values" that were not understood by Western critics, that the needs of development took precedence over "inefficient" Western-style media political discourse, or simply that critics had antigovernment agendas. In any case, policies to regulate information began to unravel as new media technology came into the consumer marketplace at the end of the 1970s.

The first challenge was offered by the humble home videotape recorder. Although on its surface not a subversive technology, video had one particular feature that distinguished it from preexisting media: it shifted control over program timing and content from media operators to consumers. Home users could chose for themselves what they watched and when. The impact of the VCR was so dramatic in Malaysia, for instance, it produced a sharp drop in over-the-air television audiences. Officials there became particularly alarmed over the foreign content of videos produced in the United States, Hong Kong, and Taiwan. These concerns triggered wholesale media restructuring. Government attempts in Malaysia to suppress VCRs first failed, then legislation on video contents proved ineffective, and finally officials had to license private media to entice viewers away from the unregulated videos.

Two additional media technologies soon appeared in the region: satellites and the Internet. Although Indonesia was a pioneer in the development of communication satellites, they initially served only as a channel for government media. By 1990, however, sales of home satellite equipment capable of receiving foreign programming soared in Indonesia, bringing programming previously unseen in the country to the archipelago's remotest islands. A few years later, the Internet arrived. At first, officials in the region seemed to regard this technology as a boon to economic development, and in most nations they enthusiastically encouraged its adoption. But, as time passed, this view became tempered by the realization that the Internet could also function as a channel for opposition voices. Then came efforts to place controls on such uses of the Internet.

Gradually and collectively the new technologies diminished the capacity of government officials to control the flow of information into their societies. This trend was accompanied by a growing public resistance to authorities' guidance on social and political issues. In three decades of independence at the end of the twentieth century, societies matured and grew in confidence. Increased wealth had produced a new generation of educated, critically minded citizens who were much less willing to defer to the judgments of political leaders than their parents and grandparents had been. The growth in new channels of information allowed these worldly wise citizens an opportunity to consider alternative perspectives. It would not be an overstatement to say that the widened access to information made possible by advancing technologies established a totally new political environment in Southeast Asia. Political leaders had to adapt to a world in which the lack of controlled information led to greater diversity of opinion and increased challenges to their leadership. Unfortunately, changes in information media occurred in ways that went practically unnoticed, and this delayed adjustments to the new realities.

Political changes came with a price, of course, chiefly in the form of greater discord across Southeast Asia. Events that might have escaped public attention in earlier times became fodder for the grist mills of the new information channels. At times, a greater political awareness prompted reactions on the street that had profound consequences. Looking back, it is possible to identify specific incidents in which failures of information control had important political ramifications. For instance, the Philippine government's inability to manage public opinion in the usual way played a major role in the collapse of the Marcos's regime—a major aspect of his ignominious departure was opposition takeover of one of Manila's popular television stations. Whether it was monitoring the house arrest of Aung San Suu Kyi in Myanmar or the last interviews of Pol Pot in Cambodia, the spotlight of international media fed local activism. Occasionally, internationally inspired activism weakened political "stability," a quality much prized by leaders because stability maintains their status quo power.

THE ANWAR CASE

The furor over the political fall from grace of Malaysia's Anwar Ibrahim provides an interesting case study of the politics that sprang from Southeast Asia's technological transformation. This incident illustrates several key principles, and its details are presented here as a general introduction to the topics discussed in following chapters. First, Anwar's trial showed that current information technologies make it impossible for governments to simply place a lid on dissemination of unfavorable information. Regardless of efforts to limit the spread of information, reports on events of public interest are bound to find their way through the multitude of channels now available. Second, the Anwar affair shows how difficult it is to block international channels. Any effort to do so can be detected, and it will tend to discredit those doing the blocking. Worse, presenting incomplete or inaccurate information tends to make authorities appear manipulative and dishonest, even if their intentions are good. The Anwar Ibrahim scandal burst unexpectedly onto the front pages of newspapers and onto the main evening newscasts of Southeast Asia in mid-1998. Like the Monica Lewinsky–Bill Clinton scandal in the United States, the Anwar story presented distasteful accounts of alleged sexual liaisons to a public unaccustomed to such things being aired in the media.

Datuk Seri Anwar Ibrahim was, in June 1998, deputy prime minister of Malaysia and the heir apparent to Prime Minister Mahathir Mohamad. Vigorous, charismatic, and comparatively youthful at 51 years of age, he seemed a logical successor to the premiership. At one point, Anwar served as acting prime minister when Mahathir took a brief sabbatical. But Anwar had served as deputy since 1993, and after five years in the post was showing signs of impatience at the slow movement toward transition. Although 72 years old and the world's longest-serving democratically elected national leader, Mahathir had given no firm signal on when he planned to retire. For several years there was rumored friction between the prime minister and his deputy, but both publicly denied any rift. The two had different power bases within the ruling United Malays National Organization (UMNO) party, and their supporters sometimes openly advocated differing positions on policy issues.

One area of apparent difference was in information policy. Anwar spoke frequently of the need for less restrictive policies, while Mahathir's public pronouncements were more likely to advance arguments for traditional ways of centralized information management. These policy shadings never rose to the level of disagreement, but observers took the contrast in outlook to be a sign that the two were not quite in harmony. In some ways, Anwar's more liberal policy views were surprising. He had risen to prominence within the UMNO Youth organization where he was considered a bit of a fiery figure and a strong proponent of traditional Islamic values. But as he later filled various UMNO positions on his way to national leadership, he demonstrated a practical, tempered style of administration and an engaging public persona.

In early June 1998, Anwar openly urged UMNO members to end "cronyism, corruption, and nepotism." His remarks were the most frank admission that such problems existed in the party, although for a number of years members had spoken about the corrosive effects of "money politics," that is the trading of political favors for financial rewards. Gossip had long held that cash kickbacks were factors in awards of official contracts and that people at the highest levels of the government profited from payoffs. In truth, Anwar's admissions were hardly new or surprising. As Crouch (1988) wrote about money politics ten years earlier,

> Government policy has made available business opportunities for Malays but it is government patronage that determines which Malays actually get the opportunities. ... Having acquired their wealth through government patronage, it is only natural that businessmen and aspiring businessmen should want to strengthen their influence in the ruling party by winning office in the party organization and eventually seats in Parliament or the state assemblies (p. 89).

Anwar's remarks about cronyism were interpreted by some as a criticism of Mahathir himself. Less than a week later, the prime minister denied overseas media reports of disaffection between himself and Anwar.

At about the same time, a book titled *50 Dalil Mengapa Anwar Tidak Boleh Mejadi PM* [50 reasons why Anwar cannot become PM] was about to be released. To stop its publication, Anwar went to court, obtaining an injunction against the author, Khalid Jafri. The book's contents, however, circulated more or less freely within political circles in Kuala Lumpur, presumably due to the efforts of Anwar's opponents. It contained lurid allegations of sexual encounters by Anwar, including a purported homosexual relationship with his wife's former chauffeur and an affair with the wife of his secretary, details of allegedly corrupt financial deals, and many other disgraceful matters. By July, Anwar announced that the book was part of an effort to oust him from his post. Indeed, within weeks he was dismissed as deputy prime minister and as finance minister. Not long afterward, he was arrested and charged with a list of crimes, including most sensationally one of sodomy.

The trial that followed was both dramatic and filled with unexpected developments. Not long after the trial opened, Anwar appeared in court with dark bruises about his cheeks and eyes. Initially, the government denied that he had been injured in custody, and Mahathir answered media questioning with the conjecture that Anwar may have inflicted injuries on himself to make authorities look bad. Eventually, the government had to admit that a senior police official Police Inspector-General Rahim Noor had beaten Anwar. This triggered a public outcry culminating in weeks of antigovernment demonstrations by Anwar's supporters, and each of these demonstrations was forcefully put down by police under the watchful eyes of international media. The trial dragged on for weeks. In the end, Anwar was found guilty of charges and was sentenced to six years in jail. As the events of the Anwar scandal unfolded, opposition groups coalesced around the former deputy prime minister's plight, forming a loose group known as the *Reformasi* [Reformation] movement. The opposition groups had divergent agendas. Among the most prominent beneficiaries of the political fallout was Parti Islam or PAS, the Islamic opposition party that had busied itself ratcheting up a national campaign in expectations of 1999 elections. After his sentencing, Anwar's wife, who had been steadily protesting the trial, announced formation of a new political party. She revealed foundation of the National Justice Party, organized to compete with the prime minister's UMNO party and with PAS for the Malay vote.

Many Malaysians expressed skepticism about the charges against Anwar, considering it a probable ploy to rid the government of a person who had become an annoyance for the prime minister. Whether this was the case or not, many believed it might be true, and this meant they had to be suspicious of reports presented by Malaysian media, nearly all of which were either directly or indirectly linked to Barisan Nasional, the ruling coalition headed by UMNO. Although as a rule these media did not suppress facts favorable to the Anwar cause, the government case against him undeniably received more thorough coverage. The belated admission by government that Anwar had been beaten in custody after consistent denials only contributed to the suspicions many in Malaysia felt. Added to this were the unexpected resignations of journalists from Malay-language dailies and the departure of a senior officer at one of the private television stations, presumably because of their links to Anwar. These developments tended to reinforce a public perception that citizens could not depend upon officially sanctioned media. According to Hiebert (1998) "the Malaysian press has not ignored the Anwar story. But many Malaysians feel that it has overlooked one side—and gone overboard in reporting the other." Dissatisfaction with the media rose to a boil in late October 1998, when demonstrators near a mosque in the old Malay settlement area of Kuala Lumpur attacked a vehicle belonging to the *Utusan Malaysia* newspaper and attempted to do the same to a *New Straits Times* car (Cordingley and Oorjitham, 1998).

Government efforts to limit and to shape coverage of the Anwar story fueled a desire for information not filtered by government-controlled media. And as the intensity of protests and allegations rose, the array of alternative news sources grew. On the Internet several sites such as www.caidmark.com.my and www.anwar.cjb.net sprang up to provide on-line reports. Chat groups and news lists also provided sharing mechanisms for exchange of observations and opinion. Political rumors, an enduring feature of Malaysian life, moved from street corners, coffee shops, and office hallways to the Internet. Knowledge of tidbits floating on the net was wider than one might expect of a country not yet fully wired to the Web; for the benefit of those not owning computers, Internet items often showed up as printed flyers. Even photographs were exchanged or downloaded in this way. Although it was commonly believed that officials could monitor actions of Malaysians on the Internet, its use increased sharply. After his jailing, an Anwar Web site was set up (http://members.tripod.com/~Anwar_Ibrahim/) devoted to snippets of information and facts about the trial, his detention, and an exchange of views on Malaysian political affairs.

Another way of getting a different point of view on the Anwar story was via international television and radio. Viewers could see foreign television channels through satellite and cable relays. Malaysia's domestic broadcasting satellite system, formally known as the All Asia Television and Radio Company (ASTRO), as well as Mega TV, the cable system operating in the vicinity of the capital, carried CNN International News, and ASTRO also offered NBC, CNBC, and Asian Business News in its lineup. Thousands more, mostly in East Malaysia, also owned illegal satellite dishes that permitted direct reception of television news from the United Kingdom's BBC and of Australian networks. Shortwave radio provided yet another route to get foreign news from many countries. BBC Radio's *East Asia Today,* a half-hour newscast devoted to news from the region, presented updates on Kuala Lumpur events each morning at 7:00 A.M. local time. These broadcasts could not only be obtained over the airwaves, but could also be picked up from Internet radio Web sites such as www.bbc.co.uk/worldservice/eastasiatoday/.

Prime Minister Mahathir was outraged by the international media coverage of the Anwar story, and he accused foreign news organizations of trying to overthrow his government. Few were surprised that government officials were said to be as unhelpful as possible when international media wished to cover the Anwar trial. Some news organizations claimed interference in their reporting of certain aspects of the case, notably prohibitions against video coverage of street demonstrations during the trials. Officially, this was done in the interest of public order and to prevent the trial from becoming a spectacle. Beyond a doubt, however, some Malaysians felt that international media were guilty of distorting the news to fit the prejudices and hidden motives of Western journalists. Visiting Tokyo while international reporting on the Anwar trial was at its height, the prime minister suggested that Japanese journalists visit

Malaysia to obtain a true picture of events. He advised them to "not trust CNN or CNBC. They have a different agenda and they tell lies to promote their agenda" (Hiebert and Jayasankaran, 1998).[1] A little earlier the prime minister had told the Commonwealth Press Union that the purpose of the Western media attacks on his administration was to "teach Malaysia a lesson, to pull it down a few pegs more" (Cordingley and Oorjitham, 1998).

Coverage by international news organizations also pushed media in Malaysia to provide more depth in their coverage of the Anwar story. Occasionally this led to surprisingly enterprising journalism. Circulation figures skyrocketed for the opposition party's newspaper, *Harakah*, giving a further boost to PAS's political credibility. The most often discussed broadcast program was one that aired on the newest private television channel NTV7 called *Dateline*. Produced by Asian News Broadcasting, an independent production company in Kuala Lumpur, it consciously set out to present viewpoints that the other channels avoided for fear of reprisals. The program provided an opportunity for opposition parties to speak out on issues, something that Malaysian television had rarely done. *Dateline* was initially a nightly broadcast, but after a few months it was cut back to air only on weekends. Objections were voiced by government officials who called producers on the carpet, demanding explanations for the program's contents. Even though plenty of frank discussions were aired, some who appeared on the program objected when their more inflammatory remarks were cut out. Producers explained that their motive in editing shows was self-protection. "What do you do if someone wants to go to jail? He can sound off and we'll get 10 lawsuits" (cited in Hiebert, 1999).

The Anwar case graphically illustrates the political transformation that occurred as a consequence of technological change. Had the incident taken place a decade earlier, it would have hardly attracted the attention of international media, and even if they had covered the story, few in Malaysia would have seen the reports. Government media would have provided the official spin on the Anwar trial, and public debate would have been quite circumscribed. But the presence of new channels uninhibited by official restrictions made it immeasurably more difficult to manage public opinion about events. Government officials tried to control the story in the usual way, but their efforts did not affect reports appearing in international media and certainly had little effect on the messages flooding the Internet. Instead, authorities were placed on the defensive, responding to news reports and rumors that circulated with ease through unregulated electronic channels.

---

[1]Many items cited in the reference lists of this text are taken from databases that do not provide page numbering. For this reason, reference lists do not contain page number information for any reference to newspapers, newsletters, or news magazines.

POLITICS OF THE ELECTRONIC TIGERS

A complex interplay of technology and politics is not particular to Southeast Asia, but policies of countries in this region encouraging use of technology undoubtedly magnified its effects. Other factors may explain why the phenomena were so exaggerated in the region. Southeast Asian nations had specifically promoted electronic technology as an avenue for economic development and had enjoyed great success, becoming suppliers of electronic components and home to major manufacturers of electronic consumer goods for world markets. For this reason, electronic technology was readily available, and because it was domestically produced it was comparatively inexpensive. Prosperity brought devices such as satellite receiving equipment and computers within the reach even of lower-middle-class workers in many countries of Southeast Asia. High levels of education fostered a political sophistication and gave people the knowledge required to use technology. All of these things made countries of the region especially prone to the influence of new information technologies in social and political realms.

In succeeding chapters I will argue that a fundamental change has occurred in the region's political landscape as a consequence of these new information technologies. This report considers the evolution of electronic media in Southeast Asia from the 1980s to the present, analyzing the political and social implications of their rising popularity. Official information and communication policies will be examined in selected countries, especially ones within the "Malay World," Malaysia, Indonesia, Singapore, and Brunei. In this account, the traditional concept of electronic media has been enlarged from conventional radio, television, and video to include all of the new information channels that materialized in the late 1990s. Most important among the latter, of course, is the Internet, which has become commonplace among the educated middle and upper classes of most countries of Southeast Asia. Other technologies considered include satellite and cable broadcasting, multimedia, and their related technologies.

IN SUMMARY

Technological changes in information media after 1980 gradually took away political leaders' ability to manage public opinion in the way they had been accustomed. With the arrival of each new technology—first VCRs, then cable and satellites, and finally the Internet—central control was further weakened. As the Anwar case illustrates, government's ability to manage public access to information was dramatically curtailed when the number of alternative information sources grew to the point that authorities could not possibly eliminate or police them all. Two conditions created this situation: technology was readily available at a cost within the reach of most middle-class citizens, and trust in conventional information channels had degenerated to the point of cynicism. In Southeast Asia, powerful, firmly entrenched figures such as Marcos and Suharto lost public confidence and were replaced, to some degree as an outcome of their loss of information control. In places such as Malaysia, the clash over public information produced mounting political conflict and turned the Anwar Ibrahim scandal into a media circus.

Similar situations can be found outside Southeast Asia. For instance, in the 1999 overthrow of the Pakistan government, army generals scrambled for days after their takeover to develop an information strategy and to make political plans consistent with these changed realities. In the Kosovo conflict of the same year and in its aftermath, opposition groups learned to utilize the Internet to rally their cause, even transmitting independent radio newscasts via streaming audio. A central aim of this account is exploration of the interconnectedness that adoption of new technologies has produced. Around the world, countries chose varied responses to media globalization, ranging from openness to stubborn opposition. A comparison of these reactions and their immediate consequences provide illuminating lessons. In particular, it is instructive to examine how Internet and satellite television came into use in the Southeast Asian region and to juxtapose different policy responses of governments there.

REFERENCES

Cordingley, P., and Oorjitham, S. (1998, November 13). How the media have fared. *Asiaweek.*

Crouch, H. (1988). Money politics in Malaysia. In Jomo (Ed.), *Mahathir's economic policies* (pp. 87–89). Kuala Lumpur: INSAN.

Fischer, S. (1998, July 17). A year of upheaval. *Asiaweek.*

Hiebert, M. (1998, October 8). Alternative news. *Far Eastern Economic Review.*

Hiebert, M. (1999, February 11). Breaking the news. *Far Eastern Economic Review.*

Hiebert, M., and Jayasankaran, S. (1998, October 29). A single spark. *Far Eastern Economic Review.*

Hewison, K. (1989). *Power and politics in Thailand.* Manila: Journal of Contemporary Asia Publishers.

Indicators 1998. (1998, December 25). *Asiaweek.*

Lee, P. P. (1988). 'Japan Incorporated' and its relevance to Malaysia. In Jomo (Ed.). *Mahathir's economic policies* (pp. 35–37). Kuala Lumpur: INSAN.

Mahathir M. (1984). Malaysia Incorporated and privatisation: Its rationale and purpose. In Mohd. Nor Abdul Ghani, B. T. H. Wang, I. K. M. Chia, and B.

Gale (Eds.), *Malaysia Incorporated and privatisation: Towards national unity* (pp. 1–7). Petaling Jaya, Malaysia: Pelanduk Publications.

Saludo, R., and Assif, S. (1998, July 17). How much longer? *Asiaweek.*

Sender, H. (1996, September 5). Bambang's Challenge. *Far Eastern Economic Review.*

Suh, S. (1998, July 3). Speaking one's mind. *Asiaweek.*

Tesoro, J. M. (1998, September 25). Descent to chaos. *Asiaweek.*

Chapter Two
State Information and Media Policy— Archetypes and Trends

When colonies gained independence, it was often the case that legislative and legal systems were kept more-or-less intact, at least for a transitional period. For this reason, present-day communication policy in Southeast Asia embodies quite a few features inherited from colonial days. Although modifications were made over time, these changes tended to be adopted incrementally and in a patchwork pattern. Obviously, this was not true in countries that fought wars for independence such as Indonesia and Vietnam; their legal systems were totally overhauled when conflict ended. Echoes of colonial practices can be found today in media policies of countries such as Singapore, Brunei, the Philippines, and Malaysia, and this has sometimes led to difficulties. Not only might such policies be outdated, but ones originally intended to protect European imperial interests might easily be redirected to uphold hegemony by dominant political figures and their political parties. How present-day policies took shape can best be understood through a historical overview.

NATIONALISM AND MEDIA POLICY

Every colonized country in Southeast Asia faced a similar problem at the time of independence: each had to fashion a distinctive identity while inventing its own particular brand of nationhood. In Southeast Asia there were many barriers to a sense of shared affinities in newly independent countries. Geography was one of these impediments. In the case of Indonesia and the Philippines, dispersed islands created natural divisions that tended to hamper unification.

Mountains served as barriers as well, isolating portions of practically all countries within the region, especially Vietnam, Thailand, Indonesia, and Burma. Steinberg (1987) emphasized three "channels of change" in the swell of nationalism in Southeast Asia: urbanization, education, and language.

> Although cities had existed long before Europeans arrived, they were altered by colonialism that turned the new towns it created inside out, so that at their heart lay not the monarchy but money—the counting houses of the Chinese and other trades, the shophouses full of consumer goods from Manchester, Marseilles, Bombay, and Hong Kong (Steinberg, p. 255).

Towns established by colonial powers such as Jakarta (originally Batavia), Kuala Lumpur, and Singapore thus became commercial outposts of European metropolitan centers and the distribution points for raw materials bound for colonial industry. The new cities also became centers of education. Although educational institutions were built as part of the machinery employed to turn colonies into efficient producers of industrial resources, they also had the effect of fostering mass societies through the popularization of link languages. Malay, Dutch, and English were introduced for administrative and strategic purposes across the archipelago, while similar developments occurred in mainland Southeast Asia. Even though instruction in vernacular languages was the principal thrust of education policy in most places, a need for local staff conversant in administrative languages developed as economic activity grew. Educational institutions that offered training to fill this demand became the most prestigious, and their graduates became the new intelligentsia. The educational systems' training in link languages thus had the inadvertent effect of creating a local political elite, one of the elements required for the flowering of nationalism.

In countries such as Malaysia and Singapore, internal social divisions were the direct result of colonial policy. Chinese and Indian immigration to the peninsula was encouraged in British times, leading to intractable cultural frictions that national integration policies have since attempted to rectify. Chinese immigration into what became British Malaya occurred in small numbers until the nineteenth century. This Chinese minority became largely integrated into the dominant Malay culture—they acquired the Malay language and adopted many Malay cultural practices, yet they still maintained a separate Chinese identity. These were part of what is known today as the Straits Chinese community, a group not fully Chinese in its cultural habits and not fully swallowed up by the larger Malay society. But in the 1800s, political uproar in China and the establishment of a generous immigration policy in Malaya provided push-pull conditions that induced a surge of population movement to the peninsula. Demand for tin by the European food canning industry led to the establishment of many mines in tin-rich Malaya. British mine owners took advantage of the abundant Chinese labor supply, setting off further rounds of immigration from the China mainland. Because of this human tide, the major cities of the peninsula became majority Chinese by the last half of the nineteenth century (Andaya and Andaya, 1982). In British Malaya, a second simultaneous inward immigration sprang up in the early twentieth century because of the sudden increase in world demand for rubber used in automobile tires. To staff labor-intensive rubber estates in Malaya, the colonial government permitted indentured workers to be recruited from Southern India. The numbers inducted for this work were huge; at its height, more than one hundred thousand entered Malaya annually. Even though most of the workers returned home at the end of their contracts, a small proportion did stay behind, and in time they constituted a substantial part of the peninsula's population (Ryan, 1976). When the first census was completed in 1911, ethnic Indians totaled about 10 percent of Malaya's population of about 2.5 million (Vreeland, 1977). Effects of these phenomena tended to be localized and dependent upon implementation of colonial policy. For instance, East and West Malaysia still have quite different demographics due to variations in colonial strategies in Malaya and in North Borneo (and eventually in Sarawak). Most Tamil workers were attracted to the peninsular region; few found their way to Borneo, where not so many rubber estates were built and the quality of life was harsher.

For these and related reasons, nations that emerged from colonialism were products of their geographic circumstance and the whims of history. Therefore these countries' populations generally lacked a unified consciousness. A vivid analysis of the making of nationalism is provided in the often-quoted work of Benedict Anderson, *Imagined Communities* (1983). In his explanatory framework, nations are purely conceived as "imagined political communities" that take shape "both as inherently limited and sovereign." In Anderson's interpretation, nationhood's tangible qualities are the product of human creation and do not arise from "naturally" bounded properties. As he noted, the nation "is imagined because the members of even the smallest nations will never know most of their fellow members, meet them, or even hear of them, yet in the minds of each lives the image of their communion" (pp. 5–6). In Thongchai Winichakul's *Siam Mapped* (1994, pp. 14–15), Anderson's perspective was further elaborated in the following way.

> A nation is conceived as a new era, a kind of community whose spatial parameters and temporal homogeneity have been *formulated* in various ways. This identification is possible only through *mediation* by certain means. … We can know about [the community] as long as we employ certain *technologies* to inscribe the possible sphere. In turn, such technologies create the knowledge of it, create a fact of it, and the entity comes into existence (emphasis added).

Media play an integral role in constructing and disseminating nations' imagined dimensions because of their capacity to extend across distances and to reach the whole of society. A key element in Anderson's argument is that the rise of print media led to formation of mass societies and to standardization of languages beginning in Europe after the popularization of movable type; both results were precursors to the modern state. Writing about newspapers' ability to inspire a shared perception among its readers, and drawing on Venezuela under Spanish rule as an example, Anderson wrote that

> The newspaper of Caracas ... created an imagined community among a specific assemblage of fellow-readers, to whom these ships, brides, bishops and prices [reported by the newspaper] belonged. In time, of course, it was only to be expected that political elements would enter in (p. 62).

In this way, newspapers performed the function of promoting a nationalist ideology in harmony with national administrative agencies and educational systems.

It was not only newspapers that encouraged nationalism; it also gained from the popularization of electronic media after 1930. Radio became a craze in every country of the industrialized world during the 1920s. Oddly, it won acceptance partly through military personnel's introduction to the technology in World War I in which it was used as a communication tool for the first time. Following the war, thousands of servicemen trained in the use of radio returned home, thus scattering their electronic skills across the world. On taking up civilian lives they continued tinkering with radios, pursuing it as a pastime by setting up small stations in their homes or in community centers. Some of these experimenters held government jobs in colonial offices overseas, where their dabbling in the medium brought radio even to remote corners of the globe. By the early 1930s these hobby operations were largely supplanted by the establishment of permanent semiprofessional stations in Southeast Asia. By this time, radio had become a worldwide phenomenon and the radio receiving set a commonplace feature of well-to-do households in the region. Simple sets could be purchased for as little as $30. Shenton Thomas, governor of Malaya, was astounded by the spread of radio set ownership among ordinary citizens of Thailand when he visited the country in 1937. He reported that "in Siam the number [of radio receivers] is astonishing. When I passed through Bangkok on my way home, I found that most houses, including small houses, houses which we should call *kampong* houses here, had a set" ("Sir Shenton Thomas," 1937). In Thailand, radio received an early endorsement from the king, who was reported to be "one of the world's most radio-minded monarchs." On a trip to the United States he visited radio stations and manufacturing facilities and brought home "a collection of shortwave sets" ("Radio in Siam," 1931). Radio stations in Manila, Saigon, and Jakarta were among the most popular of the day. Broadcasting activities tended to be carried out by government agencies or by local entrepreneurs, but in Malaya, a lack of interest among authorities limited stations on the air to those operated by hobbyists and experimenters until near the end of the 1930s.

The popularity of radio was coupled with a growth in sales of phonograph records during the same period. Then as now, radio depended heavily on recorded music to fill airtime. The first locally made recordings began dribbling into Southeast Asia's music shops in the first decade of the twentieth century. The establishment of recording and pressing facilities within the region enabled local Asian artists to popularize their music. In the 1920s and 1930s regular and frequent new record releases took place; at least one major company issued new records monthly. By the outbreak of World War II, there were thousands of recordings of local music issued in Malaya and the Dutch East Indies. Unique local music forms such as *kronchong* spread and gained popularity, building up listener interest in radio programs of recorded music. By the 1930s, practically all stations in the archipelago had begun to use these types of recordings in their musical shows. Undoubtedly, the uniquely local character of this music also contributed to a sense of cultural connectedness across the archipelago, a sense quite separate from the ideological notions that the colonial governments offered.

An interesting elaboration of Anderson's thesis, one that bears on the importance of popular music in shaping national identity, was provided in William Frederick's (1997) study of an Indonesian intellectual, Armijn Pané, of the pre-independence period. Frederick considered him ahead of his time—he called him a "cultural pioneer"—in his understanding of and appreciation for the power of mass media and the popular culture forms it inspired. Armijn was a journalist and author whose work *Belenggu* [shackles] is acknowledged as Indonesia's first "modern" novel. Frederick's analysis of Armijn's ideas about *kronchong* is insightful. This syncretistic music form drew from Portuguese and Hawaiian as well as Indonesian sources, but intellectuals of the 1930s regarded it as quite degenerate and low class. It was nevertheless wildly popular among the masses of city residents, not only in Indonesia but in nearby Malaya. Armijn defended *kronchong* and, according to Frederick (p. 61), hailed it "as a suitable foundation on which to build a modern, unified, and dynamic Indonesian culture." In Armijn's *Belenggu*, the successful middle-class protagonist falls in love with a female *kronchong* singer, and although their relationship is scandalous (he is already married), the novel's sympathetic portrayal of a lower-class vocalist helped to legitimize the popular music form from which she gained attention and appreciation.

When radio—or "wireless" as it was then known—first arrived in Southeast Asia, it projected a sense of social interaction and participation invaluable to emerging nation-states. A writer identified simply as a Sungei Lembing listener hinted at this in a letter to the *Straits Times*. The correspondent praised the newspaper.

> I think the concentration you are giving to wireless should eventually do much towards the advancement of this hitherto sadly neglected pursuit in Malaya. Particularly from an up-country man's point of view, wireless is a wonderful pastime for the many leisure hours he must necessarily face isolated from other social amenities ("Reception in Malaya," 1931).

The near-instant popularity of radio made it a natural instrument for national integration. This point was made by a radio listener in Seremban, more than 200 kilometers north of Singapore, when he wrote the *Straits Times* to complain that Malaya's first nonamateur broadcasting organization, British Malaya Broadcasting Corporation (BMBC), would not be audible in his hometown. Signing himself as Sungei Ujong, he pointed out that the organization was called "the 'British Malayan' corporation." Therefore, he argued, "they ought to provide a service that can be picked up all over the country" ("The new Singapore," 1936). The broadcasting staff had already recognized this necessity. BMBC's chairman, R. C. Giggins, made this precise point in an address his station broadcast on July 1, 1937. Speaking of his station's goals, he stated "the first move is to get a national outlook in British Malaya, rather than disjointed action or expression of opinion." To this end, he proposed setting up a chain of regional stations to back up a national service of shortwave transmitters of "reasonably high power" ("Reform of Malayan," 1937).

Coincidentally, Southeast Asia's new nationalism began to take shape in the 1920s and 1930s in parallel with expansion of mass communication, especially radio. Nationalism was similar to, yet different from, resistance to colonialism that had been evident for a century or more in many places. Osborne (1990, p. 118) has argued that those involved in the nationalist movements believed they were following the path of their forebears by "building upon the traditions already established by their countrymen, but doing so in a way that took account of changed social, economic, and political factors." Consciousness of these factors grew as a result of a convergence of developments such as the arrival of radio during the 1930s. Also important was accelerated growth in educational systems following the turn of the century. With greater access to education, a new class of literate citizens sprang up (see Ricklefs, 1981, pp. 149–152; Turnbull, 1989, pp. 192–193), and within a few decades this began to produce tangible social changes. As might be expected, the impact of educational improvements varied from country to country; by 1930, nearly one-quarter of Philippine residents were literate, while in Indonesia the proportion was estimated at only seven percent.

Perhaps because national political leadership in Indonesia was so directly in control of information and media policy making, government-operated media tended to become voices of partisan nationalists in the post independence era. Close links between political leaders and media are part of the distinctive nature of Southeast Asian politics today. Political figures frequently rose from the ranks of journalists and media professionals. Indonesia's Sukarno and Vietnam's Ho Chi Minh often wrote for newspapers. Malaysia's former Prime Minister Tunku Abdul Rahman long served as a editorialist for the prominent English-language newspaper, *The Star.* The end result of these ties was the establishment of the kind of media that did not maintain distance from politics but were identified in the public's mind with the political parties and figures for which they came to stand. Indeed, van der Kroef (1954) characterized Indonesian press as "by-products of nationalism" for the way in which media served as tools for the creation of a polity and a sense of nationhood.

Radio in particular had played a decisive role in the war of independence against the Dutch, proselytizing and propagandizing in support of independence throughout the conflict. Compared with print media, this electronic medium offered something new. As Agassi (1969, p. 4) pointed out, "radio was a rather different medium from the press. It was wholly oriented to an anti-foreign, nationalistic ideology." Official accounts of the independence later described radio's programs as "aimed at mental reforming of the population to be a free and independent nation. As the Indonesian culture has been influenced by foreign cultures ... R. R. I. [Radio Republik Indonesia] pays much attention to the National Culture" (*Almanak Pers 1954/55,* cited in Agassi, 1969, p. 55). After independence, Sukarno continued using radio to consolidate his political power, something he was able to do with great skill. He was a powerful, inspirational speaker, and his radio addresses are believed to have had a significant effect on public opinion during the early years of independence when political control of the island nation remained shaky (see, for instance, Ricklefs, 1981, p. 211). This nationalistic fervor has been maintained to the present, at least on the Indonesian government stations. For instance, policy document Declaration No. II/MPR/1983 on information and mass media stated that "information and mass media have a. To encourage the spirit of national dedication and national struggle. b. To strengthen national uniformity and national unity" (cited in Hoerip, 1984, p. 3).

Philippine nationalism was filtered initially through media that were really private American-owned corporations. As Teodoro and Kabatay (1998, p. 75) observed, "the first newspapers during the early years of the [U.S.] occupation were all owned and controlled by American nationals ... so there was a need for a Filipino newspaper." Through the efforts of independence leader Manuel Quezon, the establishment of the *Philippines Herald* in 1920 filled this need. After this, "the *Herald* assumed a nationalist position which supported the quest for independence." In this period, the same American presence could be found in radio that was exclusively operated by commercial private firms owned by expatriates (see Lent, c. 1972). Although Philippine law incorporated American-style provisions for press freedoms, in practice "the dangerous tendency rule was the test used in determining whether an utterance was seditious or not" (Teodoro and Kabatay, 1998, p. 17).

American interests also set up Thailand's first newspaper, the *Bangkok Recorder,* starting with its initial publication in 1844. Eventually this paper was transformed into the official royal publication *Government Gazette* in the late nineteenth century. Until the twentieth century, mass media were only operated by foreign missionaries or members of the royal family (see Thitinan, 1997). The beginnings of Thai radio were rooted in the national government's effort to win public support during the 1930s. As Ubonrat (1992, p. 92) described it, "once entrusted into the hands of the constitutional government [radio] very rapidly became a state propaganda machine." In the years leading to the outbreak of World War II, Thai radio served as a commanding voice of government. Radio Bangkok, which had been put on the air by the Department of Post and Telegraph, was taken over by the Department of Propaganda. By the late 1950s, the situation started to change as the pace of economic development picked up, creating social stresses and a significant urban migration. According to Ubonrat (p. 93) "during this period the need for political legitimization and national integration had never been greater." Government seized upon broadcasting as a vehicle to achieve these aims, and expansion of electronic media increased markedly, so that by 1981 Surapone (1983, p. 101) suggested that "the Thai people are overwhelmed by mass media," counting more than 250 radio stations, and 9 television stations.

POLICY MAKING IN SOUTHEAST ASIA

The development of media policy can be quite varied even in countries that enjoy common historical and political origins. It is impossible to detail the full range of policy-making customs found in Southeast Asia, but a few generalities can be offered here. First, national policy making conventionally involves central governments but may also include regional governments where a federal system exists. Foreign interests may inject themselves into the process as well, and since the 1970s, scholars (such as Schiller [1975] and Hamelink [1983], among others) have studied their influence on policy making in developing countries. Second, decision making commonly draws upon networks of informal influence: lobby groups, entrepreneurs, leadership family and friends, nongovernmental organizations, and so on. In most countries, bureaucracies play a key role in setting a policy agenda and in policy implementation. The interplay of forces such as these depends on the specific array of stakeholders in each country. Where these interests have a rough balance of power, the government must assume the role of arbitrator among stakeholders, if none of them is "powerful enough to consistently shape state action" (Rideout and Mosco, 1997, p. 83).

In Singapore and Malaysia, for instance, a central objective of all types of policy making is to balance the interests of Chinese, Malay, and Indian populations. Both countries have a governmental structure loosely modeled on a British-style parliament, made up of lower and upper houses and with the main executive power in the office of the prime minister. In addition, Malaysia has melded this parliamentary model with a traditional structure of governance in which nine of its thirteen states are made up of hereditary sultanates. The ruling sultans participate in selecting one among them who serves a five-year term as king or *Yang di-Pertuan Agong* of Malaysia. In both Malaysia and Singapore, a single political entity dominates politics—the People's Action Party (PAP) in Singapore and the Barisan Nasional in Malaysia (a coalition mainly comprising three large parties: United Malays National Organization or UMNO, the Malaysian Indian Congress or MIC, and the Malaysian Chinese Association or MCA). The government of the day generally initiates policy making in both countries. Because members of the ruling parties exclusively head the ministries in these governments and the opposition exerts little leverage over the bureaucracy, their power to define policy is largely unchecked, except of course by the prime minister himself. Singapore's opposition parties are especially toothless, lacking strength to fend off PAP's domination either in Parliament or in the courts.

Among all Southeast Asian nations, only Thailand escaped colonization, though it did lose territories in Laos, Cambodia, and Malaya to the European powers. As SarDesai (1994) explained, Thailand's rulers were adept at diplomacy and they "introduced timely reforms ... to preserve Thailand's identity and independence." Today Thailand and Brunei are the lone remaining countries in which the head of state is a hereditary monarch (Malaysia's sultanates and monarchy are titular and lack any important governmental authority). The disappearance of traditional rulers in most parts of Southeast Asia represents a turn toward Western style government—thanks in large measure to colonialism—and to regional democratic movements. However, in Thailand royal authority is shared with a legislative body that carries out regulatory and policy-making functions through ministries. The Sultan of Brunei, Sultan Yang di-Pertuan Agong Haji Hassanal Bolkiah Mu'izzaddin Waddaulah, not only serves as the supreme ruler, but also holds two ministerial portfolios: prime minister and defence. Although Brunei has a constitutional provision for an elected legislative body, no votes have been held since 1962, when an uprising against the monarchy took place and the body was suspended. Other members of the sultan's family fill additional ministerial posts. In Thailand, responsibility for media policy implementation has shifted over the years but ultimately has been in the hands of the Council of Ministers. The Government

Publicity Department (now called the Public Relations Department) long held the job of coordinating Thai broadcasting policy, but in the aftermath of the student uprising in 1992 the National Broadcasting Commission was created to carry out this function.

In Indonesia, political power from the Sukarno ouster to the mid-1990s was centralized in three power bases. These were the military, which had led the overthrow of Sukarno and maintained an influential position in the legislative process; Golkar, the army-organized mobilization organization that metamorphosed into a political party; and Suharto, the former general who led Golkar. Suharto and his supporters proclaimed this period as the "New Order" to distinguish it from the previous two-decade-long "old order" of Sukarno's leadership. Throughout this time, Parliament was under the complete control of Golkar, which remained subservient to Suharto up to the end of his time in office. Despite the apparent simplicity of authority in Indonesia, over time policy making became more and more complex, with responsibilities for information and media spread among numerous agencies at the national level, responsibilities which were frequently overlapping and uncoordinated with ones at the local, provincial, and district levels. The military provided the lone center of regulatory continuity across the nation's huge geography (see Steinberg, 1987, p. 428ff).

In the former Indochina (Laos, Cambodia, and Vietnam) and in Myanmar (Myanmar is the official name of what was once Burma, although the name Burma remains in use, especially among government opponents.), Socialist principles of policy making have been maintained, albeit in increasingly modified forms. Following reunification, Vietnam's government was faced with problems of structural underdevelopment, a somnolent bureaucracy, and an ideologically paralyzed upper echelon of national leadership. After 1986, the country began a long process of reform initiated by the Sixth Party Congress known as *doi moi*. According to Oanh (1995, p. 9), *doi moi* meant changes in thinking and mentality, as well as a restructuring of "administrative machinery of economic management" and the gradual introduction of some aspects of a market economy. Neighboring Cambodia and Laos experienced a slow recovery from the wars of Indochina, particularly in the former, a nation that suffered terribly at the hands of the notorious Khmer Rouge. In only a bit more than three years of Khmer Rouge rule, roughly 15 percent of Cambodia's residents were killed, starved to death, or made to flee the country. Finally experiencing a measure of stability following the United Nations–administered elections in 1993, the country is slowly establishing a political legitimacy needed to set up effective national policy making. Cambodia's decades of political turmoil have taken a toll. Even though the 1998 elections produced a definitive government, building publicly accepted effective policy processes will require many years. Only in 1999 did the simmering conflict with remnants of the Khmer Rouge end, finally opening the door to better economic and political conditions and to rational and stable policy-making conditions.

Myanmar's military leadership has maintained a firm grip since seizing power in 1962, despite widespread internal opposition and international condemnation. The ruling Revolutionary Council sought to fuse military rule with socialist principles by stressing self-sufficiency and by imposing stringent limits on foreign participation in the economy. So successful was it in this latter endeavor that Burma became known as a hermit nation, withdrawn and isolated even from its neighbors. It also made the country one of the poorest in Asia. In four decades of power, the government's chief challenge came not from abroad, but from within. The fight to extend Burman Rangoon's control over the nation's other ethnic groups has kept the central government preoccupied and on the defensive throughout its history. After 1988, power in the country was transferred to a body known as the State Law and Order Restoration Council (SLORC), which was not much of a substantive change because the new entity was composed of senior military officers. Although a national election in 1990 gave a lopsided win to Aung San Suu Kyi's National League for Democracy, SLORC ignored the results and refused to surrender authority. The military leadership's subsequent drive to encourage foreign investment and to gain international credibility actually led to greater global awareness of the country's sad state of political affairs. Aung San Suu Kyi's house arrest attracted additional attention and created persistent discomfort for central government. As of this writing, communication policy remains in the hands of SLORC and the narrow group of officials affiliated with its command but is being challenged through the Internet, a subject to be taken up in a later chapter.

The imprint of colonial traditions has characterized policy making in the Philippines. Under Spanish rule, political power had devolved into a rigid oligarchy headed by a wealthy landed and trade elite. As Harrison (1966, p. 133) described it, "economically, the basis of Spanish rule was the landed estate held in feudal tenure by a privileged class … on whose lands the peasant villagers laboured and lived as [they] had done for centuries." An American veneer overlaid this during the United States' half-century rule, beginning at the end of the Spanish-American war in 1902. U.S. administration of the Philippines was accepted with ambivalence at home (there was substantial public opposition to American annexation of the Spanish colony), and there was active opposition to U.S. rule in the Philippines. Nevertheless, many American values and practices were transferred to the nation during five decades of rule.

Complete independence came to the Philippines in 1946 in a quick transition at the close of the Second World War. This presented an opportunity for a new relationship with its erstwhile colonizer, yet instead of responding eagerly, Washington projected such indifference that any Philippine interest in a special relationship with the United States was extinguished. In 1965, the country elected Ferdinand Marcos as president, a figure whose personality overshadowed Philippine politics in the last half of the twentieth century. Marcos's stunningly corrupt government, tied to crony interests in the tightly woven Philippine political system, eventually led the economy into chronic stagnation. Long after Marcos's departure, politics and policy making still centers on the small clique of powerful families who hold an enormously disproportionate share of the nation's wealth. In the 1980s, 20 percent of the poorest residents owned just 5.5 percent of the wealth whereas the richest 2 percent of the population owned 53 percent of it (Steinberg, 1987, p. 442). The Aquino government, which swept into office in the populist euphoria of 1986, failed to alter the fundamental character of politics, probably because Aquino herself was a member of one of the nation's wealthiest and most influential families. As SarDesai (1994, p. 207) put it, "the local elections of 1988 witnessed the restoration of family-based, dynastic domination of regional overlords." Public pressures for more inclusive political practices have produced minor concessions but little in the way of genuine reform.

MEDIA ORGANIZATIONS IN SOUTHEAST ASIA

The nation-building enterprise pursued by developing countries produced media organizations charged with nationalism. As a rule, the organizations formed to carry out broadcasting contrasted with ones operating in print media. Radio and television institutions were more intimately tied to government power; in many cases they were nothing more than government agencies. This was true of Radio Republik Indonesia (RRI) and its television counterpart TVRI; it was also true of Radio Television Brunei, Radio Television Singapore, and Radio Television Malaysia (RTM). In other countries, the relationship between the electronic media and government was more complex. Perhaps more revealing than government control of media were the links between nations' dominant political parties and their broadcasting organizations. Information ministries in Southeast Asia have tended to be headed by members of lead parties, even in countries that are ruled by coalition governments. Presumably this is the case because this ministry is viewed as particularly sensitive and vital to the interests of political leadership. In Malaysia recently, the person filling this post has had dual appointments as information minister and secretary-general of UMNO, the lead party in Barisan Nasional. And, as I will detail shortly, privatization of Malaysia broadcasting was accomplished only after party faithful were positioned in key positions of newly formed private media organizations. Print media in the Malay-Indonesian archipelago, although privately owned and commercially supported, operate under strict government control. Regulation of these publications occurs at two levels: in each country there exists a formal framework, as for example in the Printing Presses and Publications Act of Malaysia, which is charged with oversight of newspapers and magazines. At a second level, licenses for publications tend to be awarded to commercial organizations with links to the dominant parties and to leading political figures, who hence are likely to act in concert with them.

Thailand's electronic media were restricted to eleven state agencies up until 1992, but just two of these accounted for almost 90 percent of the authorized stations, the military and the Public Relations Office. The Thai army, navy, and air force stations—a novel feature of broadcasting in this country—once constituted the majority of licenses issued in Thailand. Although they were the largest single sector of broadcasting by the end of the 1980s, they accounted for less than 45 percent of the licenses (Ubonrat, 1997). In May 1992 students rose up against the military government that had taken power in the coup of February 1991. Protests, stimulated in part by press reports and commentaries, focused on the government of General Suchinda. In response, news blackouts were forced on the state-controlled radio and television stations. News accounts from international media, and a few enterprising journalists willing to ignore government threats, brought into the open the downward spiral of political events in Bangkok. In the end, the Suchinda government was replaced and wide-ranging reforms of mass communication—including the electronic media—were enacted to correct the "one-sided reports" issued by the government-administered stations (Ubonrat, 1994). The licensing authority was reconstituted, and private corporations were allowed to obtain licenses for newly authorized UHF stations. Expansions in cable and satellite operations were accepted as well (Thitinan, 1997). A number of commentators have noted that the liberalization produced by these moves has commercialized the system. Most Thai stations now derive the largest share, if not all, of their operating revenues from advertising.

Adjacent to Thailand, Myanmar's broadcasting functions strictly as a government agency, and it is the most rudimentary system in Southeast Asia. The system is operated by Myanmar Radio and Television (MRTV) and is supervised by the Ministry of Information. Radio continues to be the main electronic medium in Myanmar with more than three times as many radio receivers—slightly more than 3 million sets thinly spread among the population of 45 million residents—as television sets, according to official estimates (Sennitt, 1996). Programs are in Burmese and English with brief transmissions in a large number of regional languages such as Karen, Shan, and Mon. Reportedly, foreign stations, especially the BBC, are popular with Myanmar listeners. The Voice of America, which maintains a comparatively extensive schedule of programming for this county, is said to be less popular because its programs contain "too much 'show business' and United States propaganda" (Lintner, 1985a). Whatever the preference, a host of other international broadcasters transmit programs in Myanmar's local languages, thus there are abundant choices available. In addition, opposition radio stations operate irregular schedules clandestinely from locations along the Thai border. The Voice of the People of Burma operated an ambitious schedule for more than a decade, and a Karen rebel station at Maw Po Kay was active in the early 1980s (Lintner, 1985b). Myanmar was the last country in Southeast Asia to set up a television service. The first telecasts aired in June 1980 from a station set up under Japanese aid in Yangon (formerly known as Rangoon). Even two decades later this was the only channel available, and only seven relay stations beamed signals to the main cities of the capital and Mandalay plus a few other areas. The television system has been maintained on a shoestring budget. In 1985, a report of the Council of People's Inspectors claimed that costs of television operation amounted to only USD $7.87 per transmission hour. At that time, the official government count of sets in the nation totaled only 17,598 ("More TV," 1985). Daily transmissions remained abbreviated, amounting to only two hours on weekdays and four on weekends in the late 1990s. Strangely, even without full national coverage, in 1998 MRTV signed a long-term contract for rental of a satellite transponder, reportedly to "broadcast [MRTV] Global TV programming to Australia and Japan as well as other countries covered by the Thaicom 3 footprint" ("Satellite footprints," 1998).

Media control in the Philippines, like other important sectors of the economy, was concentrated in the hands of the country's small network of wealthy families. In 1972, Marcos declared martial law, an action that eventually produced further shrinkage in media ownership breadth. As Rosenberg (1979, p. 152) noted, "before martial law, each major elite faction maintained its own media outlets to espouse and defend its primary economic interests; while today it has been contracted and consolidated." Even though martial law was lifted in 1982, its political and economic aftereffects lingered. Economic models instituted by the United States and strengthened during the Marcos era produced a reliance on private commercial firms for services that were provided in other parts of Southeast Asia by state-owned concerns. Among the services affected was broadcasting. In fact, the Philippines was the only nation in all of Southeast Asia to set up a broadcasting system controlled by private corporations. Its broadcasting enterprises tended to be entwined in the conglomerates that dominated the Philippine economy. Lent (1971, p. 206) reported that the daily newspaper *Manila Chronicle* also owned "nearly 30 radio stations, a half dozen or so television stations, magazines, and even comic books." Other major newspapers also had wide media holdings, but they themselves were likely to be held by one or another of the huge multifaceted corporations that underpinned the national economy. Fernandez (1989, p. 331), among many others, argued that the highly consolidated nature of mass communication eventually degraded quality of service and distorted media's purpose so that "big money meant large writing and business staffs, news presses, delivery vehicles, and nationwide circulation. It also meant control of the press by the publishers' interests, economic or political."

Nowhere in Southeast Asia is the association between media and political power as sharply drawn as it is in Cambodia. In this country, the media have degenerated beyond mere advocacy into organs of mean-spirited, sometimes vicious, political attack. In this country, every newspaper has its political patron, excepting only the *Phnom Penh Post* and a few other foreign-language publications. Private radio stations are able to survive only through the support of one or another of the main political parties. Private media depend on commercial revenues as their principal means of support, but the economy of Cambodia has not yet attained the level of consumerism to provide much income through advertising. This has made newspapers and private radio stations reliant on their political benefactors. Such conditions have debased journalistic standards, producing news reports that few believe. The practice of "brown envelope journalism" (payment to newspapers and reporters for coverage of stories, allegedly in plain brown envelopes) is reported to be common. Because journalists are partisan, they have become targets of attack in Cambodia's bitter internal conflicts. On March 30, 1997, a grenade attack on a demonstration staged by the Khmer Nation Party Phnom Penh killed one journalist and seriously wounded several other news reporters. It also led to more than fifteen deaths and to dozens more injuries among those who had the bad luck to be near news reporters. Affecting every aspect of life in Cambodia, its political history—including the tragic rule of the Khmer Rouge, Vietnam's occupation, the capricious Sihanouk monarchy, and the bizarre 1993-1998 government by two prime ministers simultaneously—has been difficult to overcome.

Elsewhere in Indochina, Vietnamese media evolved a curiously complex organizational pattern as a consequence of the country's unique political history. Here, authorities attempted to structure media according to the classical Socialist model: multilevel media organizations in which national outlets were mirrored by complementary regional, local, and even community media outlets. The media at all levels were organs of the party. This was an approach that had been refined by the Soviet Union and one that it advocated for its close allies. Vietnam faced difficulties in adopting this type of media structure—the Soviet system was highly centralized and had developed a well-disciplined bureaucracy to support agitation and propaganda activities, but nothing like this existed in Vietnam. Countries in Indochina were fighting internal wars and struggling to build their basic infrastructure; communication media were not a critical priority. Moreover, in Vietnam as in other Socialist countries around the world, official policies tended to neglect electronic media. Lenin died in 1924 before radio had become an important medium in the Soviet Union, and the principles he laid down for mass communication took into account neither its possibilities nor those of television and other electronic media. Although his brief glimpse of radio impressed Lenin, he considered it merely an adjunct to print media, referring to it as a "newspaper without paper or wires," and he proposed that "it will be possible for Russia to hear a newspaper being read in Moscow" (Paulu, 1974, p. 217). As a result, party workers continued to follow an outmoded dogma that envisioned print media as the principal channels of mass communication. This proved to be a tremendous failing in countries such as Vietnam where mass literacy was lacking.

A peculiar difficulty in coordinating Vietnam broadcasting has been its tradition of autonomy among local party councils. In many parts of the country these political entities—constituting the primary local governmental bodies—evolved from cadres that were formed during fighting leading up to unification. Their independence perhaps was a necessity while operating as guerilla units, but in peacetime they maintained their freedom from coordination by central authorities, and this proved to be an impediment to integration of national administration. There are more than two hundred radio stations and several dozen television stations in Vietnam, the majority of which are operated as "metropolitan" or provincial stations by local party units. The oversight that central mass communication officials provide is very loose. Even though the Ministry of Culture, Information, and Sports theoretically manages the national media system, its ability to control the operation of local stations has been circumscribed by the lack of resources and by internal party politics. The result has been an absence of consistent effort and much duplication of responsibilities. For example, while working on a media training project in Vietnam in the early 1990s, I was surprised to learn that the country had more than twenty separate training organizations with responsibilities in broadcast training. All groups that I encountered seemed to be underfunded, yet none were able or willing to yield their autonomy to merge with other organizations or to come under any type of unified national authority. The national organization Radio and Television of Vietnam (VNRT) is the largest component of this sprawling system. The television service originates in Hanoi and is relayed around the country by a small network of transmitters. Schedule expansion has occurred only slowly; in 1986, only ninety minutes daily were scheduled ("40 years," 1986). Although VNRT programs have the largest coverage, and therefore the largest audience, it is often accused of being boring and uncreative. Another unit is Radio the Voice of Vietnam, which acts as the principal national radio service. It maintains an ambitious schedule of programming in French and a bit of English, in addition to Vietnamese.

PRIVATIZATION OF SOUTHEAST ASIAN ELECTRONIC MEDIA

As previously indicated, Southeast Asian nations tended to give broadcasting responsibility to government agencies. In fact, this more or less had been a global pattern before the 1980s, except in the western hemisphere. In about 1980, however, a trend toward privatization began to gain wider acceptance. In Europe, countries began reconfiguring broadcasting laws to open portions of their radio and television systems to private ownership. For example, France sold some of its television channels to private investors (see Le Duc, 1987), and in Germany steps were taken to diversify investment in broadcasting (Dyson and Humphreys, 1986). Even Great Britain considered—then rejected—reductions in public media ownership, including sales or leasing of parts of the BBC's schedule, (Harper, 1988; Pine, 1987).

The logic of such policies derives purely from an economic analysis. Privatization is a strategy that assumes market forces maximize efficiency and productivity. Privatization proponents argue that state ownership of enterprises ties up scarce public capital, promotes bureaucracy, and reduces competitiveness (Coburn and Wortzel, 1986; Hula, 1988). Divestiture of many types of state enterprises can theoretically achieve such benefits, but privatizing media is more problematic than other sectors of the economy because ownership of media outlets is presumed to confer power over national information. Furthermore, according to Vasquez (1983, p. 267), the belief that "economic control is indistinguishable from political control" is commonplace among scholars. In the view of many critics, government ownership creates conditions that encourage media to "further the interests of government and … to advance the cultural and political objectives of the central authority" (Siebert, 1963, p. 35). Of course, private media can just as easily further the economic and political interests of corporate owners. In any case, privatization is bound to dilute government's ability to regulate information that flows through media to the public, and policy experts in some countries consider this a serious problem.

Research on European media restructuring raised additional doubts about privatization of broadcasting. On the basis of their study of German and French television, Wildman and Siwek (1987, p. 74) concluded that profit-oriented programmers tend to increase production budgets until audiences are optimized for advertising revenues. This contrasts with the fixed budgets usually given producers in nonprofit government media. Consequently, in their view, private media are able to use more costly production techniques, giving their programs higher audience appeal and therefore a competitive advantage over state-owned media. Greater attention to viewers' interests and tastes is just one result of private media ownership, according to Wildman and Siwek. They also suggest that privatized television initially seeks to develop new sources of programming material. These sources tend to be foreign suppliers, at least until domestic production capacity can be built up (p. 75).

At first, developing countries seemed less eager to privatize their media than Europeans and North Americans. This may have originated from the generally slower pace of government divestiture in their economies (Berg, 1987, p. 25), but the developmental role of radio and television was undoubtedly a major factor too. One justification for state ownership of media in nonindustrial countries is that governments must be able to control media to ensure their effective use in development. Planners in the developing world worried that privatization of broadcasting could lead to its domination by commercial rather than national interests. Flashy entertainment shows might be preferred over important but necessarily less exciting development programs. Development theorists pointed out, however, that government-directed development was contradictory to the aims of participatory development, an approach that had gained many adherents by the end of the 1980s. In participatory development, plans originate at the grassroots level and decisions travel upward through the administrative hierarchy, rather than in the reverse direction. The legalization of private broadcasting came about as a result of extraordinary policy changes in a number of countries. After decades of determined opposition to private ownership in Southeast Asia, commercial stations suddenly began to gain approval in the 1980s.

Malaysia became the regional trendsetter when its government ended Radio Television Malaysia's monopoly in 1983 in a move intended to divert audiences away from video. The new private channel was called TV-Tiga or TV3, Malaysia's third television channel. The Malaysian government authorized successive private channels in the 1990s, including MetroVision, which started up in February 1995. This channel targeted the lucrative, comparatively wealthy Chinese and English-speaking markets with imported shows, creating what it called a "dragon" belt at 10:30 P.M. Monday through Fridays and a "phoenix" belt at 5:00 P.M. daily, both consisting of Chinese programs ("M'sia's 4th TV," 1995). In 1998, a fifth channel was added, called NTV7, operated by business interests based in East Malaysia and intended to "foster closer relations and better integration between the people of Sarawak, Sabah, and Peninsular Malaysia" ("NTV to begin," 1996). Another private channel authorized was IMT-TV, a station that was originally planned as a regional station based in Northern Malaysia to cover that portion of the peninsula as well as Thailand and Indonesia. This ambitious plan had to be shelved in the face of financial realities after the economic downturn of 1997. As of this writing, the latest private channel to be licensed is FTA TV Channel 8, expected to begin operation in 2001.

It is important not to make too much of the diversification that media privatization produced. Although TV3 had private ownership, the station's franchise was awarded to business interests having close ties to UMNO. Even though its ownership became more diversified as time passed, majority control remained in the hands of investors aligned with Barisan Nasional (see McDaniel, 1994, pp. 158–161). The award of later licenses followed the same prototype. Zaharom (1996) argued that instead of diversity, privatization actually produced concentration of ownership. From his perspective, the entire privatization exercise in Malaysia merely converted state monopolies into "private monopolies" that extended "the tentacles of the ruling coalition and its allies even wider across the Malaysian economy, adding economic and cultural domination to what is already a virtual political domination" (p. 52). The same restrictions in ownership seem to be the norm elsewhere in Southeast Asia. In Thailand, after the free speech movement of 1992 pushed the government to license additional television channels and to deregulate cable and satellite television, media choices were expected to broaden. Nonetheless, Ubonrat (1997, p. 74) found that "although the deregulation policy for the Thai broadcast media has opened up the system to more actors, it is confined to a handful of large corporations." The advantages enjoyed by these firms made it more difficult for smaller groups to enter the competition. In Indonesia, the first generation of private stations earned their licenses mainly by offering part ownership to members of the Suharto family. It was commonly understood that any corporation hoping to gain a license for a private channel had to provide shares to one of the Suharto children. For these reasons, the diversity produced by privatization was more illusory than real. In each case, the new media corporations could not possibly function in a totally independent manner from government and from majority political party interests.

Privatization has produced unexpected headaches for policy makers. For one thing, new private networks escalated commercial competition to unprecedented levels. I found that by 1990 in Malaysia, each hour of prime-time programming on both private and government channels included about ten minutes of commercial advertising, a substantial increase from just a few years earlier. By 1997, the most popular English-language program, the hour-long *X-Files,* sometimes contained more than fifteen minutes of advertising. The heavy commercial load was apparently a by-product of RTM's intense effort to increase revenues to end the need for annual parliamentary grants. This goal was a step toward the broadcaster's eventual release from direct government management. RTM's long-term objective was to reform itself into a semiautonomous corporate organization modeled along the lines of public broadcasters such as the NHK and the BBC. Despite more than a decade of planning and study, RTM's difficulties in attaining self-sufficiency and the reluctance of some in government to surrender control held the project in check through the 1990s.

Another outcome of privatization was the growth in program importation, just as predicted by Wildman and Siwek (1987). This was definitely seen in Malaysia and Indonesia, where the new private stations simply lacked resources necessary to fill program schedules by any other means. Moreover, competition for audiences and commercial pressures also forced government channels to include more of the "blockbuster" import shows to bolster their ratings. This occurred in Malaysia, even though RTM had been given a target of 70 percent local content, including programs in English, Tamil, and Mandarin. Ubonrat (1997, p. 69) commented on this in Thailand, noting that "the share of foreign content on the cable channels is higher than on the five terrestrial channels." But as Wildman and Siwek suggested, this was not a permanent condition. As I will detail later, in Malaysia, locally produced Malay dramas have overtaken imports in popularity, and a sizeable local production industry has sprung up to satisfy demand for them.

Privatization of media became the predominant policy adjustment of the last two decades of the twentieth century. It was a component of neo-liberal economic policy reform that swept across Asia after 1980. As I have suggested, however, authorities tended to arrange privatization so that stock in the new media firms was held by corporations owned by political parties or by investors aligned with political leaders, thus ensuring continued government control. For this reason, the diversity of opinion and viewpoints in programming did not increase in the way one might expect. Nevertheless, there were changes in program content after privatization. It appears that private broadcasters tended to present information and programs from a greater variety of sources compared with state media. State stations tended to emphasize government activities and development programs. Private radio and television catered more to viewers' preferences, both in the type of shows scheduled and the packaging and styles of presentation. And, of course, private television broadcasters were initially more reliant on foreign programming, a fact that sometimes produced political repercussions.

REFERENCES

40 years of broadcasting in Vietnam. (1986). *Asia-Pacific Broadcasting Union Newsletter,* No. 3.

Agassi, J. B. (1969). *Mass media in Indonesia.* Cambridge, MA: MIT Press.

Andaya, B. W., and Andaya, L. Y. (1982). *A history of Malaysia.* London: Macmillan.

Anderson, B. (1983). *Imagined communities.* New York: Verso.

Berg, E. (1987). The role of divestiture in economic growth. In S. H. Hanke (Ed.), *Privatization and development* (pp. 23–32). San Francisco: Institute for Contemporary Studies Press.

Coburn, J. F., and Wortzel, L. H. (1986). The problems of public enterprise in developing countries: Is privatization the solution? In W. P. Glade (Ed.), *State shrinking: A comparative inquiry into privatization* (pp. 24–39). Austin, TX: Institute of Latin American Studies.

Dyson, K., and Humphreys, P. (1986). Policies for new media in Western Europe: Deregulation of broadcasting and multi-media diversification. In K. Dyson and P. Humphreys (Eds.), *The politics of the communication revolution in Western Europe* (pp. 98–124). London: Frank Cass.

Fernandez, D. G. (1989). The Philippine press system 1811-1989. *Philippine studies, 37,* 317–344.

Frederick, W. H. (1997). Dreams of freedom, moments of despair: Armijn Pané and the imagining of modern Indonesian culture. In J. Schiller and B. Martin-Schiller (Eds.), *Imagining Indonesia* (pp. 54–89). Athens: Ohio University Press.

Hamelink, C. J. (1983). *Cultural autonomy in global communications: Planning national information policy.* New York: Longman.

Harper, T. (1988, January 24). British TV opens options. *Electronic Media.*

Harrison, B. (1966). *South-East Asia.* New York: St. Martin's Press.

Hoerip, H. (1984, July). *Working paper of the Television Training Center, Jakarta.* Unpublished paper presented at the Seminar on Management of Training and Meeting of Heads of Training, Kuala Lumpur.

Hula, R. C. (1988). *Market-based public policy.* New York: St. Martin's Press.

Le Duc, D. R. (1987). French and German new media policies: Variations on a familiar theme. *Journal of Broadcasting and Electronic Media, 31,* 427–447.

Lent, J. A. (1971). The Philippines. *The Asian newspapers' reluctant revolution.* Ames: Iowa State University Press.

Lent, J. A. (c. 1972). *Philippine mass communications before 1811 after 1966.* Manila: Philippine Press Institute.

Lintner, B. (1985a, March 28). News in the air. *Far Eastern Economic Review.*

Lintner, B. (1985b, March 28). The underground press. *Far Eastern Economic Review.*

McDaniel, D. O. (1994). *Broadcasting in the Malay world.* Norwood, NJ: Ablex.

More TV relay stations. (1985, March–April). *Asia-Pacific Broadcasting Union Newsletter.*

M'sia's 4th TV channel—MetroVision channel 8. (1995). *ABU News, 1.*

NTV to begin transmission by end of 1997. (1997, November 20). *New Straits Times.*

Oanh, N. X. (1995, April). Vietnam: Recent economic performance and development perspectives. Paper presented at the Fifth tun Abdul Razak Conference, Ohio University, Athens, Ohio.

Osborne, M. (1990). *Southeast Asia: An illustrated introductory history.* London: Allen and Unwin.

Paulu, B. (1974). *Radio and television broadcasting in Eastern Europe.* Minneapolis: University of Minnesota Press.

Pine, R. (1987). Broadcasting: Public or private? A survival strategy for dinosaurs. *InterMedia, 15*(4/5), 17–21.

Radio in Siam. (1931, October 21). *Straits Times.*

Reception in Malaya. (1931, July 8). *Straits Times.*

Reform of Malayan radio policy advocated. (1937, July 2). *Straits Times.*

Ricklefs, M. C. (1981). *A history of modern Indonesia.* New York: Macmillan.

Rideout, V., and Mosco, V. (1997). Communication policy in the United States. In M. Bailie and D. Winseck (Eds.). *Democratizing communication: Com-*

parative perspectives on information and power (pp. 81–104). Cresskill, NJ: Hampton Press.

Rosenberg, D. (1979). *Marcos and martial law in the Philippines.* Ithaca, NY: Cornell University Press.

Ryan, N. J. (1976). *The making of modern Malaysia and Singapore.* Kuala Lumpur: Oxford University Press.

SarDesai, D. R. (1994). *Southeast Asia past and present.* Boulder, CO: Westview Press.

Satellite footprints with firm two contracts SSA outbid AsiaSat on two Burma projects worth $2.5 m a year. (1998, March 26). *Asia Intelligence Wire.*

Schiller, H. I. (1975). The appearance of national communications policies: A new arena for social structure. *Gazette, 21,* 82–94.

Sennitt, A. G. (Ed.). (1996). *World Radio TV Handbook.* New York: Billboard Books.

Siebert, F. S. (1963). The authoritarian theory of the press. In F. S. Siebert, T. Peterson, and W. Schramm (Eds.), *Four theories of the press* (pp. 9–38). Urbana: University of Illinois Press.

Sir Shenton Thomas opens new Singapore broadcaster. (1937, March 2). *Straits Times.*

Surapone V. (1983). Mass media, tradition and change: An overview of Thailand. *Media Asia, 10,* 101–105.

Steinberg, D. J. (Ed.). (1987). *In search of Southeast Asia.* Honolulu: University of Hawaii Press.

Teodoro, L. V., and Kabatay, R. V. (1998). Mass media laws and regulations in the Philippines. Singapore: AMIC.

The new Singapore station. (1936, November 18). *Straits Times.*

Thitinan P. (1997). Thailand's media. In K. Hewison (Ed.), *Political change in Thailand: Democracy and participation* (pp. 217–232). New York: Routledge Press.

Thongchai Winichakul. (1994). *Siam mapped: A history of the geo-body of a nation.* Honolulu: University of Hawaii Press.

Turnbull, C. M. (1989). *A history of Malaysia, Singapore, and Brunei.* London: Allen and Unwin.

Ubonrat S. (1992). Radio broadcasting in Thailand. *Media Asia, 19,* 92–99.

Ubonrat S. (1994). The development of a participatory democracy: Raison d'etre for media reform in Thailand. *Southeast Asian Journal of Social Science, 22,* 101–114.

Ubonrat S. (1997). Limited competition without re-regulating the media. *Asian Journal of Communication, 7,* 57–74.

van der Kroef, J. (1954). The press in Indonesia: By-product of nationalism. *Journalism Quarterly, 31,* 337–346.

Vasquez, F. J. (1983). Media economics in the Third World. In J. Martin and A. G. Chaudhary (Eds.), *Comparative Mass Media Systems* (pp. 265–280). New York: Longman.

Vreeland, N. (1977). *Area handbook for Malaysia.* Washington, DC: American University.

Wildman, S. S., and Siwek, S. E. (1987). The privatization of European television: Effects on international markets for programs. *Columbia Journal of World Business, 22,* 74.

Zaharom, N. (1996). Rhetoric and realities: Malaysian television policy in an era of globalization. *Asian Journal of Communication, 6,* 43–64.

Chapter Three

Home Video and the Changing Media Environment

Before 1957, videotape recorders could be found only in research laboratories. **45** Although video recording had been demonstrated as early as 1950, practical devices had proven difficult to manufacture. The aim of experimentation was solely to produce a means of making video recordings for television studio and broadcast use. Development of consumer recording was out of the question, given technical capabilities. The need for a means to record television programs was urgent, however. The closest thing then available was the kinescope recording, made by filming images displayed on a cathode ray tube screen. Kinescope recordings had dreadful picture quality. The fundamental obstacle faced by manufacturers was that to achieve sufficient bandwidth for video recordings using methods employed in audio recorders, the tape had to move past recording heads at a speed of about eighty-five miles per hour! RCA constructed a video recorder that moved tape at a speed of twenty miles per hour, but even then miles of tape were needed just for brief recordings. Eventually, the solution found by the Ampex Corporation was to move both the heads and the tape simultaneously. This was accomplished by placing the heads on a disk that rotated at a speed of 14,400 rotations per minute, while a two-inch-wide tape was pulled past the whirling heads at fifteen inches per second. The earliest commercial videotape recorders were of an imposing size (twice the size of a large kitchen refrigerator), mechanically complex, and fussy to set up and maintain. But the need was great, and within just a few years video recorders became essential pieces of equipment for every television station in the industrialized world. According to Marlow and Secunda (1991), more than four hundred stations in the United States were equipped by 1960, and that number grew to more than one thousand stations five years later.

Demand for video recorders for use in nonbroadcast settings spurred further research aimed at shrinking the equipment's physical size and driving down its cost. Many believed that video recordings would be particularly useful in training and education and in some industrial settings. By the early 1970s, manufacturers had worked out solutions to some of the biggest issues and were offering so-called "helical" formats for applications not requiring broadcast technical standards. These industrial models later provided a basic platform from which to develop formats for home use. The new industrial formats packaged tape in cassettes rather than open reels. The U-matic format, based on three-quarter-inch tape cassettes, found its way in a few well-to-do homes, even though it was expensive and no prerecorded tapes were available. Usage of semiprofessional videocassette recorders (VCRs) in consumer settings generally took place where the demand for alternative media was unusually strong and where disposable income could support the VCRs' high cost. Countries in the Arab Gulf were the types of places where semiprofessional formats were used in homes.

CONSUMER VCR ADOPTION AROUND THE WORLD

The introduction of true consumer formats by the early 1970s, in the form of open-reel half-inch tape machines, began to prove the appeal of video for home use. But machines of this type did not succeed because they were still priced well above USD $1,000, they were large and heavy, and reels of tape could hold no more than a thirty-minute recording. The turning point came in the latter half of the decade when the introduction of the Betamax and VHS formats finally brought the costs down to a level that permitted adoption of the technology by middle-class viewers. Sony founder and chief executive officer Akio Morita foresaw the importance of VCRs as an adjunct to the television set, noting that "before the development of video recording, television was too fleeting. ... once a program has gone off the air it is gone forever for the TV viewer" (cited in Lyons, 1976, p. 210). Cassettes for the new formats could record two hours on a single tape, and the machines were compact. Engineers quickly overcame the two-hour limit by adapting the VHS format to record four hours per cassette. This was done to forestall Sony Betamax's domination of the U.S. market—the United States was the prime world market for home video, but there the two-hour limit was deemed inadequate for recording such things as popular sporting events. According to Baba and Imai (1992), the greater recording capacity of VHS cassettes turned the tide, and major U.S. manufacturers chose this format instead of Betamax. Even though Betamax remained a favored format in some parts of the world through the 1980s, the power of the marketing advantages won by VHS eventually made it the global standard for home use.

The popularity of VCRs grew in some areas at an astounding rate. The production of Japanese-manufactured VCRs increased from only 2.2 million units in 1979 to more than 27 million in 1984, a tenfold increase in just five years (Usami, 1988). Countries that were known as world leaders in adoption of VCR technology were in the Arab Gulf, where estimates placed the proportion of homes equipped with a VCR at or near 80 percent by 1986 (Boyd, Straubhaar, and Lent, 1989, p. 86). Second only to the Gulf region were the wealthier countries of Asia, including Singapore. Estimates by Survey Research Singapore placed the ownership of VCRs in the republic at a little less than 40 percent in 1983, a figure that had shot up from 3 percent just three years earlier ("Video ownership," 1984). Apparently from the beginning, Sony saw the developing countries as a crucial market for consumer video. Under the guidance of Akio Morita's brother Masaaki, Sony created a division to expand sales of products in less wealthy regions. Among other initiatives, Masaaki Morita headed Sony projects for the Shah's family in Iran and Marcos in the Philippines (Lyons, 1976, pp. 213–214).

The video market's size varied from place to place in large measure according to disposable income. Initial purchase prices for VCR units were high by Southeast Asian standards; pre-tariff retail costs of VCRs hovered around USD $1,000, with Betamax recorders costing slightly more than VHS units. By the end of the 1980s, low-end VCRs had dropped in cost by about two-thirds. Nations with higher per capita gross national product generally experienced earlier VCR adoption and a quicker rate of ownership growth. In the wealthiest countries, VCRs saturated the consumer market within a few years, typically by the late 1980s. A second factor in video's popularity was the scale of demand for television and film alternatives. In countries where local over-the-air television did not satisfy viewers, video usage grew at a faster rate. Television programming tended to fall short in satisfying viewers because of censoring and import restrictions, quotas on certain program types (for instance, shows in certain languages or types of programs such as sports), or simply because of the dullness of government television. Erotic films undoubtedly contributed to VCRs' rising popularity, though it is impossible to estimate their impact because in most countries such videos moved through hidden "under-the-counter" channels.

In addition, VCRs provided an important supplement to over-the-air television, which in the early 1980s was sometimes not yet available in outlying districts. At that time in Indonesia, scattered population pockets had no access to television via terrestrial broadcasting, and the same was true in many other countries, especially in the former Indochina and in Burma. VCRs often served as the first visual entertainment medium in those areas. There is no doubt that people in the countryside wanted this kind of diversion. According to Dahlan (1987), the 1983 agriculture census reported that roughly 47 percent of Indonesians over ten years of age living in nonurban areas watched television at least once weekly. This compared with weekly radio usage of about

65 percent of those surveyed. Because of television's limited coverage, radio remained the dominant medium for Indonesians through the 1980s. A 1989 study of media use in Jakarta, Bandung, Semarang, Surabaya, Medan, and Ujung Pandang reported by Survey Research Indonesia (SRI, 1989) indicated that 58 percent of adults listened to radio daily, up from 42 percent in 1981. According to the SRI figures, growth in television viewing over the same period slowed, probably due to the effects of VCRs; 58 percent of adults watched television each day in 1989, up only slightly from the 1985 estimate of 55 percent.

Around the world, the VCR changed the balance among mass media. Film attendance dropped steadily in most places as theater goers switched to video rentals. This had a disastrous effect on film production in Southeast Asian countries where the movie industry already had been ailing. Both the Philippines and Indonesia were nations that suffered in this way. But in some countries where television did not reach the whole population, or where it was not yet implemented, the VCR created new audiences. When I visited Belize in 1980, before the start of national television, VCRs had already become important sources of entertainment. Petch (1988) estimated that in 1988 the total number of VCRs in Belize came to about two thousand. Even though few in number, VCRs spread their influence across the entire country. In both rural and urban areas, video showings in public places brought television and movies to the poorest families. In one town, I saw showings of boxing matches and collections of programs recorded in the United States that were screened in a dance hall on Saturday nights. In another place, videos were played continuously in a village tavern. Whole families and hordes of children came to watch for hours, with no charge other than the purchase of a few tidbits or drinks. For Belize and for some other Caribbean countries, the large expatriate population living in the United States provided a steady supply of recorded programming. U.S. residents would videotape hours of programs, especially movies, and bring them to relatives on home visits. Video rental shops came later when VCR ownership became large enough to make a market of sufficient size.

In some countries VCRs became tremendously influential as information channels. Shane (1994) has written about the role they played in overcoming information controls exerted by the Soviet Union's government. Video hardware crossed borders into the Soviet Union via informal means such as "truck drivers on European runs and sailors returning from Asian voyages." As Shane said, "electronic equipment seeped into the Soviet Union the way water seeps into a leaky boat, and though for obvious reasons no reliable statistics were available, by the early 1990s there was a lot of it around" (p. 205). As for videos, Shane found that even the notoriously strict Soviet information authorities could not suppress the medium; its popularity raced out of control, catching the KGB and the party off guard. A cottage industry grew up to produce videos for underground trade. "Blithely ignoring copyright restrictions, entrepreneurs bought videocassettes of foreign films from tourists and traveling Soviet citizens, paid language students to record a crude one-voice dubbing in Russian, and churned out copies for the market" (p. 207). Information technologies such as the VCR changed the course of history in the USSR, and as Shane argued they were among the media that "doomed the seventy-four year Bolshevik experiment" thus demonstrating "the power of information both to liberate and to destroy" (p. 8).

VCRs IN MALAYSIA

Because of its comparatively well-to-do population and perceived shortcomings in television programming on government owned Radio Television Malaysia (RTM), Malaysia found itself exposed to a video invasion. Malaysia's per capita gross domestic product was estimated to be about RM4,100 in 1981 (*Information Malaysia 1982-1983,* 1983, p. 149), making it one of the richest nations in Asia, behind Japan, Hong Kong, Singapore, Taiwan, Brunei, and South Korea. Malaysia imposed heavy import duties on all electronic goods, including VCRs, and initially this helped dampen video's popularity. But those who journeyed abroad could buy units for a fraction of their cost at home. Malaysians were accustomed to regular shopping trips to duty-free Singapore, where retail outlets offered every type of video machine imaginable. Tariff barriers against importation of video equipment proved hard to maintain because thousands of miles of unpatrolled beaches in Malaysia made smuggling easy and mostly risk-free. In an effort to discourage clandestine imports of video recorders, the government levied enormous fines in a number of show trials. Typical of these was one involving a Singaporean who was nabbed at a customs checkpoint at Johore Bahru trying to smuggle four VCRs from Singapore into Malaysia. The man allegedly was to be paid RM100 to conceal the VCRs in hidden compartment in his auto while crossing the border, thus evading duties totaling RM2,700. He was fined RM200,000 for the offense ("$20,000 fine for bid to smuggle video recorders," 1982).

It is difficult to exaggerate the enthusiasm that accompanied video's arrival in Southeast Asia. In Malaysia and Singapore for instance, videos provided entertainment that was a dramatic departure from that being transmitted on television. For this reason the new medium cut sharply into audiences for over-the-air channels. As Minister of Information Adam Adib explained, "housewives now return from the market with their vegetables and fish under one arm, and the weekly video fare under the other" ("South-east Asian television," 1983). For the Chinese, videos containing programs produced by the major stations in Hong Kong (and occasionally Taiwan) had immense appeal because similar programs were in short supply on local television. Malays preferred Indonesian films on video, and members of the Tamil community favored Indian musical movies. Nearly everyone enjoyed videos containing highly promoted Hollywood action movies with big-name stars. In the early 1980s, crowds of viewers formed each weekend around video shops where movies would be played on VCRs to attract customers. The number of curious onlookers gathered around video monitors in these shops sometimes grew so great, they made the sidewalks literally impassible. Estimates in 1982 indicated that one out of five homes in Malaysia having a television set also had a VCR, a remarkable proportion at that early date. Just one year later estimates placed the number of VCRs at 220,000, a growth of one-third in just twelve months ("Video cassette recorders", 1983).

Malaysia's use of import duties to throttle the growth of video was soon recognized as a mistake. It forced police to spend an inordinate amount of energy in a hopeless effort to stop contraband hardware. In addition, the policy created a black market in cheap illegal goods that drained profits from legitimate enterprises. In response to these issues, tariffs on VCRs were reduced by 50 percent in 1983, with further reductions following in a matter of a few years (Soon, 1985). Tariff barriers were replaced with a more sophisticated policy for regulating video. The new policy was aimed at the main challenge posed by this new technology—VCRs allowed viewers to choose for themselves what they would watch and when they would watch it. In the view of officials, this could impair campaigns for national unification and might even raise the possibility of political destabilization. There was no doubt that video made control over the content of mass communication much more difficult. Video's diffusion through countless rental and trading channels meant that censoring had to be carried out before films and programs entered the distribution chain. Malaysia's answer was a two-pronged "carrot and stick" strategy, first to encourage audiences to choose closely monitored media and second to impose a rigid regulatory system on video distribution.

As briefly outlined in the preceding chapter, Malaysia was among the first Asian nations to participate in the global wave of media privatization. The private network TV Tiga (TV3) was inaugurated in 1984. Unlike the rationale for media privatization in other countries, Malaysia's aim was not merely to undertake neo-liberal restructuring in one small segment of the national economy, but to create a service that would draw viewers back from video. To do this, TV3 had to present types of programs that were lacking in the schedules of state-owned RTM. Grumbling about the staid programming on RTM was heard regularly, and it was thought the new channel might add a fresh excitement to television, perhaps even jolting the government station into more imaginative ways of serving its viewers. As the general manager of Fleet Group (the private station's corporate owner) Encik Mohamed Tawfik bin Tun Dr. Ismail said, "there is a big gap between what the government wants to do (on television) and what the people actually want to experience" ("Sparks Are Flying," 1984). Privatization had other benefits. The new channel could be

equipped with up-to-date gear, and government would not have to invest a *sen*
[cent].

The key to television's privatization was that although the commercial stations were not owned by the state, the corporations that did own them were intimately associated with leading political figures and to UMNO (United Malays National Organization), the lead party in the national coalition. Therefore, the private network could be expected to harmonize its operations with the wishes of political leaders. Government announcements issued shortly after the licensing of TV3 stressed this point. A public statement issued by the Information Ministry in August 1983 stated that "conditions would be imposed to ensure the [new private] channel is operated based on the principles of the Rukunegara [Malaysia's national ideology], of Islam being the national religion, and of national security" ("Conditions for third channel," 1983). Later, speaking prior to the new station's launch, Minister of Information Adam Adib hardly veiled his government's warning, saying that "besides being required to confront the video craze, the proposed network must be viable not only in dollars and cents but also in terms of the national interest" ("Sparks Are Flying," 1984). Malaysia was not alone in adding television channels to win viewers back from video; neighboring Singapore and Thailand made plans for new television outlets at about the time. Although the motives of both countries were apparently similar to those of Malaysia, their approaches were completely different. Singapore's new service aimed to telecast highbrow programs such as symphonic concerts and serious drama, whereas plans in Thailand called for an elaborate microwave pay-TV system ("Southeast Asian television," 1983).

Malaysian policy makers' concern was that ethnic divisions might be reinforced by watching videos produced in India and Hong Kong in Indian and Chinese languages. The cultural chasm dividing Chinese, Malay, and Indian communities was clearly evident in ownership of electronic devices. Survey Research Malaysia found that in 1986, 86 percent of Malays reported they owned one or more radios; 84 percent indicated they had a television set. Among Indian and Chinese homes, the two media had significantly broader ownership—95 percent of families in the two communities had both radio and television sets. An even greater contrast was apparent in video. In 1986, VCRs were still not common in Malay homes; only 11 percent reported their families owned one. Among Indian-Malaysians, 46 percent reported having a VCR, a rate about four times higher than Malays. Among Chinese, however, the VCR enjoyed its widest acceptance; 64 percent of those surveyed said they kept one in their homes (Survey Research Malaysia, 1987).

Policy makers assumed that video was more popular among Chinese and Indian viewers because of its ability to provide culturally familiar entertainment in languages used in their homes. For these two groups, there was little of this available on broadcast television. This country is very much a multilingual society. In the Chinese community many dialects are spoken, including Hokkien, Fukien, Cantonese, and, especially among the educated, Mandarin. Among Malaysian Indians, Tamil is the most common, but Punjabi, Malayalam, and other regional Indian languages are spoken as well. For speakers of these minority dialect and regional languages, the only source of entertainment programming was video. An examination of programming during a typical week, August 18, 1985, illustrates this point. RTM's first channel that week offered not a single program in any Chinese or Indian language, although its lineup did offer a documentary on Monday at 7:00 P.M. titled *Ke Arah Pembangunan* [Towards Development], a program in the national language called *Agama Bimbingan* [Religious Guidance] each evening at 9:15 P.M., a number of locally produced programs in Bahasa Malaysia, and numerous imported shows from the United States including ones such as *Gilligan's Island* and *NBA Basketball*. RTM2 presented news in Tamil each evening at 7:00 P.M. and in Mandarin at 9:30 P.M., two hours of an imported Chinese serial beginning at 8:40 P.M. on Wednesday, and on Saturday a Hindi movie at 4 P.M. Otherwise all other programs were in English or Bahasa Malaysia (Malay). One study found that RTM2 broadcast fourteen hours of Chinese programming monthly in 1983 (Badrul, 1989). Only TV3 offered a consistent alternative with its "Chinese Belt" at 7 P.M., when it aired a Hong Kong serial drama every evening of the week. The remainder of the private station's schedule was comprised exclusively of English-language imports from the United States or Britain with a sprinkling of locally produced Malay shows; no Indian language programming was offered ("Your weekly TV guide," 1985).

An explanation of national policies on language and media may help the reader appreciate why the program schedules just described were offered. These policies had their genesis in an eruption of communal rioting on May 13, 1969. For several days after that date the country was racked with deadly clashes between the Malay and Chinese communities. These disturbances accompanied the unexpected success of Chinese political parties in an election in which Chinese and Malay parties opposed each other. Following the violence, a comprehensive set of policies was enacted to stifle frictions and to speed up social integration, including some sweeping changes in the rules for broadcasting. A code was formulated by the Minister of Information, requiring radio and television to advance "communal harmony, religious tolerance and international understanding" (K. L. Ow, personal communication, June 25, 1970). To realize this aim, broadcasters, especially RTM, are expected to emphasize programs in Bahasa Malaysia, the national language, and to give prominence to Islam, the national religion. The objective is to promote these as common aspects of the ethnically diverse Malaysian society. RTM, after the 1969 communal fighting, has been required "to foster national unity in [Malaysia's] multiracial society through the extensive use of Bahasa Malaysia" (Ministry of Information, 1989).

The introduction of the new private channel had an immediate impact on the videos available for rental. As *Sunday Mail* columnist Chew Lay See (1984) explained, "of late video offerings in the Klang region have been rather lacklustre [sic] due mainly to hesitancy on the dealer's part to import really good tapes, after having seen their takings plunge following the TV3 launch." Gigantic audiences watched the Chinese belt programming each evening, which consisted of the same types of drama that had been so popular on video. These serials were a mixture of costume and modern drama, filled with action and melodrama, and enormously entertaining. Even though these programs had Chinese settings and themes, some of the shows drew appreciable viewership from other ethnic groups. For example, in one typical week in midyear 1989, the Hong Kong series titled *Joyful Campus* aired, winning a thirty-three share among Chinese viewers, but also gaining an eleven share among Malays (Survey Research Malaysia, 1989).

The second thrust of new government policy on videos was to contain the spread of films and other programs deemed morally unsuitable or contrary to national objectives. This initiative was embodied in a new law requiring the licensing of videos sold or rented in Malaysia. To obtain the license required for a video to be circulated legally, master tapes had to be censored and approved under supervision of the Software and Systems for Industries and Enterprises (SIE) agency. Actual censoring of videos was the responsibility of the Film Censorship Board. SIE had set up seventeen centers around the country to process tapes. Master tapes imported for the purpose of making rental copies had to be screened, and once cleared, given "A" certificates. Copies made from approved masters were issued "B" certificates to show they were ready for rental or sales. Videos lacking this certificate were deemed illegal and subject to seizure by police and to stiff fines levied against their owners. Each copy had to carry the name of the company duplicating the tape and the registration number of the master videotape. The Home Ministry had responsibility for overseeing video imports. It charged between RM12 and RM26 (USD $4.80 to $10.40) for every "B" certificate issued, depending on tape length, a sum that added substantially to the cost of each video. Beyond this, firms that copied and sold legally certified videos also had to be licensed. Each of these licenses required a deposit of RM2,500 (USD $1,000) and an annual fee of RM400 (USD $160). Failure to obtain this license subjected dealers to fines of RM50,000 (USD $20,000) or two-year jail terms ("'No' to video raids," 1984).

Several justifications were offered the public for this elaborate system. One explanation was that licensing blocked "pornographic tapes and those of excessive violence" ("Police crackdown," 1983). Another was the need to protect "legal" video operators. According to Encik Ahmad Haji Zainuddin, manager director of SIE, there were twenty to thirty thousand employed in the trade, and it was necessary to "legalize" the industry to keep it from "going down"

("Video centres," 1984). To bolster officially sanctioned video enterprises, SIE encouraged establishment of standardized rental fees. In the states of Kelantan and Terengganu, an association formed among rental operators with the support of SIE tried to enforce a standard rental rate of RM5 for a three-hour tape and RM3 for a two-hour tape.

To force compliance with the new system, highly publicized police raids were staged beginning in March 1983. Reportedly, in the first day of a nationwide crackdown, more than 33,000 uncensored tapes were taken by police ("Police crackdown," 1983). The pressure was sustained for many months by mounting regular raids. In another splashy national sweep, thousands of videos were seized in thirty-two coordinated police raids across the country on a single evening in September 1984. Police claimed in that action to have taken about 3,300 master tapes worth approximately RM300,000. Police expressed surprise at the breadth of the tapes' distribution, noting that some of the videos were found in outlying towns far away from the coast. It appears that the target of these raids were not pornographic film distributors but operators who were renting uncensored Chinese language imports. A police spokesman in Kedah, Aziz Harun, reported that none of the videos taken in his state were "X rated," but he also revealed that some operators had closed on the day prior to the raids because they had "smelled us" ("2,034 video tapes," 1984). Officials indicated that the tapes probably were smuggled into Malaysia by ship from Hong Kong.

The fact that early raids were targeted at distributors of Chinese programs, rather than of sexually explicit films, suggests that the main motives behind these arrests were not moral or religious but ideological in nature. This is not to say that pornographic videos were of no interest to police, however. As the raids on video copying and distribution centers continued sporadically over succeeding months, they occasionally netted individuals involved in production of pornography. These enterprises tended to be small and scattered. An example was an arrest in Penang in July 1987 in which a man was found to have stored about 230 sexually oriented videos in the apartment from which he operated. Officers believed that the materials were rented through a bookstore that also sold adult books and magazines. The man apparently rented videos for RM3.50 per week. According to police the films were "produced in foreign countries," reportedly Hong Kong, Singapore, India, Australia, and Japan ("Porn video," 1987). Police raids on video centers became an enduring feature of Malaysian efforts to stamp out illegal distribution. In the first three months of 2000, there were about a half-dozen police strikes. In one, a sixteen-year-old youth was held after police found "obscene" video recordings in his possession ("Teenager pleads," 2000), and in another as many as one hundred thousand recordings were seized from a shopping complex ("Pirated VCDs," 2000).

In the late 1980s, I had the experience of clearing videotapes through this system. A family member sent me a package containing, among other things, a video recording of an American professional football game. The videos were shipped by mail, so it could only be claimed at a postal office specializing in express mail and foreign packages. On arrival, I had to open the parcel for a postal inspector. When he saw the contents, I was told that the cassette could not be released until I presented a video import license. To obtain this, I had to pay fees and file appropriate documentation, which I decided to do. In due course, I was able to present the required license, whereupon postal authorities turned the video over to the censoring board maintained by FINAS, a government agency supporting Malaysia's film industry. I then had to pay fees and provide further documentation for it to be screened and issued proper certification. The entire process was not especially cumbersome and fees were modest, but about six weeks were needed to negotiate all the steps required to import the cassette. And yes, censors seemed to have viewed the entire (tedious, as it turned out) three-hour football match.

It should be stressed that early 1980s video regulations were intended purely to ensure that videotapes in circulation had been censored; laws had no effect on distribution of noncopyrighted materials. Unauthorized reproduction and rental of copyrighted videos were entirely separate issues, ones which government officials at first were reluctant to tackle. By 1986, the availability of videos copied without permission had become so pervasive, Derrik Khoo observed that "pirate video programs are as common as legitimate videotapes in Malaysia" ("No hope," 1986). Through the early part of the 1980s, Southeast Asia had become a place where copies of films, music records, and computer software were produced without consideration of international copyright. Not only were unauthorized copies of such materials available locally, but the region also developed a brisk international trade in pirate tapes and floppy disks. In Malaysia, this happened because copyright laws had an important proviso: unless films, video, and other types of software were released by the copyright holder in Malaysia within 30 days of release elsewhere, there was no right to protection. This arrangement was common in other Southeast Asian countries as well, and it meant that the majority of English-language movies could be copied freely there since only a small portion could be screened profitably in local theaters. To protect the most popular films, distributors shipped them into Southeast Asia for one showing per country before the expiration of the 30-day deadline. Sometimes, the screening would be scheduled at an odd hour such as 1:00 A.M. or 2:00 A.M., after which the film would be sent onward by air to the next destination. Later, when more prints could be made available, films would return for their regular run of one, two, or more weeks. Films not lucky enough to gain protection in this way were likely to end up on video store shelves, copied by local entrepreneurs from master tapes acquired without permission. Videotapes like this often carried copyright warnings identifying the recordings as made for internal use by the movie studios.

Malaysia, Thailand, Singapore, and Indonesia were often mentioned as countries where wholesale pirating of videos, music, computer software, and even books were tolerated in the 1980s. The underground industry flourished in these countries because regulatory frameworks lagged far behind production technologies, and because the issue of intellectual property rights had little saliency among policy makers at the time. Nonetheless, the unflattering attention brought about by illegal duplication of recordings eventually aroused sufficient international pressure so that one by one countries agreed to rewrite copyright laws. In Malaysia, the Copyright Act of 1987 led to an immediate reduction in availability of cheap unauthorized computer software and videos. Such items disappeared from shops literally overnight. Retailers did not necessarily see firm enforcement of the new law's provisions as undesirable. The manager of one of Kuala Lumpur's largest computer shops, Alan Choy, observed at the time that "while the act will stabilize the computer industry, it will also in the process, weed out the weak [retail firms]." He was emphatic that his company would dissociate itself from unauthorized software suppliers pledging "we will not deal with pirates. The stakes are too high" ("The morning," 1987). Although enforcement of the new law was initially forceful, before long copied items began to be sold again, and a wide array of pirated software continued to be available.

POLITICS ON VIDEO

When recordings are used to project political themes, they can become enormously powerful persuasive tools, and videos frequently have been employed for this purpose. Perhaps one of video's most striking attributes is its capacity to animate and give undeniable authenticity to its messages. For instance, it is one thing to hear about violent military clashes but quite another to see carnage and blood spilled on the screen. Much has been written about this in the United States, where during the war in Vietnam viewers were confronted with a cavalcade of disturbing images from the front lines on each evening's television newscasts. Many observers believe this ultimately brought antiwar demonstrations onto streets and U.S. diplomats to the negotiating table. The fact that videos can present ideas compellingly and also can be distributed without much interference make them doubly attractive to political opposition groups.

There are many examples of the political use of videos in Southeast Asia, but one of the earliest occurred in Indonesia. Although video was only minimally troublesome to Jakarta authorities in its early years, one incident offered a glimpse of official concern about the medium. Indonesia's military launched a large-scale campaign dubbed Operation *Sapujagad* in 1980 against presumed subversive elements that were accused of spreading their ideas by videos. The drive reportedly was aimed at Communist agitators who were trying to revive their party on Java and Sumatra. Skeptics said that the drive was an indication of "the government's own paranoia," nevertheless government pointed to rising crime rates as evidence of the political movement's ill effects. The specific claim about video use centered on the distribution of cassettes containing purportedly "anti-government political propaganda" in the city of Bandung, West Java's capital, although no copies were shown to journalists or to scholars (Sacerdoti, 1980).

In Malaysia, opposition parties are essentially cut off from mainstream electronic media. Their spokespersons are rarely seen on television, and when they do appear it usually involves their presentation in a less than favorable light. These political parties therefore consider videos an important means of reaching their potential constituencies and as a tool for rallying their cause. One example of this is the Parti Islam (PAS) video portraying the Memali incident on November 19, 1984. Distribution was said to be extensive within Kelantan and Trengganu, two states where PAS enjoys strong support. The video claimed to show how residents of the tiny village of Memali were massacred as a result of government efforts to suppress a small religious movement. Claims made by PAS were, of course, denied by government officials. Deputy Information Minister Kassim Ahmad denounced the video as an effort to distort the incident, declaring that bodies of women and children were shown "scattered all over the place like they had been killed by the police." He proposed that the same could happen anywhere unless the public was not "vigilant against groups who tried to inflame the people to hate government" ("Pas distributing," 1986). A spokesperson for PAS, deputy president Haji Fadzil Noor responded that the video proved village residents did not attack the police and that the government was indeed responsible for the bloody outcome.

One of the most bizarre political uses of videos came to light in 1989 when opposition parliamentarian and long-time government critic Karpal Singh asked Home Ministry officials during parliamentary debate for clarification of allegations about Malaysian Indian Congress (MIC) party leaders. He claimed that deputy speaker of Parliament and MIC secretary-general D. P. Vijandran lodged a complaint with police about a break-in at his home. Following the complaint, according to Karpal Singh, police had arrested several suspects who had in their custody tapes containing pornographic scenes involving "an MIC leader, wives of some personalities, and typists and clerks of Maika Holdings [an investment firm associated with MIC]." An excited debate over the truth of the report and the proper handling of the scandalous accusations ensued in Parliament, during the course of which another of the opposition representatives asked, "if the tapes can be found, can they be shown [in Parliament]?" This suggestion was immediately overruled by the presiding speaker, saying there "was no provision for such a procedure" ("Repartee over," 1989). Later, the prime minister, in speaking to the press, wondered aloud how Karpal Singh knew so much about the tapes if "he did not have the tapes and had not seen them" ("Tape issue," 1989).

For weeks speculation about the Vijandran story swirled around the capital city. Finally, in early January 1990, police acknowledged that they had indeed received the tapes but that officers had destroyed all materials recovered from the burglary. According to police officials, they followed advice from legal counsel and burned eleven videocassettes and six envelopes of photos and negatives that they had confiscated. Police also revealed that they had declared the case "closed" and had released the six persons held in connection with the theft. Although police may have destroyed the tapes, someone had apparently made copies. Over the following year I was twice offered copies of the tape (an offer I naturally declined), but numerous informants said they had seen or knew others who had seen the tape. Prime Minister Dr. Mahathir accused Karpal Singh himself of planning the robbery "after obtaining information from certain people that there were pornographic videos in the safe in Mr. Vijandran's house." The Prime Minister observed that "sometimes there are people who are perverts who like to stand naked in front of mirrors. Now with the latest technology available, there might be some who like to tape themselves in the nude" ("PM: Karpal," 1990). The full story of how the tapes came to be taken from the politician's home and copies distributed through a network of video operatives has never been revealed, but few doubt that the caper had any other motive than damage to the MIC leader's political career. The case had an unhappy ending for Vijandran, who had to resign his post, a man who, through the political use of video recordings, had been turned into a national object of disgrace and the butt of off-color humor by his political enemies.

SINGAPORE AND THE SPEAK MANDARIN CAMPAIGN

Singapore was another nation that experienced a rapid influx of video recorders in the early 1980s. One source claimed that in 1983 the country had one of the highest penetration rates in the world, 62.7 percent of television homes ("Video cassette recorders," 1983). Survey Research Singapore (SRS) found in November of the same year that 38 percent of all households owned a VCR, a figure SRS reported had climbed from just 3 percent in three years ("Video ownership," 1984). Singapore had the highest per capita income in Southeast Asia, except for Brunei, and VCRs were available at remarkably low prices. They were sold in the innumerable shops in tourist areas along Orchard Road at such low prices that visitors from places such as Australia and Pacific islands came just to purchase them to take home.

Like Malaysia, Singapore tried to draw viewers back to television with a
greater variety of programs, but unlike its neighbor, it opted to expand state
broadcasting activities rather than establish private television. As part of the effort to augment broadcast choices, Singapore Broadcasting Corporation
(SBC) announced plans in 1983 to enlarge its drama offerings and to
strengthen and increase programming for children and teenagers on all channels ("Eyes on increased," 1983). Strictly speaking, SBC was not a government
organization; it had been converted to a public corporation as a statutory
board in 1980. The third Singapore channel, which signed on the air in 1984,
was intended to offer a service quite different from the mass-appeal programs
on the first two channels. Minister of Foreign Affairs and Culture Dhanabalan
said the new station, known as Channel 12, would "help to stimulate an increase in art and appreciation of finer things in life, as well as act as an infor-
mative source to widen the intellectual vistas of the people of Singapore"
("Third channel," 1984). Among other programs, the new channel was set up
to transmit performances by the Singapore Symphony Orchestra, quality doc-
umentaries, and serious dramatic performances. Channel 12 began with only
a brief daily schedule, on the air from 8:00 P.M. to 10:30 P.M. nightly. The new
channel did not meet with the positive response expected, however, and by the
end of 1984 viewership slumped to just 17,000. This forced SBC to revise
plans to include more popular offerings in its schedule. Among the changes
made were transfers of some of the more highly rated shows from the main
channels to Channel 12 and the addition of several sports shows, Asian films,
and Chinese opera, all of which necessitated an expansion in transmission
hours ("More sports," 1986).

Like their Malaysian counterparts, Singapore policy makers had complicated motives for their efforts to stifle video. Until the mid-1990s, the government supported broadcasting. If video became popular enough to erode
broadcast audiences, cuts in advertising revenues would surely follow, and this
would transfer a greater share of television's cost to the national budget. Unlike Malaysia, there was none of the distrust of foreign ideology that influenced public officials to steer viewers away from the popular Chinese programs from Hong Kong. Instead, in Singapore official opposition to the
"dialect" Cantonese found in videos from Hong Kong was probably a greater
factor. The drive to suppress dialects began with the "Speak Mandarin" campaign starting in 1979.

The importance of the dialect issue lies in the fact that more than three-
quarters of Singapore's population is ethnic Chinese. With the exception of the
peranakan (Chinese whose families migrated to the region before European
colonialism, also known as Straits Chinese), most Chinese Singaporeans still
retain an identity and a language affinity for the region of China from which
their families originated. Most immigrants in the nineteenth and twentieth
centuries came from Southern China and therefore they spoke the dialects as-

sociated with that region. These included Hainanese, Cantonese, Hakka, and the like. Although somewhat similar, these dialects are mutually unintelligible. Because of this, each language group devolved into its own community within Singapore, creating sets of subgroups that partitioned the city-state. Obviously desirous of eliminating these barriers, the government sought a suitable link language around which to achieve unification. Although English was (and is) spoken by the majority of Singaporeans, the language was not seen as a solution to the dialect problem. Many Chinese felt a strong attachment to their Chinese identity, and the imposition of a Western language would have created additional resistance to the adoption of a new language. Consequently, the choice was Mandarin, a language that had served as the language of educated Chinese for centuries. Beyond this, Kuo (1984) noted two additional reasons for the choice of Mandarin: making this a common language for the Chinese-speaking community would eventually reduce the burden on the school system to educate all students in the language. It would also enhance Singaporeans' ability to interact with social and commercial contacts in the People's Republic of China, where Mandarin is called *pu tong hua,* the "common language."

In a country of many social campaigns, the Speak Mandarin offensive became unusual in its high profile and its endurance, lasting through the 1980s and 1990s. Basically, the campaign aimed to eliminate all public use of dialects, replacing them with Mandarin. It should be emphasized that there was no attempt to restrict English usage or to replace it with Mandarin. Through the 1980s and 1990s, signs reminded visitors to "Speak Mandarin instead of dialect" as they entered government buildings or stepped to an enquiry counter. These urgings were backed by regular pronouncements by officials who called on residents' national pride and patriotism to learn and use the common language in the Chinese community.

The "Speak Mandarin" drive had an immediate impact on broadcasting, as Radio Television Singapore began dubbing dialect-Chinese television programs into Mandarin in 1979. Since that time only limited schedules of dialect programs were permitted on radio—as a "service to the elderly"—and traditional performance arts on radio and television where use of dialect was an integral part of the presentation. Essentially all other Chinese-language programming was converted to Mandarin. After 1979, the easiest way to view television programs of the popular Hong Kong television serials in the original language was via video. Video shops stocked these shows, and they were very popular with cassette renters. This provided officials a motive to squelch videos. But video had a strong hold on Singapore. By 1987, VCR ownership was reported by three-quarters of Singapore households ("Singapore leads," 1988).

Singapore's video experience foregrounds a critical aspect of what came to be known as cultural globalization—as popular culture forms began to travel across national borders with fewer restraints, media's effectiveness as a tool for building unified national identities was reduced. Governments wanted to use broadcasting to build national cohesion. Viewers and listeners, on the other hand, wanted media for entertainment, and the sources of the entertainment were not their principal concern. Hollywood, Bollywood (in India), London, and other of the world's popular culture production centers had the resources and knowledge to create entertainment that could move freely across cultural divisions. Films and television shows from these centers were especially challenging to countries having large immigrant populations, such as Singapore and Malaysia, where allegiances were divided between the local culture and their homelands. In these two countries both Indian and Chinese residents still retain a sense of being connected with the societies from which their parents and grandparents originated.

Few other aspects of culture seem to capture the essence of cultural identity as fully as language. It is because of this that language policy has assumed such exaggerated significance in Southeast Asia, and Singapore's Speak Mandarin campaign provides a useful case for study. Ironically, this campaign had served to continually remind Singaporeans of identity issues, that despite the rhetoric the republic's population is not yet fully unified. As Birch (1992) noted, the campaign keeps "the issue of Singapore identity—what it is that makes a person Singaporean, and therefore willing to sacrifice for the good of Singapore—constantly in focus." Singapore's Chinese community is not only split by dialect languages, there is a social gulf between English- and Chinese-speaking subgroups. Of course nearly every Chinese Singaporean can speak some of both, but individuals tend to have a predisposition for the language they use at home. This preference reinforces itself in the language people choose for their family's education; both English and Mandarin education are options available in Singapore.s

VIDEO CDs

At the end of the 1990s, videos began to be distributed in the new video compact disk (VCD) format that swiftly overtook videocassettes' popularity. These CDs look like DVD recordings but are computer CDs containing MPEG video files, encoded in so-called "White Book" standard, usually version 2.0. video CD player units designed to be connected with conventional television sets became available for as little as RM300 (USD $80). Even fancy miniature portable units could be obtained for under RM550 (USD $150). Any up-to-date computer using Microsoft Windows 95 or later could play the files using the Active Movie features built into the operating system. Macintosh computers could play the CDs as well, although only a small proportion of Southeast Asians users owned Apple products. Video CDs suffer from serious imperfections. To squeeze a full-length movie onto two CDs, with their limitation of 640 megabytes per disk, high levels of digital compression is required. The resulting video lacks resolution and sometimes suffers from artifacts of digital processing such as blotchy colors, poor lip sync, and stuttering movements. These effects are compounded when the computer employed is not fast enough to keep up with the strenuous processing demands of simultaneous video and audio streams.

VCDs practically eliminated sales and rental of videocassettes by the end of the 1990s. At that time in Malaysia, the cost of legal VCD or video copies of individual movies ranged from RM20 to RM40 (USD $5.20 to $10.40). But unauthorized pirate versions were equally easy to buy on street corners and in lobbies of shopping malls where hundreds of titles were on offer. These typically sold for RM8 (USD $2.10) or less per film. At these prices, videocassette rental suffered badly; for little more than a rental fee, a VCD providing unlimited use could be purchased. Cost was not the only factor in favor of pirate copies; most were not censored. As explained by journalist Zainal Alam Kadir (1999),

> Pay RM10 for a heavily-censored film at the cinema or spend as low as RM5 for a "full-length" unedited version of the latest movie title on counterfeited video compact disc (VCD). This is the kind of decision a Malaysian has to make every time a new movie title comes to town. The most "logical" solution is (no matter how perverse it is), for an average Malaysian, is to go for the second choice.

The resurgence of pirating spawned by this new distribution medium was phenomenal. As in the heyday of videocassette copying, titles appeared on the street even while films were in their first run showings at local theaters. Even movies banned in Malaysia, such as *Schindler's List*, were easily obtained from sales kiosks in busy shopping centers. By 2001, pirate copies of movies had become so plentiful that distributors were forced to reduce pricing of legal copies. The new price scheme lowered costs from RM40 to RM17, about USD $4.50. According to the Video and Film Industry Association of Malaysia (Vifim), the industry group that represents the major studios in Hollywood, 80 percent of the market was held by the pirate VCD producers. This resulted in an estimated loss of USD $40 million, a figure that placed Malaysia second only to China as a pirate marketplace (Lau, 2001). Police sweeps against pirating yielded progressively larger hauls of illegal copies as VCDs grew in popularity. In 1995, the number of videotapes and discs seized was re-

ported to be 99,445, increasing to 231,482 in 1996, and to 949,351 in 1997
(Asiah, 1998).

All across Southeast Asia, VCDs had a similar impact. Pirate VCDs sold for P100 in the Philippines, roughly USD $2, a figure that seems to have been common across the region. In Indonesia, the decision was made to stamp out pirate distribution in early 1999. The pervasiveness of VCDs can be inferred from official estimates that as many as 33,000 persons would be put out of work if pirate distribution were stopped by the drive. The *Jakarta Post* suggested that the crackdown be focused on the major suppliers of illegal VCDs, citing one source that claimed "there are only three or four big VCD pirates here. They are not invisible but just untouchable because of the power of their money." The newspaper reported that only three suppliers "own 85 percent of the country's total annual production of 17 million copies of pirated VCDs" ("Indonesia's plan," 1999). Facing mounting international pressure to halt production of illegal videos, measures were adopted to put pirate operators out of business in the major supply countries of Taiwan, China, Hong Kong, Macao, and Thailand. Nonetheless, moves in those countries appeared to have simply caused pirate firms to relocate their operating bases in countries such as the Philippines and Malaysia. In 1999, a report from the International Intellectual Property Alliance (IIPA), a group representing U.S. copyright interests, identified Malaysia as "one of the world's leading exporters of illegal optical media products throughout Asia and, increasingly, to other markets worldwide" (Oh, 2000). Optical media products include audio CDs, CD-ROMs, DVDs, as well as VCDs. Singapore was one country where police raids appeared to have significantly shrunk pirate VCD distribution. Kang (2000) reported a decline of half in the number of illegal copies seized by police between 1999 and 2000, the reduction attributed to a smaller number of outlets selling them.

An insight into Southeast Asian attitudes toward the proliferation of pirate video CDs can be gained from a news analysis piece by Shareem Amry (2000). Her piece considered the appeal of inexpensive VCDs, which she admitted was "difficult to resist." In her view, the problem was that "Ministry officials not only have limited resources" but that legal action was "stymied by the intellectual property owner's reluctance to show up and testify in court." By this she meant that production houses in Hollywood or Bombay were expected to appear in Malaysian courts to testify against pirate manufacturers and distributors to gain redress. Although such testimony would be critical to prosecute cases, one can sympathize with producers' reluctance to accept the costs involved in sending representatives to Malaysia to participate in cases for a market of marginal importance in their global distribution plans. Shareem noted that "additional intellectual property laws are in the process of being enacted to supplement the Government's arsenal against this scourge" and proposed that an "autonomous body" be created to take charge of actions against pirating. Another perspective on the protection of intellectual property rights was revealed in a bitter editorial appearing in the *New Straits Times*. In it, the editorialist asserted that the WTO's patent regime by "US and her allies" in the Marrakesh Agreement on Trade-Related Aspects of Intellectual Property Rights "will deprive the developing countries of the option of reverse engineering, as was done by Japan, Taiwan, and Korea in their early industrialized days" ("What's new," 2000). In other words, the editorial argued that Malaysia and other developing countries were deprived of their right to achievements attained earlier by other Asian tigers. No explanation was offered in the piece to justify equating "reverse engineering" with unauthorized copying of intellectual properties.

REFERENCES

2,034 video tapes seized in raids. (1984, September 3). *New Straits Times.*

$20,000 fine for bid to smuggle video recorders. (1982, August 2). *New Straits Times.*

Asiah B. (1998, October 12). Country loses RM500m annually to CD pirates. *Business Times* (Malaysia).

Baba, Y., and Imai, K. (1992). Systemic innovation and cross-border networks: The case of the evolution of the VCR systems. In F. M. Scherer and M. Perlman (Eds.), *Entrepreneurship, technological innovation and economic growth* (pp. 141–152). Ann Arbor: University of Michigan Press.

Badrul Risham Naruddin. (1989, September). RTM2 mahu ke mana [Where is RTM2 headed]? *Dewan Masyarakat.*

Birch, D. (1992). Talking politics: Radio Singapore. *The Australian Journal of Media and Culture, 6*(1), Retrieved February 10, 2000 from the World Wide Web: kali.murdoch.edu.au/~cntinuum/6.1/Birch.html.

Boyd, D., Straubhaar, J. D., and Lent, J. A. (1989). *Videocassette recorders in the Third World.* White Plains, NY: Longman.

Chew Lay See. (1984, September 2). Gloom after the raid by the cops. *Sunday Mail.*

Conditions for third channel. (1983, August 12). *New Straits Times.*

Dahlan, M. A. (1987). The Palapa project and rural development in Indonesia. *Media Asia, 14,* 28–36.

Eyes on increased sales. (1983, May–June). *Asia-Pacific Broadcasting Union Newsletter, 28.*

Indonesia's plan to eliminate pirate VCDs gets good response. (1999, February 26). *Xinhua News Agency.*

Information Malaysia 1982-83. (1983). Kuala Lumpur: Berita Publishing.

Kang, J. (2000, December 19). Fewer porn VCDs seized this year. *Straits Times.*

Kuo, E. C. Y. (1984). Mass media and language planning: Singapore's Speak Mandarin campaign. *Journal of Communication, 34*(2), 24–35.

Lau, L. (2001, February 21). Cheaper videos, VCDs in KL to beat piracy. *New Straits Times.*

Lyons, N. (1976). *The Sony vision.* New York: Crown Publishers.

Marlow, E., and Secunda, E. (1991). *Shifting time and space.* New York: Praeger.

Ministry of Information. (1989). *Radio Television Malaysia.* Kuala Lumpur: Department of Broadcasting.

More sports slots on SBC-Singapore. (1986). *Asia-Pacific Broadcasting Union Newsletter, 4.*

No hope for video chains. (1986, September 3). *New Straits Times.*

"No" to video raids. (1984). *Asia-Pacific Broadcasting Union Newsletter, 6.*

Oh, E. (2000, March 16). Change in tack. *Malaysian Business.*

Pas distributing distorted tapes. (1986, January 15). *New Straits Times.*

Petch, T. (1988). Belize. In M. Alvarado (Ed.), *Video world-wide: An international study* (pp. 311–322). London: John Libbey.

Pirated VCDs to be destroyed. (2000, March 18). *New Straits Times.*

PM: Karpal was behind it. (1990, March 9). *New Straits Times.*

Police crackdown on video centres. (1983, No. 2). *Asia-Pacific Broadcasting Union Newsletter.*

Porn video center smashed: Suspect held. (1987, July 29). *New Straits Times.*

Repartee over alleged obscene video tape. (1989, December 7). *New Straits Times.*

Sacerdoti, G. (1980, October 9). Enter the communist bogey. *Far Eastern Economic Review.*

Shane, S. (1994). *Dismantling utopia: How information ended the Soviet Union.* Chicago: Ivan R. Dee.

Shareem Amry. (2000, January 23). Anti-piracy initiative to sound death knell for counterfeiters. *New Sunday Times.*

Singapore leads in VCR ownership. (1988, March–April). *AMCB.*

Soon, P. Advertising expenditure to drop? (1985, August 10). *The Star.*

South-east Asia television. (1983, October 8). *The Economist.*

Sparks are flying over TV3 in Malaysia. (1984, June 26). *Asian Wall Street Journal.*

Survey Research Indonesia. (1989). *Establishment survey.* Jakarta: SRI.

Survey Research Malaysia. (1987). *Media Index.* Kuala Lumpur: SRM.

Survey Research Malaysia. (1989, No. 25). *50 Leading Programmes by people ratings and audience composition.* Kuala Lumpur: SRM.

Tape issue: Karpal asked to explain. (1989, December 8). *New Straits Times.*

Teenager pleads guilty to possession of obscene VCDs. (2000, August 2). *Sarawak Tribune.*

The morning after. (1987, December 2). *Malay Mail.*

Third channel in the offing. (1984, January–February). *Asia-Pacific Broadcasting Union Newsletter, 40.*

Usami, S. (1988). Japan. In M. Alvarado (Ed.), *Video world-wide: An international study* (pp. 71–82). London: John Libbey.

Video cassette recorders: National figures. (1983, July–September). *Inter-Media, 11,* p. 39.

Video centres which are run illegally. (1984, September 3). *New Straits Times.*

Video ownership increased. (1984, May–June). *Asia-Pacific Broadcasting Union Newsletter, 28.*

What's new from a bully. (2000, January 24). *New Straits Times.*

Your weekly TV guide. (1985, August 18). *New Straits Times.*

Zainal A. K. (1999, November 17). Fuzzy picture still for cinemas. *New Straits Times.*

Chapter Four

The Competition for Satellite Dominance

International satellite television emerged as an important medium in South- 67
east Asia only in the 1990s, even though the technology had been available in
the region since the 1970s. In satellite television, signals are relayed from the
Earth to a satellite 22,400 miles above the equator. Equipment onboard then
retransmits the broadcast back toward the Earth, but because of the satellite's
height, the returning signal can cover up to one-third of Earth's surface.
Through satellites, broadcasters can reach audiences that would be far beyond
the reach of Earthbound television signals. This capability comes at a price.
The distance to be traveled and the limited power of the transmitters onboard
the satellites makes signals weak as they arrive back on Earth. This means that
specialized antennas and equipment are required to receive broadcasts properly. Signals from most broadcast satellites are intended for reception by spe-
cially equipped sophisticated receiving stations. From these Earth stations,
programs are routed onward for retransmission through conventional broadcast stations or distribution via cable systems. Some powerful satellites relay
signals that can be received directly on home sets equipped with comparatively
simple antennas and converters, however. Southeast Asia helped introduce this
technology to the world when Indonesia placed in operation the first satellite
system constructed by a developing country. Built and launched with the help
of Canada and the United States, it was called Palapa.

Drawing upon the expansive national vision characteristic of the early Suharto years, plans were formulated starting in 1970 to join Indonesia's 13,000 scattered islands through a satellite network. Political wrangling and regional frictions in the years following Sukarno's ouster underscored the importance of a modern communication infrastructure for national integration, and the only practical means of constructing a countrywide system for telephone, telegraph, and broadcasting was through satellite technology. The microwave and undersea cable facilities Indonesia had been building gradually would have taken many decades to complete. Moreover, a truly national microwave and wire network would have been much too expensive to construct and maintain, given Indonesia's island geography. After the decision to go ahead with a satellite network was made in 1974, plans were implemented quickly, and Palapa began relaying television signals on 16 August 1976. For the first time, Televisi Republik Indonesia (TVRI) in Jakarta had the capacity to cover all of the country's major cities using Palapa.

The Palapa system was based upon U.S. technology supplied by American space industries and the National Aeronautic and Space Administration (NASA). The physical installation, both Earth and space segments, amounted to an initial cost of US$100 million and annual recurring costs of about US$35 million. Indonesian planners expected that fees for telephone usage would cover these expenses, and seven years after construction, the system would return a profit ("Satellite communications," 1976). This confident outlook apparently led to overcapacity in the satellite system and made it necessary to lease transponders (receiver/transmitter equipment onboard the satellite) to foreign users. At the time, some observers expressed concern about the dependence on U.S. equipment suppliers and about the local sustainability of the project. Some also objected to the patron-client relationship that Indonesia would be forced to accept with U.S. government agencies and corporations. U.S. suppliers were heavily involved in equipping the broadcasting relay system built around Palapa. In particular, the Harris Corporation held a contract of USD $20 million to supply transmitting facilities for the first round of expansion of TVRI, involving thirty-six sites. NASA provided the launch on a Thor-Delta rocket, and the prime contractor was Hughes Aircraft. Hardware and launch costs alone totaled USD $47.9 million.

The spread of television in Indonesia through Palapa satellite relays has been well documented and researched, thanks to the efforts of a team of East-West Center researchers. Their major works, *Satellite Television in Indonesia* (Alfian and Chu, 1981) and *Social Impact of Satellite Television in Rural Indonesia* (Chu, Alfian, and Schramm, 1991), chronicle the adoption of television in rural areas of the country's outer islands in the provinces of Sumatra, Bali, West Kalimantan, North Sulawesi, and South Sulawesi. Work was carried out under cooperation between Indonesian Institute of Sciences (LIPI) and the East-West Center. The research describes a range of social and cultural changes researchers attributed to television exposure, including improvements in general knowledge and learning about modern health practices and birth control. The research team found that Palapa television viewers

> learned approximately three times as much about eight principal development programmes as did non-viewers. Television helped narrow the knowledge gap between the lower and upper social and economic strata. It contributed to the learning of the national language. . . . Television promoted the adoption of family planning and modern health care, encouraged greater participation in village social organizations, and facilitated more active use of rural markets and public financial institutions. . . . Rural Indonesia has apparently become more closely integrated into the national scheme. (Chu et al., 1991, pp. xi–xii)

Without a doubt these glowing results solidified government policy makers' intention to rely on satellite television for rural development, and Indonesian television was characterized in the 1980s by programming focused on issues such as health care, education, agriculture, and so on.

But researchers concluded that there were also harmful aspects to television's adoption. They pointed specifically to advertising of foreign consumer products. They found that "where there is no existing demand, the commercials have been able to create demand. The phenomenal increase of soft drink consumption is an example" (Chu et al., 1991, p. 262). As findings in this research became known among government policy makers, options to mitigate the social and economic effects of commercialism began to be weighed, especially ones that would reduce the growing demand for imported goods in rural areas. In the end, officials chose to completely suspend advertising on TVRI. According to researchers, television advertising had whetted consumer appetites for items such as foreign cosmetics and toiletries, and this had raised alarm that exposure to commercial appeals would harm village life. It was thought likely that advertising would introduce a cycle of "rising frustration" mentioned by Lerner and others, and it would contribute to an imbalance in foreign trade. The ban on advertising remained in place for more than a decade.

Several researchers have issued cautions about the findings of this research, notably Holaday (1996) who critiqued the broad conclusions offered in the study. He described how in-depth research methods showed that the actual social processes were much more complex than ones portrayed in the East-West/LIPI findings. For instance, he proposed that the social interaction of village life was not readily accessible to outsiders, and misinterpretations by researchers were likely to have resulted from their broad-brush approach. In addition, he pointed out that unification of Indonesia's thousands of islands demanded more than mere hardware—that the country's citizens were separated by more than geography. Within its borders there were more than a dozen languages and an equal number of cultural divisions.

The Palapa system employed a network of Earth stations to pick up TVRI's television programs from the satellite, after which they were retransmitted via conventional television transmitters. Within a decade, however, some entrepreneurs began building their own TVRO (television receive-only) equipment for direct sales to home users. Consumer-owned receiving stations of this type were quite inexpensive. A three-meter diameter parabolic antenna, together with all other required electronics, could be purchased for less than USD $400 in the early 1990s. These receiving systems allowed viewers to pick up not only Indonesian television, but also Philippine, Malaysian, and Thai programs relayed on Palapa. Larger units, capable of receiving signals from weaker or more distant satellites, could be purchased for about USD $2,000. The total ownership of the smaller home units was estimated to be about six thousand in late 1988 ("New signals," 1988), and it nearly doubled to ten thousand two years later. By then, one could find satellite equipment sales outlets even in villages; total national sales were said to be as high as one thousand receiving dishes per month. Although initially the use of home receiving gear increased access to TVRI and thus seemed harmless to officials, the growing attention given to the foreign television programs delivered through the satellites eventually became a concern to policy makers.

STAR TV AND THE CULTURAL INVASION THREAT

By the early 1990s, government officials' unease about the impending cultural threat of satellite television reached a peak throughout the Asia-Pacific region. An article in *Asiaweek* described an alarming scenario typical of warnings being issued by many observers at the time.

> Soon Asians will be "Surfing U.S.A." on their TV sets. The likes of Madonna and American television's most famous single mom, Murphy Brown, will be seen in millions of homes across the region— whether anyone likes it or not ("Values under," 1993).

Because of predictions like this, policy makers braced themselves against the coming of what was proclaimed to be the age of global telecasting. The launch of a number of satellites relaying programs to Asia appeared likely to create difficult competition for terrestrial broadcasters and film distributors. As described in the preceding chapter, the video fad had already cut into television audiences in a number of countries and had produced a big drop in film attendance practically everywhere. This phenomenon had already sensitized authorities to the possibility that the media's status quo could be challenged by new signal delivery technologies.

Although the medium's negative aspects gained the attention of critics and public officials, not all observers forecast troubles as a result of satellite communication's development. Jussawalla (1991, p. 47), for instance, proposed that new technologies actually could offer significant benefits by accelerating development outside the major urban centers of Asia.

> The economic and social benefits of improved telecoms through satellites will be realized when the vast hinterlands or remote islands are not cut off from metropolitan centers. In turn this helps to stem the growing migration from rural to urban areas and will stimulate economic activity in the remote regions thereby improving the quality of life.

From Jussawalla's perspective, expanding communication technology could not only become a springboard for participation in the powerful new economies of the Pacific rim, but could, as in the case of Indonesia, build "a sense of national identity and [integrate] diverse peoples" (p. 48). If these positive results were to be realized, however, the systems would have to be planned and operated within the developmental framework of countries where signals would be received. In the case of new satellites being launched in the 1990s, most foreign owners showed little inclination to cooperate with development agencies of their target regions.

Undoubtedly the foremost example of regional satellite television in the early 1990s was Satellite Television Asian Region Limited, more commonly known as STAR TV. This multichannel satellite television system began operations from its base in Hong Kong in December 1991. At its startup, the system was largely devoted to the relay of Western television programs via AsiaSat 1. The satellite broadcaster was founded by a partnership of Hutchinson Wampoa of Hong Kong and its chairman Ka-Shing Li. Four of its five channels were transmitted in English and the other carried Mandarin programs. The STAR TV system sent signals to a wide span of Asia through two separate satellite "beams." The Northern beam covered East Asia as far West as China's Western border and as far South as Thailand. The Southern beam covered an extended region from East Malaysia on Borneo, across Southeast and South Asia, up to the Middle East as far as Western Turkey. Shortly after its inauguration, STAR TV claimed coverage of 680,000 households, but within three years this number grew to 54 million (*STAR TV 94*, 1994). The rapidly expanding audience for STAR TV and its concentration on foreign program imports provided credible evidence to critics that a cultural invasion by satellite television was well underway.

The operation of STAR TV took a major turn, however, when Rupert Murdoch's News Corporation acquired a 63.6 percent share of the system in July 1993. The new owners shifted the emphasis of the satellite broadcaster from European and North American shows to ones based within the region. This move necessitated a change in operations from a wide regional spread of the services to more narrowly targeted relays. According to company documents this was done "to develop a sub-regional focus, where each major market will have a tailored package of international and Asian-language channels" (*STAR TV 94*, 1994, p. 8). To accomplish this goal, a collection of acquisitions and co-production agreements were negotiated to provide the local content needed. STAR TV made deals with ATV in Hong Kong, Media Asia Films, and Dubai Radio Television, among others.

A critical element in the success of STAR TV was a drive to capture Indian television markets. India had postponed development of television until the 1980s, but in the middle of the decade the government began a dramatic expansion of the state-owned Doordarshan network. Within a few years, television audiences multiplied spectacularly, and by the end of the decade the Indian television audience had become one of the world's largest. But viewers found the government channel less than satisfying, and alternatives were desired. Doordarshan had acquired a reputation for mediocrity so familiar in state broadcasting organizations. Its news programming avoided controversy and ignored government opposition parties. Consequently, videos and pirated satellite television channels gained great popularity among Indian city residents. The satellite programs were distributed via impromptu neighborhood cable systems that sprang up in urban areas in the early 1990s. The Indian television market, with its low level of competition and its large and growing middle class, represented a rich opportunity for advertisers and entertainment entrepreneurs. In late 1993, STAR TV purchased a 49.9 percent interest in Asia Today Ltd., owner of the highly successful private Indian television producer ZEE TV. Once added to the Southern beam, STAR TV gained entry to the entire subcontinent, where almost overnight it became the dominant cable channel. ZEE TV's Hindi language programs immediately challenged government's Doordarshan channel for urban audiences across India. One report claimed that ZEE's audience in the three largest cities of India rose to 37 percent during viewing peak times, compared with only 39 percent for the two main Doordarshan channels combined, and 8 percent for all other STAR TV's channels combined (Karp, 1994).

A steady growth in audiences for all its channels was reported by STAR TV. By 1997, it claimed to reach 260 million viewers in more than 61 million homes across its satellite footprints. STAR TV figures, based on a variety of independent studies, suggested that its viewership expanded by 8 million homes in the first six months of that year. By 1999, estimates had climbed to 300 million viewers in fifty-three countries. The largest concentration of viewers was in "greater China" where more than 50 million households were reported to be tuned in. South Asia and the Middle East accounted for about 20 million homes. Meanwhile, Southeast Asia had a comparatively small viewership, only about 1.3 million homes, with more than a third of these in the Philippines (STAR TV, 1999). These results were modest even though STAR TV began transmitting on Palapa's system by 1997, the coverage of which extended across all of Southeast Asia. As I will show, rigid restrictions on satellite reception in certain parts of Southeast Asia kept STAR TV's audience figures from growing as quickly as in neighboring Asian countries.

POLICY RESPONSES TO SATELLITE TELEVISION IN SOUTHEAST ASIA

Like video, space communication permitted viewers to bypass the obstacles that government authorities had set up to limit exposure to foreign television programs and films. These barriers were set up to keep viewers tuned into domestic channels, mainly state-owned networks, to ensure that government political and development messages reached intended audiences. Nevertheless, in practically every country of Southeast Asia, dissatisfaction with viewing choices mounted through the 1980s. In the absence of competition, government television programs became increasingly viewed as patronizing and generally lacking in popular appeal. There were several related factors that contributed to this situation. Political interference was commonplace. Government officials who had little knowledge of broadcasting frequently meddled in the day-to-day operation of networks. Broadcasting staff in government organizations tended to assume a bureaucratic mentality that led to unimaginative programming and scheduling. Finally, and most importantly, the main aim of broadcasting organizations in Southeast Asia was mobilization of mass participation in development programs, not serving the tastes of viewers.

Satellite television's challenge to government television drew varied responses as the number of signals available in Southeast Asia grew. Broadly speaking, two strategies were available—to outlaw use of satellite receivers, a simple tactic but difficult to enforce effectively, or to build up domestic channels to compete on an equal footing with the foreign programs. Which of these choices a nation preferred was largely based on political considerations.

Indonesia

While Indonesian officials felt uneasiness over the growth of satellite television in the 1980s, home satellite receiving equipment sales rose so quickly that the technology spread before government policy to regulate it could be put in place. Owners of the home receiving setups tended to be the wealthy and to have political connections, and because they had a large investment in hardware, they were opposed to any restrictions in their use of it. By the time authorities finally drafted regulation of satellite television, they were unable to prohibit ownership and instead were forced to institute licensing of receiving equipment.

Consequently, there was an unplanned but logical progression of policy on satellite television in Indonesia. First came establishment of Palapa to augment the government broadcaster's wire and microwave relay system. Palapa's signals were transmitted to Earth-based television relay transmitters in the TVRI network, but of course anyone with an appropriate receiving setup could watch the programs directly from satellite. As Palapa began to relay programs for other nearby countries, however, Indonesia viewers with the satellite equipment could now tap into these shows as well. Even television owners in remote locations who purchased parabolic dishes to receive TVRI discovered they also had a range of foreign channels from which to choose. Among these were three from Malaysia in Malay, a language easily understood by the majority of Indonesian viewers. As sales of receiving equipment gained momentum, Indonesia moved from a situation in which there was a single-channel monopoly over broadcasting held by the government broadcaster to one in which the range of options was comparatively wide. And for those whose incomes permitted more elaborate receiving stations, it was possible to purchase more sophisticated systems capable of tuning in more distant and lower-powered satellites. By the early 1990s, equipment of this type could bring in dozens of channels of foreign television.

With the growing numbers of home parabolic antennas in Indonesia, local private broadcasters sought and were given permission to use satellites to extend their signals to a national viewership. Even if government could not enforce a ban on satellite reception, it could at least make it possible for domestic channels to compete with the foreign channels on an equal footing. First, it was Rajawali Citra Televisi Indonesia (RCTI), then later Televisi Pendidikan Indonesia (TPI), and so on. It is common knowledge that these channels were able to win approval to relay their programs through Palapa because each of the private stations was partly owned by one or another of President Suharto's family members. Typical of state television across Southeast Asia, government programs on Televisi Republik Indonesia (TVRI) bore a heavy developmental motif, as previously described, and were the frequent targets of criticism. Private stations drew large numbers of urban viewers away from TVRI by airing well-produced mass entertainment shows, mainly imported from the United States. So, when the private stations extended their reach to Indonesia's outer islands via satellite, their emphasis on foreign content contributed to the globalization of Indonesian media.

Satellite television seemed ready to be spread to an even wider audience with the introduction of Indovision, a subscription television service, beginning in 1993. This cable service did not immediately win popular acceptance, however; estimates by 1997 suggest that there were fewer than twenty thousand subscribers. Explanations for this lack of success vary. Some observers said that availability of good local channels reduced the appeal of satellite television, whereas others blamed the high cost of hookup fees. In light of this, Indovision revised its lineup of programs, providing an array of new channels in 1997, mostly of foreign origin. The new package also offered a favorable payment arrangement, including a plan through which the cost of descramblers (which subscribers were required to purchase) could be spread out by an extended payment plan. Despite these measures, the pace of growth remained slow.

Malaysia

While Indonesia accepted and embraced satellite television, Malaysia was wary. A simple difference in geography between the two countries explains their contrasting policies. Indonesia lacked the capacity to cover anything approaching its whole population by terrestrial television in the 1970s. There were too many islands with a population too scattered to be reached by a network of wire-interconnected relay transmitters. For its situation, satellite television was ideal. On the other hand, Malaysian television could reach more than 90 percent of residents by ground-based transmission, so its broadcasters did not need a satellite to provide coverage to the majority of the country.

Unlike Indonesia, Malaysia initially imposed a total ban on private ownership of satellite receiving equipment, except for embassies and members of its royal families. Apart from these exceptions, for many years the only legal satellite Earth stations in the country were owned by either Syarikat Telekoms Malaysia, the private national voice and data service, or by Radio Television Malaysia (RTM), the national government-owned broadcasting organization. Because of this, and because cable television systems were prohibited, there was little or no public access to the international television program networks. Malaysian Information Minister Datuk Mohamed Rahmat expressed uncertainty about these services. Commenting on the popularity of STAR TV in 1991, he said, "We don't know whether the programs transmitted by satellite are good or bad for us" ("Tuning in," 1991). But a year later, his ministry announced plans to fine illegal satellite users USD $40,000 and to dismantle any receiving stations it found. According to the minister, the equipment might be used to pick up pornography, communist propaganda, or programs with other types of unsuitable values ("Taking care of values," 1992).

Malaysia's position on satellite reception was in step with other policies limiting public exposure to Western media products. For example, in 1992 the government announced its plans to "drastically" cut television-show imports and to gradually decrease the number of Western films imported. The director of the National Film Development Corporation Zain Hj. Hamzah said that his organization was considering instituting "regulatory measures so that by the year 2000 only a minimal . . . number of films of exceptional quality . . . will be imported" (Lee, 1992). Information Minister Mohamed Rahmat reiterated this goal several years later, proposing that foreign materials would be cut to only 20 percent of broadcast programming by the year 2000 ("Only 20pc," 1996).

Admittedly, efforts to ban satellite reception had not been completely effective. In East Malaysia on the island of Borneo, there were many illegal parabolic receiving installations in homes, in spite of government threats of fines and prosecution. Under a 1996 law, fines as high as RM10,000 (USD $2,600) could be levied upon conviction of owning satellite receiving gear. In East Malaysian communities bordering on Indonesian Kalimantan, it was a simple matter to travel across the border to purchase the affordable hardware in Indonesia where it was legal. One report in the *Far Eastern Economic Review* claimed that as many as 22,000 home satellite systems were in use in East Malaysia by 1994. The same source mentioned a split between Syarikat Telekoms, which thought that satellite broadcasting "does not interfere with local culture," and the Ministry of Information, which took an opposite stand (Vaikiotis, 1994). By 1997, estimates placed the number of unapproved satellites in East Malaysia at "more than 30,000" ("The *Asiaweek* Newsmap," 1997). On hearing of government threats to crackdown on illegal dishes, one owner responded defiantly, "I have spent quite a sum on getting this parabolic dish. I am not going to take this down. . . . The VIPs and the rich and famous also have it. I hope the authorities will go after those people" ("Owners of parabolic," 1997).

Even at an early date, Malaysia had already begun to rethink its decision forbidding home satellite reception. This was evident when Malaysia began making tentative plans for domestic satellite television. An announcement by the then–RTM deputy director-general (engineering) in 1989 revealed that RTM was looking forward to delivering its programs by direct broadcasting satellites. Eventually, he predicted, "before the 21st century," the terrestrial transmission system would be replaced by home satellite receiving set-ups ("RTM to introduce," 1989). The likelihood of the eventual introduction of the technology was acknowledged in 1992 by the minister of telecommunications and posts, Samy Velu, who indicated that "there will come a time when Malaysians can get licenses for parabolic satellite dishes" ("Govt needs," 1992). By blocking satellite television viewing, the country had limited options to only three channels (eventually more in the vicinity of the capital city). This had created a pent-up demand for more entertainment choices. The problem was thought to be especially acute among youth, whom government authorities suspected were falling into bad habits, possibly because they did not have enough wholesome recreational outlets. Karaoke lounges and video arcades were examples of pastimes that were frowned on by officials. Writing about this problem, *New Straits Times* columnist Faezah Ismail (1993) commented that many youngsters "go to these arcades and only come home to sleep. Is it any wonder they acquire such habits as smoking, drinking, and gambling?"

The first sign that Malaysia would open the door to global television came with the announcement that a new wireless cable system would be opened in the vicinity of the capital city, Kuala Lumpur, starting sometime in 1992. Originally, this system was to be operated by Radio Television Malaysia, but after years of delay and review it was finally inaugurated by Mega TV, a subsidiary of the private television station TV3. From a policy perspective, the introduction of cable was a sound strategy. The cable systems could carry satellite programs but limitations could be placed on the choice of channels available to viewers. The programs distributed by the cable systems could be censored or the timing of their schedules altered locally. Finally, by their very nature these systems were practical to operate only in high-density population districts, hence politically and culturally sensitive rural areas would be free from exposure to the medium. If cable television became popular, it would depress viewers' appetites for less easily controlled program relays seen on illegal satellite receivers. Mega TV's cable system did not begin operation until 1995. It offered subscribers only five channels of international television programming: CNN, Discovery, HBO, ESPN, and a channel that provided segments from NHK Japan, Indian and Chinese movies, and relays of the Cartoon Network.

By the time Mega TV started operations, it was clear that Malaysia was having trouble maintaining its policy of restricting international film and television. By then, Malaysia had signed contracts for the launch of its own satellite system Measat-1 (Malaysia East Asia Satellite). This provided substantial capacity for television relays, ones that would be managed by a Malaysian corporation and therefore subject to national content regulations. By 1996, the shape of Malaysia's entry into global television competition became clear. Borrowing a page from STAR TV, Measat was designed to carry a service called ASTRO—the All Asia Television and Radio Company—providing dozens of television channels not only to Malaysia, but also to countries within the transponder's footprint. Among these were India, Vietnam, Indonesia, Taiwan, and the Philippines, to name a few. Although Paul Edwards, chief operating officer of ASTRO, said the company wouldn't necessarily be active in all these countries, he stressed that "we believe we can turn Malaysia into an Asian broadcasting hub" (Suraya Al-Attas, 1996). Reportedly, the Malaysian satellite broadcaster expected to derive more than half of its earnings from foreign subscriptions (Nirmala, 1997).

The reversal in policy on satellites in Malaysia produced a real expansion in the media choices available to viewers. Low (1996, p. 6) commented that things had changed "from a skimpy collection of state-controlled programmes to a vast array of channels providing a virtual wonderland of viewing options." Although the number of alternatives widened, surprisingly few took advantage of the new cable and satellite choices. Mega TV, the cable channel available in urban districts, claimed to have one hundred thousand subscribers after nearly two years of operation. This figure was a definite disappointment, representing less than 4 percent of the total households in the country. ASTRO's results were somewhat better, with more than fifty thousand subscribers signing contracts with the satellite system in the first six months of operation ("Astro received," 1997).

Singapore

Singapore's situation is quite different from other Southeast Asian nations. A tiny country surrounded by Malaysia to the North and Indonesia to the South, media from neighboring nations are readily available throughout its territory. Nevertheless, the country does not permit satellite receiving dishes to be privately owned. Until establishment of the cable system, imported shows were limited to those that could be seen on its own domestic channels and on channels from Malaysia and Indonesia. Singapore has been characterized as having a highly controlled communication environment. This is one of the few countries to institute a system for screening and censoring access to Internet Web sites, and there have been a series of disputes about press freedom involving foreign media such as the *Far Eastern Economic Review* and the *Asian Wall Street Journal*. Singapore's restrictiveness should not be overstated, however; the country opened itself to foreign media by allowing the BBC's World Service to broadcast locally on the VHF FM band. This service is uncensored and covers all of Singapore, as well as Southern Johore in Malaysia.

A cable system was authorized in Singapore in the 1990s, but its installation proceeded slowly. Expansion lagged because of the difficulties of installing cable in the many apartment towers across the island. Most Singaporeans live in these multiunit dwellings, the majority of which are maintained by the Housing Development Board (HDB). Some portions of the country did not receive cable service until after the end of the century because of the glacial speed of project construction.

As in Indonesia and Malaysia, Singapore has attempted to position itself as a regional center for global media. Minister for Information and the Arts Brigadier General George Yeo asserted in 1993 that Asia would challenge the West's domination of news media "within 25 years." At about the same time, Singapore Press Holdings corporation began recruiting staff for an "Asian News Network" ("Media group," 1993) intended to compete against CNN. Singapore has so far had the best results in its campaign to become an Asian media hub. The Discovery Channel relocated there from Hong Kong at the end of 1996, joining more than a dozen other satellite channels already based in the country. The reasons for Singapore's success were spelled out by Kevin McIntyre, senior vice president and general manager of Discovery Channel Asia.

> As the republic grows into the media hub of Asia, Discovery Channel will be able to take advantage of the excellent technical and communications infrastructure in place here. . . . Additionally, the cost of up-link and post-production facilities is considerably less here than in other cities in the region ("Singapore closer," 1996).

Another coup was the relocation of ESPN's joint service with STAR TV Sports to Singapore in 1997. This new venture combined the two major satellite corporations' sports activities in programming for Asian viewers and employed 250 persons at its Singapore headquarters ("Sports TV," 1997). Although Singapore enforces strict laws on local broadcasters, they are not imposed on the satellite channels located within its boundaries.

THE RESULTS OF SATELLITE TELEVISION'S GROWTH

Intense efforts by governments to gain control over satellite television signaled that a new phase of media development had arrived in the region. Misgivings began to be expressed, based on concerns that space-based broadcasts could upset delicately balanced domestic media policies. Each country's particular concerns arose from its politics, demographics, media structures and so on and thus were specific to its own national situation. A wide range of potential problems were discussed, but two main categories emerged: cultural conflicts caused by globalized content and an undermining of terrestrial broadcasting. The following is a brief overview of whether apprehensions about these issues have—or have not—been borne out in Southeast Asia.

Cultural conflicts

The most persistent fear about satellite television was that national cultures would be overwhelmed by a flood of foreign television from media globalization. This was a particularly sensitive matter in Islamic Southeast Asia and in Singapore, where the topic raised not only questions about commerce and identity but also about religious and social values. As noted earlier, growth in the number of new satellite television channels covering Asia in the early 1990s convinced many critics that the flow of cultural products from the West would become an uncontrollable avalanche. Conventional wisdom of the day held that the proliferation of television satellites would inundate Asian countries with channel upon channel of shows loaded with alien values and other kinds of objectionable contents and that national policy makers would be helpless to limit access. The end result of satellite usage was predicted to be (depending on one's point of view) cultural degradation, cultural pollution, or cultural suicide.

Improbably perhaps, none of this happened. Marshalling resources swiftly, a majority of countries in Southeast Asia built domestic media production capacity that enabled local television to solidify its hold on audiences. How this occurred can be seen in Malaysia. In the early 1980s, Malaysia's weekly listing of the ten most popular television programs consistently included at least two U.S.-produced shows. But by 1990, no foreign series made the list, although a few miniseries specials and hit movies won large ratings. Malay-language dramas produced locally by independent Malaysian firms began to replace English-language series as top-rated shows. For instance, in June and July 1990, each week there were at least three of these domestically produced shows among the top ten programs, and in one week there were six. Audiences for programs in the national language grew primarily because of an expanded audience among ethnic Malays who constituted the majority. This trend was especially evident in audiences for the main newscast in Malay. In sample periods of 1983–84, this news program never appeared as one of the top ten shows of the week, but by July 1990, it appeared at least once among the top ten shows every week. Viewing among Malays grew so much because ownership of television sets in rural areas increased during the decade of the 1980s, and the better local Malay-language programming raised the popularity of television within the Malay community. As local television's hold on domestic audiences became more secure, the threat of foreign cultural products by satellite faded. Indeed, production capacity built to counter the popularity of imported programs gradually began to be redirected to the creation of programming that could compete as exports in the global market.

Terrestrial broadcasting in a satellite era

Some observers warned that satellite channels could destroy terrestrial broadcasting systems by stealing their audiences and by undercutting their national development mission. It is true that in Southeast Asia the main government channels have been challenged as never before by the new competitors. But pressure was created not merely by competition from satellite broadcasters; it also came from the increasing strength of private channels and of the ever-expanding range of other entertainment options. All three countries mentioned in the foregoing discussion have undergone some degree of privatization in broadcasting. This alone has cut sharply into audiences for the main government television channels in Indonesia and Malaysia. In Singapore, the heart of the government broadcasting organization, Singapore Broadcasting Corporation, had already been sliced apart and sold off in pieces to private firms before century's end.

Despite the heated competition, or perhaps because of it, domestic television audiences grew rapidly in Southeast Asia. For instance, in 1985 merely 53 percent of Malaysian adults watched television on any given day, but by 1989 this figure had grown to 74 percent—despite a substantial increase in VCR ownership (Survey Research Malaysia, 1989). Even if cable or satellite television reduced the proportion of viewers watching local channels, the overall number of persons watching television continued to creep upward. This is likely to be the case for the foreseeable future throughout Southeast Asia (excepting possibly Singapore, Brunei, and Malaysia where the potential viewership already makes up nearly the entire population). The new viewers covered by expanded transmission areas and wider set ownership have tended to prefer locally produced programs in local languages.

The rivalry between government and private stations across Southeast Asia brought new interest to the medium and may have contributed to higher levels of television viewing. Private broadcasting has different motives than those that guide government television, however. For these stations, commercial realities have to be the foremost consideration, whereas public service stations as a rule give priority to informational and developmental objectives. In practice, this means that private stations in Southeast Asia tend to concentrate on wealthier viewers in the urban centers and on programs that appeal to upscale families, leaving government stations with an audience of predominantly lower-income rural viewers. But satellite-delivered television targets the same kind of viewer as the private channels. Because of costs of receiving satellite channels and because of the nature of their programs, their greatest popularity has been achieved among highly educated city residents who have a command of English or one of the other regional link languages.

The fact that locally produced programs have been more popular than imports in Southeast Asia suggests that the availability of imported shows via satellite will not necessarily dominate television's audiences. For this reason, and because of satellite television's restricted viewership, the mass popularity of the main broadcast television channels seems unlikely to be overturned soon. The experiences of terrestrial broadcasters in North America and Europe tend to support this view. In the United States the main commercial networks for land-based broadcasters of CBS, NBC, Fox, and ABC together retained the largest share of viewers throughout the 1990s. They achieved this result by utilizing the broadest possible program appeals. Although the commercial networks' audiences are declining, they remain the most popular channels in the country. For example, in the opening week of the television season in 1996, the average combined rating for the four broadcast networks was only 38.8, down from 41.6 the year previous. Still, ABC, CBS, and NBC each maintained average audiences at or near 10 percent of the country's television homes—larger by far than any cable or satellite network ("TV ratings," 1996). Similar patterns were evident in succeeding years.

A few Southeast Asian governments have attempted to provide a measure of protection for their public television organizations by requiring that satellites under their control relay government television stations, along with the usual selection of international channels. Malaysia's RTM is included within the menu of options available to ASTRO subscribers, and Indonesia's Palapa still carries the broadcasts of TVRI. This strategy may be successful in these two countries because the majority of home satellite systems within their borders are set up to receive signals from the national satellite. Elsewhere—especially in areas where services such as STAR TV are popular—such an approach may not be effective.

In the final analysis, over-the-air television's continued viability depends on its ability to sustain advertising revenues sufficient for its operational costs. As satellite television has spread across Southeast Asia, broadcast advertising strategies have had to be modified to accommodate significant changes in official policies and in business conditions. This can be noted in Indonesia where advertising on satellite television was first eliminated, then restored only a few years later. The globalization of television advertising as a by-product of satellite television is likely to produce two simultaneous and different consequences. The first result is an intensification of competition for advertising revenues, something already observable in several Asian countries, particularly Indonesia. Second, at the same time, more advertisers are being drawn into the television game because their specialty products can be more efficiently marketed through the more narrowly targeted—and thus more cost-effective—global channels. Advertisers who previously opted for specialized print media over television may find a niche-oriented satellite and cable television approach more efficient. So, although advertising revenues will be divided among more channels, the overall expenditure for television will rise. This was evident in Indonesia soon after satellites began relaying private television nationwide. Media consultant Ernst Katoppo pointed to the "advent of commercial television as an advertising medium" as the source of growth in total advertising revenues (cited in Kerk, 1994). Between 1990 and 1995 overall spending on advertising increased sixfold from about 500 million rupiah to more than three trillion rupiah. By the mid-1990s, television claimed 48 percent of Indonesian total advertising expenditures (Oetama, 1996).

On the other hand, satellite television poses technical difficulties for advertisers. As channels are relayed to a wide swath of geography, cutting across a major portion of Asia, how can advertisers identify appropriate target audiences? Conventionally, market research determines the prospective consumers of advertised goods and services in any country, but in many countries such research is difficult to carry out because of legal restrictions, accessibility of populations, language issues, and so on. On a global scale the costs of marketing research of this type become prohibitive. Likewise, assessing advertising's reach may be one thing in Malaysia (where services such as ACNielsen provide quality ratings information) but quite another when products are being marketed in multiple countries or in countries where such research is unavailable. Even in Indonesia, television audience figures are only available for five major cities, a fact that makes intelligent advertising planning an impossibility.

POLITICS OF BROADCASTING SATELLITES

Jostling for political and commercial advantage has characterized the space race from its beginning, and disputes on international principles to control satellite broadcasting technology erupted first in the 1960s. In 1963, long before the first broadcasting satellite was placed in orbit, the United Nations' Committee on the Peaceful Uses of Outer Space considered the possibility that satellites could relay unwanted broadcast signals into countries within their coverage areas. This issue was of particular concern to Brazil, though other countries including the Soviet Union expressed their fears about the potential abuses of a medium that could reach across national boundaries so easily. Early satellite systems launched by the United States, Canada, and the Soviet Union showed that television could be relayed effectively to large areas. In Southeast Asia, the Japanese launch of a broadcasting satellite for domestic relay of its NHK network's programming was seen as vaguely threatening (see Queeney, 1978, p. 224).

INTELSAT, the global consortium established in the 1960s for operation of a worldwide system of communication satellites, provided a further lesson on the political dimensions of this technology. The preliminary agreement for the consortium permitted COMSAT, a United States corporation, to operate the system in behalf of the other members. When the time came for a permanent agreement, dissatisfaction with domination by the United States emerged, and a long negotiation process to resolve the conflicts in interests between the United States and other member countries resulted. The process seemed stymied for long periods because, as one researcher noted, "the United States attempted to retain its position of economic power by controlling the decision-making processes of INTELSAT" (Day, 1973, p. 467). The end result was heightened suspicions about the motives of developed nations in the use of satellite technology. As Day correctly predicted, "INTELSAT represents a lost opportunity to create a model for international commercial cooperation. The scars from the difficult two years of negotiations will not heal rapidly" (p. 472).

As the decade of the 1990s closed, satellite television had become a major segment of mass communication in a number of countries of Southeast Asia. Each of the three countries examined in this chapter set out to become a regional production and distribution center. Their goals are commendable, but whether any can succeed remains an open question. Competition within the popular culture industries of Asia has gotten fierce, and other countries of the region have a wealth of experience, as well as capital and program resource advantages. Already, there have been clashes over Southeast Asian leadership in the field of communication satellites. Malaysian Telecommunications and Post Minister Samy Velu claimed in 1992 that other Asian countries discouraged his nation from launching its own satellite to promote use of theirs instead. He suggested those countries objected to a launch of a Malaysian satellite "because they are afraid of competition." Indonesian Director-General of Posts and Telecommunications Cacuk Sudarijanto responded to Velu by declaring that "we are prepared to face competition from other countries and we are not worried of even 10 Malaysian satellites" ("Satellites: Indonesia gears," 1992).

The reason countries of the region wished to play a leading role in the growth of satellite television was, of course, the perception that this could become the most important and economically powerful form of mass communication in the twenty-first century. But there was more than this. The political stakes in the dueling over satellite control were even greater than the potential financial benefits. The entire Pacific Rim had become a zone of technological enterprise during the latter part of the twentieth century, and demonstrating leadership in fields such as satellite communications could strengthen claims on regional political leadership. If any country were to gain technological superiority in Southeast Asia, it would not only achieve an economic advantage, it would also enhance its status as a political and technological power within the region. The leaders of these three countries—Dr. Mahathir Mohamad, Goh Chok Tong, and Suharto—acted as if their national standing, and in some ways their personal prestige, were at stake in their race for space supremacy. As Singapore Prime Minister Goh Chok Tong argued, "getting ready for the future is not a choice. Getting used to technological changes is not a choice. It is a must. Only then will we maintain our relevance and value in this fast-changing world" ("Singaporeans told," 1997). Similar views were echoed by Malaysian Prime Minister Mahathir Mohamad who urged his countrymen to prepare for technological competition, proposing that "we have the best opportunity now . . . if we miss it, others will proceed and they'll be so far ahead that it'll be difficult for us to catch up" ("Understand power," 1997).

Beyond Southeast Asia there were many competitors that had designs on control of satellite television in Asia, mainly corporations based in North America or Europe. Competition from these areas tended to be framed by Southeast Asian opponents as a conflict between the Northern and Southern global regions, between colonizer and former colonies, or as yet another example of East-West conflict. This theme played consistently in Malaysian Prime Minister Mahathir Mohamad's analysis of international dynamics. For instance, he expressed dismay when Rupert Murdoch's News Corporation purchased a majority share in STAR TV. He complained that the satellite television operator might "create friction and instability in this region so that the West can compete with us" ("Murdoch outfit," 1993). Mahathir's feelings about the power of media in developed nations emerged clearly in his speech before the plenary session of the United Nations in New York on September 27, 1996. In his view,

> the growth and influence of electronic, satellite, and information technology is astounding. But its impact poses one of the biggest political and ethical challenges of our time, subverting and distorting our social consciousness. The elites of the North and South have become blind to the enormities of reality. . . . Monopoly of the electronic media by the North should be broken. In the past Western missionaries spread the gospel. Today the media has taken over and all our cherished values and diverse cultures are being destroyed. ("Inequities of power-sharing," 1996)

The solution to this challenge according to the Malaysian government was to gain a technological advantage, and through this to avoid dependence on foreign nations. To this end, Minister of International Trade and Industry Datuk Seri Rafidah Aziz, advised Malaysian universities to become involved in the "hunt" for technology. She said universities could act as a "technology sponge," absorbing it from abroad then "squeezing it out" to local industries ("Act as 'technology sponge,'" 1996).

Proponents of satellite broadcasting were forced to negotiate a thicket of political issues at every level—domestic and regional, as well as international, and this frequently led to inconsistent policies within the region. The view of satellite technology as emblematic of political and economic leadership was in apparent conflict with the severe restrictions placed on the use of satellite television within national boundaries. Southeast Asian countries wanted to play a role in the technological development of satellites and to be seen as an important player regionally, and possibly even internationally, but at the same time some were unwilling to provide their own nation's television viewers free access to satellites. For example, although Malaysia did not allow direct reception by satellite, officials certainly recognized the potential value of global television. Its information minister announced in 1990 the signing of agreements with three broadcasting organizations: CNN International, the European One World Channel, and a West Asian broadcaster. The agreement allowed program exchanges between broadcasters from around the world with Radio Television Malaysia. Without a trace of irony, Information Minister Datuk Mohamed boasted that "I received many letters from Papua New Guinea and Australia praising RTM productions," in explaining the benefits of satellite television ("RTM seeks," 1990).

Satellites, like certain other "new" technologies, had a capacity to undermine the ability of nations to control domestic access to foreign information sources. This had many political implications: it weakened the authority of political leaders who wanted perhaps to shield the public from news about their behaviors and decisions; it stimulated debates about policies that had previously been taken for granted; and it reduced the secure grasp that some political figures had on political power. Atkins (1995) analyzed this phenomenon in the civil uprising of 1992 in Bangkok and concluded that direct broadcasting satellite services

> acted as vital two-way conduits of information, both at a mass level and an interpersonal level among the elites. Demonstrators were emboldened by the coverage, perhaps knowing it was airing across the world. CNNI and BBCWST [BBC World Service Television] were able to be juxtaposed with the military-backed regime's overtly propagandist coverage of the unrest, further undermining the legitimacy of the government and later forming the basis of calls for broadcasting reform in Thailand (p. 64).

A similar phenomenon occurred in Malaysia in 1998 when Deputy Prime Minister Anwar Ibrahim was charged with sex crimes and corruption. As detailed in the first chapter, many Malaysians were skeptical about the charges. They and other curious viewers tuned into international newscasts from the BBC and CNN International to get story details not filtered through Malaysian news services. Of course, news reporting is not merely about facts. Atkins also argued that "the arrival of international news and information services—as part of wider cultural and economic exposure—has the potential to disperse Western liberal values among audiences previously shut off from the material" (p. 65).

Yet despite early predictions, satellite television did not become a conduit for predominantly Western values. Instead, local and regional programming had become the main attraction for the medium. Programs produced within the region in the major link languages of Asia—Mandarin, Hindi, Malay, and English—comprised a major portion of the schedules. The changes in media habits brought by satellites and other new media led broadcasting organizations to revise their operational strategies. Malaysia, Singapore, and Indonesia, not to mention Thailand and the Philippines, scrambled to be players in the regional and global media markets that emerged over the decade. Even so, for these countries, cultural issues remained in the foreground: how to participate in global media markets while preserving social values and cultural integrity.

As domestic television producers in Asia started flexing their muscles and took charge of their own markets, they increasingly saw themselves as potential entrants in the global market. In India, whose movie industry has enjoyed great success, the strength of local television productions quickly swamped program imports. Kumar (1999) quoted United Television (India) producer Zarina Mehta who observed that "Mahabharat has 60 percent of Indian audience, [while] Santa Barbara is half a percent. Sometimes it reaches even 0 percent. I rest my case." As *Asiaweek* author Susan Berfield (1996, p. 38–39) noted, "international satellite operators were supposed to change Asia. Instead, Asia has changed them." This revised perspective on media globalization presents a totally new scenario for Asia. Like other Pacific Rim nations, Malaysia, Singapore, and Indonesia currently intend to become sources rather than passive receivers of international films and television programs. Nevertheless, the strategy of creating television programs to vie in the global market with ones produced by Western popular culture industries may not prove successful for all. Pauling (1999) reported that deregulation in New Zealand intended to promote domestic producers on the world stage actually caused a huge increase in program importation. Despite such experiences, the optimism of Southeast Asian producers encourages them to think they can seriously challenge established players in international programming markets. As Malaysian television columnist S. Indra Sathiabalan (1997) wrote,

> Good series are hard to come by but to give credit where it is due, there is a whole lot of potential out there. What is important is that we shouldn't sell ourselves short . . . Equating local TV productions with those from the West is no longer a pipe dream.

With this apparently in mind, Malaysian Minister of Information Datuk Mohamed Rahmat announced his intention to convince Marketing International Programme-Asia (MIP-Asia) to hold its festival in his country. He noted that "many South-East [sic] Asian countries have expressed their desire to host the programme, and I am determined to get the organizer to choose Malaysia" to "introduce Malaysia as a development and growth centre for television programmes" ("Bid to host," 1997). Malaysian television production house HVD Entertainment's motto nicely captures Southeast Asia's sentiment on globalization: "Go global or fail locally."

REFERENCES

Act as "technology sponge," Rafidah urges universities. (1996, August 2). *New Straits Times.*

Alfian, and Chu, G. C. (1981). *Satellite television in Indonesia.* Honolulu: East-West Center.

Astro received 50,000 subscriptions in less than half a year. (1997, April 11). *New Straits Times.*

Atkins, W. (1995). *Satellite television and state power in Southeast Asia: New issues in discourse and control.* Perth, Australia: Edith Cowan University, Centre for Asian Communication, Media and Cultural Studies.

Berfield, S. (1996, November 8). *Asiaweek.*

Bid to host TV marketing programme. (1997, April 21). *New Straits Times.*

Chu, G. C., Alfian, and Schramm, W. (1991). *Social impact of satellite television in rural Indonesia.* Singapore: AMIC.

Day, L. A. (1973). *An analysis of the proposals submitted by the United States to the plenipotentiary conference on definitive arrangements for the International Telecommunications Satellite Consortium, 1969-1971.* Unpublished doctoral dissertation, Ohio University, Athens.

Faezah Ismail. (1993, August 18). Zapping the video game habit. *New Straits Times.*

Govt needs to plug satellite dish loopholes first: Samy Velu. (1992, October 6). *The Straits Times.*

Holaday, D. A. (1996). The social impact of satellite TV in Indonesia: A view from the ground. *Media Asia, 23,* 100–106.

Indra Sathiabalan, S. (1997, March 27). *Sun Megazine.*

Inequities of power-sharing intolerable. (1996, September 28). *New Straits Times.*

Jussawalla, M. (1991). Privatization and national priorities in the Asia-Pacific region. *Asian Journal of Communication, 1,* 41–51.

Karp, J. (1994, January 24). Cast of thousands. *Far Eastern Economic Review.*

Kerk, C. (1994, January 21). 31pc jump for Indon ad spending. *Business Times.*

Kumar. A. (1999, Spring). Localizing the global in India: New imperatives for international communication scholarship in the satellite era. *Transnational Broadcasting Studies* [On-line]. Retrieved May 20, 1999 from the World Wide Web: http://www.tbsjournal.com.

Lee, M. (1992, May 4). Malaysia takes aim at film, TV imports. *Variety.*

Low, L. (1996). Social and economic issues in an information society: A Southeast Asian perspective. *Asian Journal of Communication, 6,* 1–17.

Media group to set up Asian network. (1993, February 20). *New Straits Times.*

Murdoch outfit assures Dr M on STAR TV. (1993, August 6). *New Straits Times.*

New signals in Jakarta, (1988, December 23–30). *Asiaweek.*

Nirmala M. (1997, January). Ruling the air waves. *Malaysian Industry.*

Oetama, J. (1996). Economic development, electronic media and the survival of the newspaper industry, the case of Indonesia. *Media Asia, 24*(1), 5–11.

Only 20pc foreign material for our TV by year 2000. (1996, December 13). *New Straits Times.*

Owners of parabolic dishes ignore deadline. (1997, July 2). *New Straits Times.*

Pauling, B. (1999, April). *Deregulation and the increase of television imports into New Zealand.* Paper presented at the Broadcast Education Association meeting, Las Vegas, NV.

Queeney, K. (1978). *Direct broadcast satellites and the United Nations.* Alphen aan den Rijn, The Netherlands: Sijthoff and Noordhoff.

RTM seeks global link to boost image. (1990, January 29). *New Straits Times.*

RTM to introduce direct broadcast satellite within 10 years. (1989, April 14). *New Straits Times.*

Satellite communications: The answer for Indonesia; bonanza for suppliers. (1976, September). *Television/Radio Age International.*

Satellites: Indonesia gears for competition. (1992, July 15). *New Straits Times.*

Singapore closer to becoming a TV hub. (1996, October 10). *New Straits Times.*

Singaporeans told to embrace new technology. (1997, May 29). *New Straits Times.*

Sports TV stations move to Singapore. (1997, January 23). *New Straits Times.*

STAR TV. (1999). *STAR TV viewing homes April 1999* [On-line]. Retrieved April 29, 1999 from the World Wide Web: www.startv.com/full_version/full_set/info/dist.html.

STAR TV 94. (1994). Hong Kong: Satellite Television Asian Region Ltd.

Suraya Al-Attas. (1996, October 4). Astro-nomical expectations. *New Straits Times.*

Survey Research Malaysia. (1989). *Media index.* Kuala Lumpur: SRM.

Taking care of values. (1992, September 25). *Asiaweek.*

The *Asiaweek* newsmap. (1997, July 4). *Asiaweek.*

Tuning in the world. (1991, October 25). *Asiaweek.*

TV ratings for ABC, Fox drop. (1996, September 27). *New Straits Times.*

Understand power of multimedia. (1997, February 27). *New Straits Times.*

Values under siege. (1993, December 15). *Asiaweek.*

Vaikiotis, M. (1994, May 12). Outlook: Partly cloudy. *Far Eastern Economic Review.*

Chapter Five

Technology
Infrastructures

A number of Southeast Asian countries profited from the efforts of multina- 91
tional firms to geographically diversify their production sites for electronic
goods. The growth of electronic industries in Korea, Hong Kong, Singapore,
and Malaysia, and to a lesser degree in Thailand, Indonesia, and the Philippines, followed a pattern that began with Fairchild's investment in its first offshore production facilities in Hong Kong in 1962. Hong Kong served as the
favored site for offshore production for most of that decade, but by 1968 Mex-
ico had supplanted it. After this, the global center for production of electronic
goods moved to Southeast Asia, and Singapore took over as world leader in
1969. Then, according to a study conducted by Singapore Economic Research
Center in the mid-1970s, Malaysia surpassed Singapore as top offshore site by
1974 (Pang and Lim, 1977). Their study also showed that during this period
the electronic industry in Singapore enjoyed explosive growth, expanding
from just 700 workers in 1968 to more than 42,000 six years later, even after
retrenchment of some 17,000 employees during a brief economic downturn in
1974–1975 (p. 16). Then as now, electronic manufacturing output was predominantly intended for overseas markets, typically more than 90 percent of
production. Pang and Lim found that U.S. firms concentrating on semiconductor production dominated the Singapore electronics industry and that electronic firms had become the largest employers in the country's manufacturing
sector. But Singapore's position had already weakened because of competition
from "cheaper labour countries"—especially Malaysia. The industrial formula
that Singapore and Malaysia employed was to capitalize on a low-cost labor
force but to enforce technology transfer policies to build human capital. The

knowledge workers that resulted were perfectly suited to spread the gains in industrial production to related information technologies.

By the 1990s, it was comparatively easy for Asian nations to fashion a compelling global information technology (IT) strategy based on superior electronic know-how produced by decades of leadership in manufacturing. Mathews and Cho (2000) found in their analysis of the East Asian semiconductor industries that Korea, Taiwan, and Singapore—and to some extent Malaysia—had become global leaders in "production, consumption, trade, and investment in integrated circuits and in products based on them such as computers." By the end of the decade, these four countries had become "mainstream rather than marginal players … [competing] at the most advanced levels of technology" (p. 31). These economic and industrial strengths gave the tiger economies the leverage needed to build their information industries into major players in regional and possibly global markets. Many countries on the Pacific Rim, and particularly ones in Southeast Asia, fashioned grand schemes to mobilize their labor force and to attract capital from investors overseas.

As countries turned from manufacturing to information-based economies, each had to contend with disagreements about their information policies. All countries had traditionally placed restrictions on certain kinds of information access that partners from the industrial countries found troublesome. The largest share of investment in Southeast Asian technology had come from the United States, but this country promoted the most extreme restriction-free information policies. Immediately, the plans hatched by entrepreneurs had to face objections of potential investors not only on questions of infrastructure development and human resources, but ones about public access and freedom of information. The contraction between information control and information technology investment was not lost on any of the countries, and each set out to modify their legal frameworks to make their claim on regional leadership more plausible to investors.

CONVERGENCE AND THE CHANGING MEDIA SCENE

The idea of what constitutes mass media seems to have been evolving steadily for well more than a century, thanks to more or less continual technological change in the production and delivery of information and entertainment. The development of rapid shipping and transportation, particularly in the creation of global postal systems, beginning in the mid-1800s enhanced the pervasiveness of newspapers. The arrival of radio in the 1920s and the development of television in the 1940s were other turning points. As described in this work, the establishment of satellite distribution systems, the capability of low-cost video recordings, digital recording and distribution, fiber-optical transmission networks, and of course the Internet each spelled a redefinition of mass communication. Sometime within the past decade, however, the reconstitution of media concepts became codified as "convergence," the notion that many different kinds of electronic technologies, including some not obviously communication media, were merging into unitary integrated systems. Convergence led to technologies that encompassed existing media while adding features such as interactivity, time shifting, easy storage, multipoint delivery, and so on. As Verhulst (1999, p. 2) described it,

> The changes, initiated largely by digitalisation and compression, affect all levels of the media value chain—content, distribution and interface—and lead to the so-called media convergence. The electronic storage, manipulation and display of text, pictures and sound in a common digital form makes possible new forms of media—"multimedia"—and thus new products or services and new markets.

Convergence therefore suggests not just transformed versions of previously existing media, but wholly new sorts of information and entertainment. The emergence of computer gaming as a diversion provides a good example of what this means. These games enjoy particular appeal among young adolescents, but many adults are enthusiasts as well. These games take some of the concepts of board and card games and add realism and the ability for single players to compete with artificial computer opponents. Some of these games draw from traditional versions (Risk, Monopoly), whereas others present entirely new games (Doom, Age of Empires). Computer gaming was made possible by the emergence of software markets resulting from two decades of the personal computer's popularity.

Convergence embodies not merely technological change but also economic and competitive change. The latter offered opportunities for enterprises outside the developed world, especially ones within the Pacific Rim, where technical development was relatively high and labor costs relatively low. As just noted, Southeast Asia enjoyed a strong competitive position because it had become one of the world's largest production zones for electronic components and for consumer electronics.

MALAYSIA'S MULTIMEDIA SUPER CORRIDOR

In the colonial period, broadcasting in the Asia-Pacific region mainly consisted of government monopoly radio and television. As we have seen, this model, which was maintained after independence, started to break down with the arrival of video, and it came under further pressures when satellite television arrived. Malaysian policy makers were very much aware of global satellite television's growing popularity. This consciousness was the chief reason for inauguration of the nation's own Mega TV and ASTRO television services. Because of the ban on ownership of satellite receiving equipment, Malaysia was spared from the chaos that occurred during satellite television's early years. Even as satellite parabolic antennas became commonplace elsewhere in Asia, Malaysia held to its promise to protect terrestrial television services. The prohibition against parabolic receiving antennas was also based on the fear that harmful influences might come from exposure to foreign media via satellites. Malaysia's decision to bar development of electronic technology that might weaken government information control presented a problem, however, when the country sought to assert its technological leadership. The Malaysian government envisioned itself as a regional leader in technical services and imagined this as a path toward status as a developed nation by the year 2020. It intended to achieve this goal through prominence as a manufacturer of technical products, a center or "hub" for IT in East and Southeast Asia, and a value-added transshipment point for various types of regional high-tech goods.

Possibly the most ambitious information technology project launched anywhere in the world took shape in Malaysia during the mid-1990s with the establishment of the Multimedia Super Corridor (MSC). This grand plan was developed with the stated goal of projecting Malaysia into the forefront of global computer technology. This "corridor" was both a physical location in the central Peninsular region and a set of policies providing protection and support for technological enterprises operating within national boundaries. During the last half of the decade, the project grew and developed through the creative vision of political and corporate leaders, producing a remarkable set of policy initiatives.

Observers agree that although Malaysian Prime Minister Dr. Mahathir Mohamad did not personally conceive the MSC concept, he was definitely the driving force behind its implementation. He was an enthusiastic proponent of MSC and an indefatigable spokesman on its behalf. His support was based on reasoning that "if the MSC is set up in this region, we can learn new technology and we may even be involved in the technology and be more adept in its application than others" (Ashraf, 1997). The prime minister stressed again and again MSC's value in legitimizing Malaysia's claim on regional and global leadership. As he explained it,

> We have succeeded in becoming an industrial nation. But today we are entering an era of information technology, an era in which the workforce consists of knowledge workers. ... Let us focus on our national development. Once we have become a developed nation, we only need to whisper and others will pay heed to our whispers ("Acquiring IT," 1997).

Calls such as these seemed to have had a public resonance, and enthusiasm among ordinary Malaysians grew rapidly during 1997. That is to say, it grew until the economic recession set in late that year.

Even opposition parties found themselves on the side of information technology development in the country. Democratic Action Party (DAP) leader Lim Kit Siang complained about Malaysia's tardy response to the opportunity. Speaking in Parliament at the May 6–7 session in 1996, he asserted that "Malaysia had been quite slow in realising the critical importance of IT in enhancing both our competitive advantages in the global marketplace." Comparing the plan with the country's neighbor and main competitor, he continued, "Singapore, for instance, established its National Computer Board in 1981 … it now aims to build up a pool of some 35,000 IT professionals by the year 2,000" (Lim, 1997, p. 94).

In Malaysia, the term "multimedia" assumed a larger meaning than it has usually had elsewhere. Generally, the term is used to denote computer-based audio, video, and graphics applications such as Internet radio, presentation graphics, and various types of sound recording techniques, including MP3. In Malaysia, use of the term multimedia encompasses these and adds all types of digital information technologies, including text and data. Multimedia there has become equated with almost anything to do with computers and electronic technologies, both hardware and software. One government briefing document proposed that the technologies included within the scope of multimedia embraced ones employed in business, at home, in school, and while traveling (Multimedia Development Corporation, Briefing Document, 1997, cited in Zainab, 1998).

The MSC is a strip of land about ten by thirty miles (fifteen by fifty kilometers, a territory of 270 square miles) running from the Kuala Lumpur City Center to Putrajaya—the new city chosen to be the new government administrative center—and to the Kuala Lumpur International Airport (KLIA). This narrow band of land lies between the two major national highways that extend southward from the capital, the North-South Expressway and the Coastal Link Highway. Within these boundaries resources for computing and information technology are to be concentrated, making the MSC, it is hoped, a rich center that will attract research and commercial enterprises from around the world.

At the heart of the MSC is the new government center, Putrajaya. Two motives seem to have been behind establishment of the planned city. First, there was a real need for expansion of government offices, many of which tended to be concentrated within or near the business district of Kuala Lumpur, where land costs had shot up sharply during boom times in the early 1990s. The concentration of government offices close to the city center contributed to congestion that had become more and more intolerable. Kuala Lumpur had taken comfort in the fact that its traffic mess was at least less serious than ones in Manila, Bangkok, or Jakarta, but by the end of the decade travel via city streets and arterials had grown much worse. Establishment of an administrative district in Putrajaya was generally welcomed as a partial solution to the capital city's traffic problems. In keeping with the goal of exemplifying advanced multimedia capability, Putrajaya would be built to exploit every imaginable benefit of technology. Original plans for the center called for "paperless offices," electronic record keeping, video conferencing, digital archiving, and so on.

The MSC concept drew upon the notion that the country's largest international airport would be based within its boundaries. KLIA was inaugurated just before Malaysia's hosting of the Commonwealth Games in 1998. After this, Subang International Airport, which had served as the principal air gateway for more than twenty years, was scaled back, and its traffic was restricted to domestic flights. The sprawling KLIA facility was located deep in the central region, in a site of former oil palm estates and rain forest jungle. Construction of the airport produced complaints because of its high cost and because of its distance from the capital city. A taxi ride from the city center to the airport grew from a maximum of less than thirty minutes to more than an hour with the opening of KLIA. Like many other projects mounted by the government during the 1990s, this new airport was intended to symbolize Malaysian preeminence as the region's technological and commercial leader. It was intended to serve as the logistics hub for transportation of people and goods into and out of the country via its integrated electronic information networking. The networks would be a key to the IT infrastructure of the entire Multimedia Super Corridor. Today the airport itself projects an ultra-modern "space-age" appearance and boasts eighty gates on two parallel runways that can accommodate more than seventy-two flights per hour (Zainab, 1998).

The connection between the airport location and this MSC technology oasis might seem strange, but it fits the central motive for the government project—to push Malaysia into the ranks of developed countries using technology as an economic springboard. The MSC project was part of a larger initiative known as "Vision 2020," that is, a vision to become a developed nation by the year 2020. The Vision 2020 project, associated with Prime Minister Mahathir and his close associates in government and in United Malays National Organization (UMNO), was formulated in the mid-1990s. Vision 2020 was less a carefully crafted concept than it was a loosely coordinated set of economic principles meant to inspire the Malaysian public toward lofty but achievable goals. And it was genuinely inspirational, even to many who were disinterested in politics and economics; the idea that Malaysia could rise to the same level of achievement as Japan, or as nations of Europe and North America, truly captured the imagination of Malaysian citizens.

Another facet of the MSC concept was the planned city Cyberjaya, touted as the region's "intelligent city." This showplace city was planned to be a twin of Putrajaya, and together—according to Multimedia Super Corridor promoters—they would be known as Megajaya. As enraptured *New Straits Times* reporter Carolyn Hong (1997) explained it,

Cyberjaya's name says it all. This will [be] a city devoted heart and soul to the wonders of information technology. It will be a zone to link Malaysia to the world, in a big way and the MSC's backbone of development in IT and multimedia technology.

The city was allocated seven thousand hectares to the west of Putrajaya, where the government promised to create a center containing information hardware and software of the highest technological order. The city would contain the hub of the MSC's 2.5-10 gigabit telecommunications network. Responsibility for construction of the required infrastructure was given to Telekoms Malaysia without bid and as an exclusive license.

The success of the corridor hinged on garnering investment from abroad, and officials worked tirelessly to spread the word to computer and information communities in industrialized countries. The prime minister, in particular, maintained an unceasing effort to enlarge support among firms from Japan, Europe, and the United States. At the end of the 1990s, the outspoken critic of Western corporations and governments found himself pitching the Multimedia Super Corridor to his erstwhile antagonists. In one notable visit he called on entertainment industry leaders in Hollywood and spoke to them at a reception at the Beverly Hills Hotel. The very individuals he singled out so frequently in complaints about U.S. cultural products heard Dr. Mahathir say that as the developing countries raised their economies, "they would be looking for deeper fulfillment" and this demanded a "cultural context that went well beyond American pop culture" (Goh, 1997). In this meeting the prime minister reiterated his government's pledges to investors. Among these were freedom of ownership in IT firms in the MSC; unrestricted hiring policies, especially freedom to recruit expatriate workers; the best physical technical infrastructure available anywhere in the world; no censorship of the Internet; and a promise that Malaysia would be a regional leader in the protection of intellectual property rights and cyberlaws.

The issuance of "cyberlaws," that is, laws offering legal protections against abuses of e-commerce and intellectual properties was a cornerstone of the MSC. According to Datuk Leo Moggie, minister of energy, telecommunications and post, the laws would be embodied in legislation to be brought to Parliament before the end of 1997. Called the Multimedia Convergence Act, it would "be in tune with the rapid technological convergence of telecommunications, broadcasting, and computers" (Ahmad, 1997). The cyberlaws would have four objectives: (1) to create means under law for digital equivalents to personal signatures; (2) to establish a set of laws protecting against hacking, tampering, and other attacks against computers; (3) to protect intellectual properties; and (4) to establish protections for the practice of medicine over public digital networks.

In 1997, as activities on the MSC reached a crescendo, Zainab Nordin (1998) carried out a study on attitudes toward the project among government employees in all Malaysian ministries. Her research presented a number of interesting findings. She used self-administered questionnaires to collect data on staff perceptions, and in a few selected ministries she gathered in-depth interviews as a supplement to the survey. At that time, Zainab found a high degree of engagement in the MSC effort; only 24 percent of respondents admitted they did not understand what the project was, although this awareness varied considerably from ministry to ministry. She found that 42 percent had no opinion on whether "entering the Information Age" was a good thing, and 8 percent foresaw problems in the initiative. Fifty percent did agree that the MSC was a "good" thing. Zainab found striking differences among Malaysian ethnic groups in their technical capabilities. In her sample of government workers, only 18 percent of Malays rated themselves as "expert" or "very familiar" with computers, but among Chinese the figure was 46 percent. Only 22 percent of Indian respondents claimed expertise or familiarity with computers, and 50 percent admitted that they were "not familiar" with them. Despite shortcomings in expertise, 69 percent of the government staff claimed that they did use computers in their jobs. Zainab concluded that additional training would be needed to prepare staff for the Multimedia Super Corridor. Although staff members were aware of project requirements, the MSC could be effectively implemented only if more workers became skillful computers users.

SINGAPORE—TECHNOLOGY POLICY IN THE INTELLIGENT ISLAND

By no means was Malaysia alone in seeking economic development through technology leadership. Singapore fashioned itself as the "intelligent island," a city-state built around an infrastructure of cutting-edge information technology. This notion was laid out in a government document published in 1992 called "A Vision of an Intelligent Island." The paper summoned Singaporeans to join in a national undertaking not unlike the Multimedia Super Corridor, proposing that "some 15 years from now, Singapore, the Intelligent Island, will be among the first countries in the world with an advanced nationwide information infrastructure. It will connect virtually every home, office, school, and factory" (cited in Yeo and Arun, 1999). Consisting of an island of roughly twenty by eleven miles (forty-two by twenty-three kilometers)—in total an area of 224 square miles—Singapore presented appropriate dimensions for the enterprise zone described in the Intelligent Island concept. Singapore had another advantage as well. It had one of the strongest economies in Asia, and therefore it could muster financial resources needed for costly infrastructure development.

Singapore's infrastructure was already the best developed in South and Southeast Asia. According to the Information Society Index produced by the International Data Corporation, Singapore's economy was the world's fourth most information driven, and the survey forecasted that it would jump to second place by 2002 ("Singapore—data," 1999). It had the widest reach in telecommunications, with more than fifty-five telephone lines per one hundred population, more than double the twenty-one lines per one hundred population established in Malaysia ("When India," 2000). In fact, this figure was the highest in all Asia, even higher than the figure of forty-nine in Japan and slightly higher than Hong Kong ("Wired China," 2000). Comparable figures in Indonesia and Philippines were less than ten per one hundred inhabitants. The advantage enjoyed by Singapore in Web access was even greater. The number of Internet users per ten thousand population in 1999 was an astonishing 2,946—about eight times greater than Malaysia's 368 and a figure well beyond even Taiwan's level of 1,373. Indonesia at 14.5 and the Philippines at 20.6 were far behind. According to the Information Society Index, about half of Singapore's adults carried a pager, and almost one-third of residents carried a cellular telephone. About 41 percent of Singapore households owned a personal computer, and based on this, the National Computer Board set as a goal adoption of electronic commerce by 50 percent of all firms by the year 2003. In an attempt to meet this goal, information enterprises worked feverishly though the end of the 1990s to wire Singapore's business and residential districts.

National ambitions in technology development were spelled out in detail by Senior Minister and former Prime Minister Lee Kuan Yew when he spoke at the Asian Media Conference in Los Angeles in October 1998. He began by noting the inevitability of technological change, suggesting that "the new media technology is here to stay and will become more all-embracing with time. It will change the governance of Asian societies." He then voiced a positive view of the future, "these societies will adjust, adapt and adopt the new media technology while retaining their traditional core values." Yet he accepted the potential threats, proposing that

> in the coming years, regulators around the world will have to act together to combat cross-border crimes in cyberspace. The new technology is a force for both good and evil. … Although it may take some time, morality and wisdom must find a way to control and tame the new technology to preserve the fundamental values of society by which parents bring up their children to be good citizens. In responding to this challenge of new technology, Asian societies will seek solutions different from those of the West. ("Media will stay," 1988)

Restating the Asian cultural values thesis, Lee ended his speech by proposing that "despite advances in technology, the media in the various countries of East Asia will remain different from the media in America."

To support the drive for technology leadership, Singapore created a program called "Singapore ONE [One Network for Everyone]" in 1997. Under this plan, the country installed wired technology across the island, making it available to nearly all homes, businesses, and institutions. The project provided for 95 percent of residences to be connected electronically to government, telecommunications, and computer services. The Singapore ONE project is based on an asynchronous transfer mode (ATM) optical fiber network that when fully implemented will amount to an estimated 186,000 miles (300,000 kilometers) of fiber. Although the project's initial goal was to have 400,000 subscribers by the end of 2001, eventually about 90 percent of the country's population would use the network (Tort, 1999). Meanwhile, the country made a gigantic investment in hardware to support voice and data services, something close to USD $1.2 billion in 1998 alone. Starhub, a private firm, was awarded a license to begin operations in 2000 providing fixed and mobile telephone service in the project. It announced plans to invest about USD $1.2 billion in its networks by 2009. The new company was formed by a partnership of Singapore Technologies, Singapore Power, British Telecommunication, and Nippon Telegraph and Telephone ("Singapore—data," 1999).

To set the stage for infrastructure development and for industrial restructuring needed for regional technological leadership, the legal framework for telecommunications was redesigned. For the first time, the Telecommunications Act of 1992 provided for competition and liberalization in the IT field. The legislation also separated the regulatory and service components of Singapore Telecommunications, creating the Telecommunications Authority of Singapore (TAS) as the agency responsible for supervision of information technology sector. But, as Ang (1999, p. 102) pointed out, the TAS not only regulates telecommunications but promotes Singapore's technology "to ensure that Singapore telecommunications infrastructure ranks with the best in the world in terms of accessibility, quality, service, and price." In the end, the Singapore government decided that an integrated policy structure made more sense. In March 1999, it announced that TAS, the National Computer Board (NCB), and portions of SBA would be merged into a new "streamlined" agency to be known as the Information Technology and Telecommunication Authority (ITTA) of Singapore. At the same time, it also renamed the Ministry of Communication as the Ministry of Communication and Information Technology.

Practically every aspect of Singaporean society was touched by the emphasis on technical advancement, but Singapore's wholehearted embrace of IT had a particularly pronounced impact on education. Utilization of computer technology in the classroom was one of three government priorities for the education system in the twenty-first century. According to Chia (2000), the Information Technology Master Plan for Education aimed to allocate 20 percent of classroom time to activities related to information and communication technology (ICT). In a survey of twenty-seven nations, including many industrialized nations in Europe and Japan, Singapore had the highest level of access to modern personal computers in primary and secondary schools. Among these countries, Singapore ranked third, behind only Canada and Norway, in the number of computer workstations per student ("IT survey," 1999). Some experts have voiced reservations about the inactivity and isolation that heavy use of computer technology may cause, yet Chia described Singapore's plans for computers to be used even in physical education classes. Although he noted that this possibility had "not received much attention," he suggested that "as ICT use in all curriculum subjects becomes pervasive, it is important for physical education teachers to be thinking and reflective users of the technology" (p. 98). Soong (1997) was one researcher who pointed out negative aspects of the drive toward educational technology in Singapore. She foresaw social, political and economic drawbacks, and noted the special pressure this placed on the government. She was particularly worried about family problems that technology adoption might introduce, and she urged school counselors to take up such problems in meetings with families.

As in Malaysia and elsewhere, the stress on technology leadership was coupled with industrial policies providing at least a semi-open field for competitive enterprises. By April 2000, Singapore Telecom's service monopoly ended, opening the door to other players. By that time, and partly because of restraints on SingTel (the landline voice and data provider), the cellular telephone market had grown to whopping proportions. By 2000, there were three major mobile telephone operators, StarHub, MobileOne, and SingTel. United States companies were the dominant foreign communication and data equipment manufacturers in Singapore. Among the largest of these were Hewlett-Packard, 3COM, and Cisco Systems. Unlike the expansion occurring in the equipment manufacturing sector, however, the process of economic liberalization was extremely cautious in the fields of information media content providers and Internet service providers.

SingTel's business strategy was similar to ones employed in Malaysia's MSC—it reached out for foreign assets to strengthen its regional position. In early 2000, SingTel faced the disappointing failure of its proposal for the purchase of Cable and Wireless HKT. In fact, Hong Kong's most well-established telephone company was snatched away by Pacifc Century CyberWorks' takeover bid, an audacious move by a comparatively little-known Internet startup. As part of its overall plan, Singtel, which was 76 percent owned by the

Singaporean government, did manage to form a business alliance for regional broadband services with News Corp, the Rupert Murdoch media conglomerate ("Wake-up call," 2000). Singtel's drive to finalize partnerships like these came from a realization that competitiveness demanded strong regional and global alliances—ownership by the Singapore government would not alone ensure strength in the marketplace.

Malaysia's Multimedia Super Corridor program undoubtedly acted as a spur to Singapore's technology development policies. As Senior Minister Lee Kuan Yew explained it, "We will face stiff competition from Malaysia. ... Policies that we adopted which have made for our success are now followed by our neighbors" (cited in Hiebert, 1997). The competitive dynamic between the two nations resembles sibling rivalry, certainly a by-product of their intimate joint history. Prime Minister Goh raised eyebrows on both sides of the causeway in 1996 when he remarked, "Singaporeans will have no choice but to work smarter and harder. If we fall behind and cannot make a living, we may have to rejoin Malaysia." Although he seems obviously to have been making a joke, there was a flurry of speculation in Malaysia about the real intentions of the prime minister's remarks. As a tiny country surrounded by giants, Singapore does sense its disadvantages acutely. Prime Minister Goh Chok Tong expressed national sensibilities this way.

> We are like someone being chased by tigers with a cliff in front. The tigers are closing in fast but the cliff is difficult to scale. The tigers are the dynamic economies like Thailand, Malaysia, Indonesia, and China. The cliff is the formidable challenge posed by the developed countries ("Chasing the lion," 1977).

Much of this anxiousness is misplaced. Singapore does have a disadvantage in population and geographic size, but in technology achievement it far outstrips other tiger economies of Southeast Asia. A study reported in the *Far Eastern Economic Review* suggested that among a group of forty-nine countries worldwide, Singapore ranked second in technology infrastructure whereas Malaysia ranked nineteenth; whereas Singapore ranked second in computer literacy, Malaysia was ranked twenty-eighth (Hiebert, 1997). In any case, competition between Malaysia and Singapore does not imply that if one wins, the other must lose. On the contrary, because the two countries have closely linked economies and because of their geographic proximity, if industrial technology policy in one succeeds, the other is bound to benefit as well.

THAILAND AND INDONESIA

Like Malaysia and Singapore, Thailand has also tried to employ technology as an engine of national economic expansion and growth. Its efforts have not produced the results experienced in either of those countries just discussed, however, despite Thailand's great potential. The reasons for this are instructive. Unlike Singapore and Malaysia, Thailand did not have the benefit of regional leadership in the electronic manufacturing industry, even though the country was making good progress in that direction until the economic collapse of 1997–1998. The recession devastated large electronics corporations, leaving them on the verge of collapse. Because big firms were unable to give Thailand impetus in the regional battle for technical advantage, it became necessary for the smaller firms to serve as the foundation of a renewed initiative (see Mathews and Cho, 2000, pp. 58–59). Unfortunately, this drive had to be mounted under conditions in which foreign direct investment was stagnant or declining (see Lall, 1997, p. 66).

The lack of industrial leverage afforded by electronic industries forced Thailand to choose another route to develop its information and entertainment technology. Thailand put into place government and quasi-governmental agencies to nurture development of domestic IT firms. The National Electronics and Computer Technology Center (NECTEC) was assigned broad responsibility for technology development in the information field. The specific responsibility for information technology policy formulation was delegated under NECTEC authority to the National Information Technology Committee (NITC) in 1992. NECTEC, together with NITC, issued a white paper on future priorities in information technology in 1995. Titled *IT 2000*, the document laid out areas of need, such as education, economic development, and quality of life. The plan foresaw information technology as a logical means to address these important issues in Thailand. The policy document claimed to be offered in response to changing conditions such as "ending of the larger conflict in Indochina, the conclusion of the General Agreement on Tariffs and Trade (GATT), the formation of NAFTA and AFTA." Although the plan praised Thailand's achievements in areas such as implementation of a digital telecommunications infrastructure, it pointed to weaknesses in service quality, unmet demand, and a weak regulatory framework.

Three major "agendas" were set forth in the plan: (1) to "invest in an equitable information infrastructure to empower human ability and enhance quality of life," (2) to "invest in people—build a literate populace and an adequate information technology human resource base," and (3) to "invest for good governance" (Pairash, Reinermann, Goodman, and Pipe, 1997, p. 268ff). The motives of the plan seemed to be equally divided between economic and social issues. Like policies of other countries nearby, the paper proposed to make Thailand into a regional technology center, and it argued that "Thailand now stands at a crossroads. We must set out to develop the country into a modern regional hub in Southeast Asia." (Pairash et al., 1997, p. 267). Specifically mentioned as sectors to be exploited were financial services, manufacturing, transportation, tourism, and human resource development. At the same time, the document envisioned the use of information technology as a tool to develop social well-being, rural development, wealth redistribution, improved environment, and social harmony.

Policy documents such as *IT 2000* set Thailand's course to join other Southeast Asian countries in connecting its development and industrialization plans to technological superiority. Thailand's efforts to maintain its technical edge, however, were hampered by inaction in multiple bureaucracies charged with oversight of media and information development. In addition to NECTEC, the National Science and Technology Development Agency (NSTDA) had responsibility for policy making. Other key bodies included the Telephone Organization of Thailand (TOT), Communication Authority of Thailand (CAT), and the Ministry of Transport and Communication, each of which played roles in setting the national IT agenda. These and related agencies faced serious shortcomings in properly assessing conditions in the field, however.

According to Palasri, Huter, and Wenzel (1999), Thailand pioneered the development of networking in Asia when researchers at the Asian Institute of Technology in Bangkok established a telephone link to colleagues in Japan and Australia. Using ordinary personal computers and modems, during 1986 Kanchana Kanchanasut and Tomonori Kimura accessed university networks at foreign universities as far away as the United States. Thailand had an opportunity to assume a leadership role in IT through these early successes, but the window of opportunity soon closed as other countries responded more quickly. Although Thailand experienced rapid increases in per capita gross domestic product (GDP) over the last two decades of the twentieth century, there was not a commensurate growth in information technologies. At the time of the most explosive growth in the Internet during the mid-1990s, the official view of government policy was that the network was mainly for the use of government offices and for academic research and communication purposes. Consequently, Thailand soon fell behind its neighbors in the race for technology leadership. By 1996, Thailand's ratio of Internet hosts to GDP was only 49.4, just slightly better than Philippines (44.6) and Indonesia (41.7), but well below 165.0 in Malaysia and 284.2 in Singapore (Palasri et al., 1999). According to Busakorn (1996), by the end of 1995 there were only sixty corporate nodes connected to commercial Internet service providers in the country.

Of course, Thailand was better positioned than some countries in Southeast Asia. Indonesia, by virtue of the nation's size and enormous population, was another contender for the regional technology leadership prize. Indonesia might seem an unlikely candidate for technical leadership, yet at least one project aimed to place the country squarely in competition with Singapore and Malaysia. Indonesia has hosted electronic manufacturing firms, but like Thailand, the industry has never been at the same size or at the same level of technical development as its neighbors. Indonesia's candidate for regional cyber supremacy resembles Malaysia's MSC, but on a much smaller scale. Called "CyberCity" by its main backer and chief architect, Edward Soeryadjaya, it is planned as a technology center of only forty-four hectares located in an abandoned airport near Jakarta. The site would serve as an incubator and operating base for newly formed companies or high-tech firms lured to the site. Although judged by some observers to be hopelessly optimistic, the venture did attract backing by the Japanese government and a grouping of Japanese companies (Caragata, 2000). By early 2000, a few companies (such as an Internet service provider, a computer systems firm, and the Jakarta Multimedia Academy) were operating from CyberCity. For this plan to grow into a major force, great changes in the legal framework for information media will be needed, and improvements in infrastructures such as telephone and data services will have to be implemented. At the time of this writing, no firm plans for these improvements were under consideration.

SIZING UP THE CORRIDOR

As intimated in the foregoing description, national technology development initiatives had their critics and skeptics. Predictably, some opposition arose from persons who saw the plans as overreaching, extravagant, and wasteful. Others, technology experts and academics, privately expressed doubts about their feasibility and about proposed benefits. Criticism of the Multimedia Super Corridor was especially harsh, and a brief analysis of the complaints about this project reveals the factors at work here. His support of the MSC placed Malaysia's prime minister in the uncomfortable position of advancing compromises to attract foreign, mostly Western, investment. As one who frequently used international venues to criticize Western governments and enterprises, Mahathir was forced, somewhat awkwardly, to defend tax holidays and other concessions his government offered to international firms that invested in the MSC. His response to a query on this point was that "it is a reality that foreign investments had made the nation much richer now and the people are enjoying more income than before." But he stressed limitations placed on overseas investors, saying, "We do not know what is coming. What we know is that if it is done elsewhere, we will still feel the negative effect. That is why we restrict them to the designated zone … this is our precaution. We take precautionary measures so as not to expose the whole of Malaysia" (cited in Ashraf, 1997).

As the country slipped into recession in late 1997 and the downturn deepened in the following year, questions about the policy of granting concessions to foreign companies grew more insistent.

The criticism from at least one of the opposition parties was not that the

MSC was overly ambitious but that the policy failed to address human aspects of IT. The DAP's leader Lim Kit Siang admitted that "the MSC may be the crown jewel of the National Information Infrastructure (NII) which Malaysia must build if we are to make the transition to the Information Society." But he continued, "In the ultimate analysis, the IT revolution must be about people, how it would completely change the way people work, live, learn and not about the power of microprocessors or bandwidths" (Lim, 1997, p. 11).

Even government authorities had to acknowledge the importance of doubts that critics had raised. MDC executive chairman Tan Sri Othman Yeop Abdullah, in explaining early deadlines set for Cyberjaya, admitted the dates were "aimed at instilling confidence among investors. They are a bit impatient because they see nothing happening" (Hong, 1997). The original deadline for the city's founding was set for 1999 but was moved ahead to 1997 to reassure investors. Even so, by the middle of that year, the city was only a bulldozed site in the middle of a palm oil plantation.

By the year 2000, skepticism about the logic of the Multimedia Super Corridor had begun to creep into reporting on the project. By then, the political atmosphere had changed subtly by reporting on the Anwar affair and by a sequence of events that hinted at the vulnerability of national leadership. These events included a challenge to Mahathir's control over UMNO, the rising popularity of alternative information channels such as on-line newspapers, and unease over Mahathir's frequent sometimes confrontational public clashes over his government's policies. Gloom over the negative atmosphere cast a pall over all official campaigns, and especially the MSC, because it had been seen as grandiose from the beginning. As *The Economist* saw it, "Many of the billions of dollars Asian countries are spending to reproduce Silicon Valley's high-tech hum will be wasted. Asia does have a high-tech future—but it is not the one its governments are hoping for" ("Asia online," 2000).

On the one hand, by 2000 more than 360 companies had been awarded official recognition as MSC participants. Included among those participating were some large multinational firms, including Nippon Telegraph and Telephone, Arthur Anderson, and McDonalds. On the other hand, most of the important international technology firms such as Microsoft, Intel, and Sun Microsystems had set up only small offices in the MSC. Microsoft, for instance, had set up a tiny facility in Cyberjaya, housing only a staff of seven, and allocated a five-year budget of $2.6 million (Omestad, 2000). According to figures from the Multimedia Development Corporation (MDC), nearly two-thirds of the companies accorded official MSC status were domestic Malaysian firms. Of the remainder, only 8 percent were from the United States, 13 percent were European, and 3 percent were Japanese. According to MDC's senior manager for special projects, Zait Isa, the corridor aimed to host fifty "world class" companies by 2003, with that number rising to 250 in 2010 and ultimately to 500 by 2020 (Trina, 2000).

Regardless of optimistic projections for growth in the future, most observers considered foreign investment in the MSC by 2000 to be disappointing. The purpose of the project was to attract funds from leading technology firms to make Malaysia a regional center for information and technical leadership. But with the predominant investment coming from Malaysian sources and with similar efforts mounted in Singapore, Hong Kong, Taiwan, and even Thailand, the prospects for achieving the project's aims are highly uncertain. The reasons for slow growth in investment appear to be more than just regional competition. Lall (1997) suggested that Malaysian policy differed from that of highly successful Singapore in at least one important respect. According to him, Malaysia "retained a protected import substitution regime" but "the import-substituting sector did not have many technology-import interventions, and little help was given to local enterprises in searching for and buying foreign technologies" (p. 71). Finally, as suggested above, Mahathir's own public persona and government policies have been impediments. His advocacy of "Asian values" and repeated criticisms of "globalization and purported Western plans to recolonize developing nations" appeared to have dampened investors' willingness to commit capital to the Multimedia Super Corridor.

ACROSS THE REGION

Economists often discuss Malaysia and Singapore as if they were a single entity, even though they are totally independent nations. It is true their economies are so intertwined that both are forced to act more or less in parallel. Both countries followed similar industrial policies in the field of electronic technology, characterized by Lall (1996, p. 18) as "interventionist … combined with free trade." Their guided economies grew into globally successful electronic production centers that served as a platform for each to launch further development projects, Malaysia's Multimedia Super Corridor and Singapore's Intelligent Island.

In the information field, technological competence and industrial capacity are essential, but they are not sufficient. It is one thing to manufacture hardware components but quite another to process sensitive information and cultural products. Skeptical investors from the West—especially the United States—found the information policies conventionally pursued by the tiger economies deeply troubling. There were attempts in each country to set aside these concerns through clarifications, assurances, and new "cyberlaws" designed to spell out guarantees for venture capitalists. Nevertheless, reassurance such measures offered tended to be upset by events within these countries; all were set back badly by the economic "Asian flu" of 1997–1998. Thailand was particularly harmed by 1998 revelations of corruption on a previously unsuspected scale and Malaysia was haunted by Western capitalists' distrust of its prime minister.

Competition among the tiger countries cannot be conducted in isolation, however, and eventually there will need to be some degree of coordination and cooperation among regional information centers. MDC executive chairman Tan Sri Othman Yeop Abdullah acknowledged this when he called for common legislation to define standards for e-commerce. Noting that electronic commerce must be conducted across national boundaries, he said this required "a high level of secure transactions and we have to work very hard on this if we want to be there" ("Asia's cyber hubs," 2000). He indicated his desire for the Asia Pacific Economic Co-operation Forum (APEC) to address this issue.

REFERENCES

Acquiring IT for a better tomorrow. (1997, January 11). *New Straits Times.*

Ahmad K. (1997, March 24). Cyberlaws to be tabled by year-end. *New Straits Times.*

Ang P. H. (1999). Information highways—policies and regulation: The Singapore experience. In V. Iyer (Ed.), *Media regulations for the new times* (pp. 97–114). Singapore: Asian Media Information and Communication Centre.

Ashraf A. (1997, April 12). Dr M: Nation can gain directly from MSC. *New Straits Times.*

Asia online. (2000, February 5). *The Economist.*

Asia's cyber hubs require common code. (2000, July 17). *New Straits Times.*

Busakorn S. (1996). *A critical perspective on Thai Internet policy making: Commercialization and public access.* Retrieved April 8, 2001 from the World Wide Web: http://www.busakorn.addr.com/thaitcom/ThaiInternet-all.htm.

Caragata, W. (2000, March 10). Bricks before clicks. *Asiaweek.*

Chasing the lion. (1997, February 27). *Far Eastern Economic Review.*

Chia, M. (2000). Information and communications technology and physical education in Singapore. *Media Asia, 27,* 94–98.

Goh, C. (1997, January 16). PM: Hollywood could gain from MSC. *New Straits Times.*

Hiebert, M. (1997, February 27). Future shock. *Far Eastern Economic Review.*

Hong, C. (1997, May 17). Intelligent city brain of MSC. *New Straits Times.*

IT survey ranks Singapore tops. (1999, November 21). *Straits Times.*

Lall, S. (1997). *Learning from the Asian tigers.* New York: St. Martin's Press.

Lim K. S. (1997). *IT for all.* Kuala Lumpur: Democratic Action Party.

Mathews, J. A., and Cho, D. (2000). *Tiger technology: The creation of a semiconductor industry in East Asia.* New York: Cambridge University Press.

Media will stay different. (1998, November 2). *Straits Times.*

Omestad, T. (2000, September 25). Building a high-tech magnet. *U.S. News and World Report.*

Pairash T., Reinermann, H., Goodman, S. E., and Pipe, G. R. (1997). Social equity and prosperity: Thailand information technology policy into the 21st Century. *The Information Society, 13,* 265–286.

Palasri, S., Huter, S., and Wenzel, Z. (1999). *The history of Internet in Thailand.* Eugene: University of Oregon Books.

Pang E. F., and Lim, L. (1977). *The electronics industry in Singapore: Structure, technology, and linkages.* Singapore: Economic Research Centre, University of Singapore.

Singapore—data communications equip market. (1999). *FT Asia Intelligence Wire.* Washington, DC: U.S. Department of Commerce.

Soong, C. (1997, May). *A vision of an intelligent island.* Paper presented at the International Conference on Counseling in the 21st Century, Beijing.

Tort, M. A. (1999, August 30). These are part of this big effort to become an intelligent island. *BusinessWorld.*

Trina T. R. (2000, July 7). MSC-status firms will be big contributor to GDP. *New Straits Times.*

Verhulst, S. G. (1999) Coping with the new communications environment: Are regulations still relevant? In V. Iyer (Ed.), *Media regulations for the new times* (pp. 1–2) Singapore: Asian Media Information and Communication Centre.

Wake-up call. (2000, March 16). *Far Eastern Economic Review.*

When India wires up. (2000, July 22). *The Economist.*

Wired China. (2000, July 22). *The Economist.*

Yeo, S., and Arun M. (1999, August 15). Censorship: Rules of the game are changing. *Straits Times.*

Zainab N. (1998). Government staff attitudes toward the Multimedia Super Corridor of Malaysia. Master's degree professional project, E. W. Scripps School of Journalism, Ohio University, Athens.

Chapter Six

Internet Policies

Experts agree that the Internet has been a technological development of transcendental importance. It has altered human lives, particularly in the way that people interact and, increasingly, the way they get information about their world. These developments have been remarkable in the developed countries but even more dramatic in developing countries, where the Internet has become familiar even in the least developed areas. There are two dimensions of the Internet's popularity. First is the ease of access to information it provides. In vast regions of Africa and Asia, libraries and other kinds of information centers are rare, and those that exist frequently are poorly financed. The Internet can help fill the information deficit by bringing resources located around the globe to users in underdeveloped regions. This access is generally without intermediation or other controls. As will be described shortly, authorities in some countries of Southeast Asia have tried to restrict the Internet, but these efforts were never more than partially effective. It is the free, unrestrained opening to massive information and entertainment that makes the Internet so powerful in this region of Asia. The second property of the Internet is its enormous capacity for personal communications. Conventionally, distance has moderated communication between two parties—the greater the distance, the longer the transit and the greater the cost. But on the Internet, the time factor practically disappears; messages travel from the originating computer to the receiver within a few seconds or less. The cost is the same whether the distance is a few feet or around the world. The ability to communicate via the Internet has brought together people separated by great distances in a way no other technology could achieve. This capability produced headaches as well as benefits for policy makers. For instance, the Internet made it possible for dissidents living abroad to remain in nearly constant contact with their compatriots at home.

The Internet grew out of a project of the U.S. Defense Department called ARPANET (Advanced Research Projects Agency Network), based on a plan first published in 1967. The essence of the network was a new concept—packet switching, which evolved in parallel with the networking. This technique attached addresses to batches of data so that they could move across complex networks to arrive at their destination quickly and efficiently, without the need for hardware redirection. Four host computers were connected to the original ARPANET by 1969, but within a few years the number of interconnected computers rose rapidly. The number grew large enough so that by 1972 electronic mail capabilities were introduced to the network. For more than a decade afterward, e-mail was the most popular network application. A paper published by the Internet Society (on the Internet, of course) described the core characteristics of the network: "Internet was based on the idea that there would be multiple independent networks of rather arbitrary design, beginning with the ARPANET as the pioneering packet switching network, but soon to include packet satellite networks, ground-based packet radio networks and other networks" (Leiner et al., 2000). The technique for communicating among the diverse collections of networks was a set of standards called the transmission control protocol/Internet protocol (TCP/IP).

The universal acceptance of this TCP/IP protocol and the network-to-network structure produced a vast, unified interconnection system eventually linking together most of the world's principal computers. Even though the Internet was devised as a tool for academics and researchers, almost from the beginning other applications for the network emerged. Simple software used in early linkages among computers began to be replaced by more user-friendly packages for file sharing and for person-to-person communication in the early 1990s. As the Internet Society's unofficial history indicates,

The Internet has now become almost a "commodity" service, and much of the latest attention has been on the use of this global information infrastructure for support of other commercial services. This has been tremendously accelerated by the widespread and rapid adoption of browsers and the World Wide Web technology, allowing users easy access to information linked throughout the globe. Products are available to facilitate the provisioning of that information and many of the latest developments in technology have been aimed at providing increasingly sophisticated information services on top of the basic Internet data communication (Leiner et al., 2000).

Also, as the Windows operating system grew in popularity in Versions 3 and 3.1, a different kind of computer user—less technically savvy, more concerned about results than methods—began to appear. The introduction of Windows' enhanced visual and intuitive operating system established computers as commonplace tools of clerks, secretaries, and any others who needed to communicate in a written form or who needed to maintain records. As time passed, more computers entered homes where they provided better methods of personal communication and record keeping. Computers also became popular through entertainment software such as games, electronic photography, and—as Internet access grew—music, news, sports, and a range of other recreational activities.

In Southeast Asia, the Internet was an instant phenomenon. In the more developed countries, the potential of the global network as a business tool was perceived at once. Seizing on the opportunity to set the standard for the region, several countries embarked on ambitious plans to expand access to the Internet and to encourage development of local technical resources for the network. In Singapore, Thailand, Malaysia, Brunei, and the Philippines, public receptiveness to the Internet was high; these countries had large numbers of residents with enough wealth and technical know-how to make use of the Network. For instance, Malaysia's entrepreneur development minister Datuk Mustapha Mohamed spoke to the attendees of a Kuala Lumpur conference on the subject of opportunities in electronic commerce in 1996. Mustapha's thrill over the Internet's prospects was clearly evident.

> Imagine a captive global market of educated, literate professionals then multiply that by the number of computerised corporations. Think of new products and services required to develop and sustain their ever-growing needs and the east in which business will be facilitated. ... Asia is ripe for electronics commerce as a means for Malaysian companies to compete effectively on a global platform (cited in Fadzil, 1996).

Such excitement was common among national leaders at that time. Malaysian Institute of Microelectronics Systems (MIMOS) director-general Tengku Datuk Dr. Mohd Azzman Shariffadeen effused that "the market for electronic commerce could be huge. This will be the virtual mall ..." (cited in Lee, 1996).

Frankenstein (1997) reported results of a survey on Asia-Pacific business use of Internet in the *Far Eastern Economic Review*. The findings underscored the Network's importance to commerce along the Pacific Rim. For example, Taiwan and Singapore respondents were the most avid users, with 41 percent in the former and 36 percent in the latter stating that the Internet was essential to their work. Across Asia, the majority of managers found the Net either essential or occasionally useful, from a high of 71 percent in Japan to a low of 63 percent in Indonesia. The survey pointed to a contradiction between respondents' beliefs and their actual behavior. The level of actual Internet use was substantially lower than indicated by their perception of its usefulness. Only 26 percent of managers surveyed in Singapore used it frequently, the highest figure in the region. At the same time, 28 percent of executives in Malaysia admitted they never used the Internet; the comparable figure from the Philippines was 21 percent and from Indonesia 20 percent. Interestingly, more women than men (by a ratio of 17 percent to 11 percent) believed that the Internet had contributed to efficiency.

One of the most powerful features of the Internet was e-mail. In 1992, only 2 percent of Americans used e-mail but within five years the proportion grew more than sevenfold to 15 percent. The business world of Southeast Asia was a little slower in adopting e-mail, but interest in it was high. A commentary in the *Far Eastern Economic Review* in 1997 urged its use, admitting that e-mail "is lagging in Asia, [but] it is available in most places. You don't need special phone lines or fast modems for e-mail messages. The clunkiest computers alive will send and receive e-mail just fine" (Fluendy, 1997). Once again, the availability of low cost (or often free, as in the case of Eudora Lite or Netscape Communicator) software encouraged use of e-mail. Anyway, in most countries of Southeast Asia, the cost of software was not an important issue because unauthorized copies of popular software were available, typically at a cost of less than USD $10 per CD-ROM. For a while, Southeast Asia was a center for global pirating of software, and the availability of inexpensive software stimulated greater adoption of computers across the region. Also contributing to the public interest in computers and e-mail was a plentiful supply of information on hardware and software. In Malaysia, all the major daily newspapers began publishing weekly computer supplements beginning in the early 1990s. In the English-language *Star* and *New Straits Times,* these are large tabloids inserts that appear twice weekly.

To accelerate Internet adoption, governments in Southeast Asia encouraged Internet providers to offer easy, inexpensive connection options. This was true in Malaysia where Jaring (a Malay word meaning net, as in fishing net) had been the pioneering Internet service provider (ISP), operated by MIMOS. To obtain a Jaring account in 1996, there was a one-time registration fee of USD $20—or in the case of students USD $8. Then, on-line charges were levied at the rate of USD $0.50 per hour—or for students USD $0.25 (Foo, 1996). Unlimited usage was also offered for a flat fee of USD $20 per month. Telephone access was available across the country with dial-in telephone numbers in more than twenty cities. Beginning in 1997 Jaring introduced an international roving service; users could dial in to local ISPs in many dozens of countries and the charges would be applied to their Jaring accounts. Other ISPs in

Malaysia soon began operation, notably one offered by Telekom Malaysia that started up in September 1996. The Telekom service was to be priced "attractively" according to Telekom CEO Datuk Mohamed Said Mohd Ali ("September launch," 1996), but some criticized the pricing schedule that emerged as too costly for home users ("Telekom Malaysia should," 1996). The growth in Internet users during the mid-1990s was extraordinary. MIMOS Director-General Datuk Tengku Azzman Shariffadeen claimed that "MIMOS had a growth rate of 22 percent per month [in 1995] which was very fast and we couldn't handle the number of subscribers. This year [1996] our growth rate dropped to 15 percent a month and managing the growth with partners has made it easier" (Ang, 1996).

Over following years, Internet service providers developed a range of specialized services to enlarge their subscriber bases. In Singapore, SCV (Singapore Cable Vision) offered Internet browsing via television beginning in 2000. Through the service, viewers could receive Web pages on their television screens. Officials did not claim their browsers were a full substitute for conventional browsing but rather a complement to existing connections via personal computers. As Desmond Poon, assistant manager of Broadband Engineering Services, SCV, explained it, "if you are at home, for example, after a day of work, you have enough of computers, you probably want to sit down and just relax and maybe go through some web pages" ("SCV's Internet," 2000). One clever feature of the SCV browser was hyperlinking; viewers could click on URLs (uniform resource locators) displayed on television shows and be switched immediately to the selected Web site. In Malaysia, government announced plans in late 2000 to build a wireless Internet system to extend coverage to the most remote areas of the country. The plan was estimated to cost approximately USD $83 million to bring coverage to an additional 120,000 rural residents. By 2000, efforts like these raised the level of Internet access to almost 9 percent of the population in Malaysia. This compared with about 39 percent in Singapore and 33 percent in Japan ("Wireless Internet," 2000). Brunei's strategy for the encouragement of Internet usage seems to have stressed in-school training. Khine (1994) reported that as early as 1992, the national curriculum included computer studies at the lower secondary level. The plan involved three years of classroom training to develop computer literacy.

In addition to a lag in the number of regional users, the availability of Southeast Asian resources on the Internet trailed developed countries in Europe, North America, and Australia. One study of library Web sites found that "the largest gateway on Southeast Asia is actually located outside the region at Leiden University in the Netherlands" (Lim, 1999). This Web site can be found at *http://iias.leidenuniv.nl/wwwvl/southeas.html*. The same study found that Singapore's own library gateway was maintained by the South/Southeast

Asia Library Service of the University of California, Berkeley. Another researcher found that "homepages exist for all the major academic libraries" for each country in Southeast Asia, and identified twenty-eight such library Web sites. But this study also noted that access to on-line library catalogs was only via Telnet in most cases, suggesting that merely a "handful" of libraries had Web-based catalog access (Rashidah and Wong, 1999). Both studies urged greater training of library personnel in Internet use so that better services could be offered to answer the increasing demand for library Web resources.

Despite the overall sense of enthusiasm, there were Internet detractors. In Malaysia, Prime Minister Datuk Seri Dr Mahathir Mohamad warned against potential dangers in unlimited access to the Web. He urged Malaysians to develop a "moral fortress" as protection against "undesirable information." He said that "without the moral fortress, people would become victims and use their information sources for the wrong purposes, such as viewing pornography." Ironically, he made these remarks at the opening of the on-line edition of the Malay-language newspaper *Utusan Malaysia.* He conceded that the Internet could be useful, but noted that "the Internet is like a knife which can be used either to kill or to carve a beautiful sculpture" ("Beware dangers," 1996). It is also clear that pornography and cultural content were not the only concerns motivating officials in Singapore and Malaysia. In 1996, the Singapore government had announced creation of a national Internet Advisory Committee. This body was set up as the agency responsible for devising techniques and standards for censoring Web content. The minister for information and the arts and health, Brigadier-General George Yeo, said at the time the purpose was "not to impede the growth of Internet, but rather to promote its healthy growth. … Clash of ideas is good but we do not want ideas that are extreme" (Kaur, 1996). When asked what he thought would be objectionable, he mentioned pornography and content that would promote religious and racial hatred. But by this time, even in placid Singapore, the Net's political content had become a worry. In September 1996, the Singapore Broadcasting Authority enacted rules governing "subversive" Internet Web sites that might "incite disaffection against the government" (Gordon, 1996). Based on this, it seems the government's greatest concern was over the airing of domestic political issues on the Net, not politics beyond its borders. Through the period from 1997 to 1998, a prime example of the growing political power of the Internet was presented by events in Indonesia.

THE INTERNET IN INDONESIA—AN EXAMPLE FOR THE REGION

Beginning in July 1997, the economies of a number of East and Southeast Asian countries began to weaken. Reasons for the decline were complex and differed in each country, but the catalyst seems to have been collapses of financial banking institutions in Korea and Thailand. Swiftly expanding insolvency among large government-backed corporations in those countries sent shockwaves throughout the region. This tended to further weaken economies that were already fragile, and for a time there was a downward spiral that affected the whole region. Indonesia was one of the most vulnerable countries. Its economy was in danger because of mismanagement and grossly corrupt government-business practices. These problems were only magnified by the economic squeeze that occurred when foreign investment was frozen or withdrawn in response to large losses being absorbed elsewhere in Asia. The declining financial situation rippled across the archipelago, placing overwhelming pressures on Indonesian financial institutions. The Indonesian rupiah's value plummeted from about 2,000 to USD $1 to less than Rp 10,000 to USD $1 at one point. Many with modest savings found what little they had to be worthless because of the rupiah's diminished value and because many banks closed their doors or froze depositors' accounts.

A belief common in Southeast Asia is that political stability rests on economic good times. This theory was put to the test in Indonesia during the failure of confidence for the rupiah. Public anger over the financial collapse translated into a reaction against Indonesia's President Suharto. Events began to race out of control in 1998. In January it became known that Suharto had selected B. J. Habibie as his vice president. This unsettled investors, many of whom considered him an unrealistic technology maven who had squandered hundreds of millions of dollars in a nonsensical struggle to build an Indonesian aircraft industry. Both stock valuations and the rupiah plunged. From February through May, student street protests grew in intensity, ravaging Jakarta and several other cities. During this time the Internet became the central communicative tool for dissidents and student protests. On May 12, five students were killed in protests at Trisakti University. Reaction to the killings produced an explosive furor across the country; protests peaked in the days after May 15 when more than 500 protesters were killed ("Indonesia awakes," 1998). Support for Suharto crumbled rapidly thereafter as even his trusted longtime supporter Harmoko, Speaker of Parliament, called for him to step down. On May 21, Suharto abruptly announced his resignation.

Indonesian media under Suharto were subject to tough restrictions on political reporting, making it impossible for activists to get up-to-the-minute information through state-controlled outlets. Government officials tried to quell the unrest by sending soothing messages via state broadcasting media—TVRI and RRI—and by bullying private television broadcasters into projecting the government viewpoint. Freedom House, a U.S.-based human rights group concerned with information access, published a report titled *Survey of Press Freedom* in 1996. This report evaluated information policies in countries around the world, presenting comparisons of data showing how policies in each nation affect information available to its citizens. The survey rated seven of the ten countries of Southeast Asia "not free." These were Singapore, Malaysia, Indonesia, Cambodia, Laos, Vietnam, and Myanmar (Gordon, 1996). Such judgments were based largely on internal constraints placed on reporting of events such as those that unfolded in Indonesia.

As the political situation came to a boil in Jakarta and across the archipelago, opposition forces not only took to the streets but also redirected their information campaigns away from leaflets and other printed materials—the only channels available a generation before—to the Internet. Anti-Suharto groups found the Internet provided an inexpensive, ubiquitous means of staying in touch with others who had similar political objectives. It was also useful as a means of staying informed on events, reports of which were being suppressed by the government and military censors. Internet chat rooms, mail lists, and Web sites provided activists an opportunity to promote their causes without interference from government. These channels were beyond the reach of authorities. Some snippets from the news group soc.culture.indonesia provide examples of the rhetoric. One writer identified as Ferry Winokan argued against the government: "Do you still need ABRI or Indonesian army to rule the country? … This is not wartime and who needs the army to roam around the country to partake in bribery and corruption?" Another proposed new national leadership: "Mr. Rais has got what it takes to run Indonesia, Inc. Mrs. Megawati is more like Cory Aquino." Of course the Internet has no political bias of its own, and some of the respondents on the Net spoke in support of Suharto. One proposed "if [Suharto] is wise, listens to US officials and the IMF [International Monetary Fund], Indonesia is safe. But, his family and friends will lose their companies. If not, Indonesia will be doomed because of someone's arrogance" ("Taking it," 1998). Among the most influential of Internet information sources was the U.S.-based Indonesia mail list "apakabar." According to journalist T. Basuki, the list "helped accelerate Indonesian society's awareness of the need for change as it encouraged open and democratic debate on issues" (Pabico, 1999).

The Internet's critical contribution to political actions taking place in Jakarta was the unification of disaffected Indonesians everywhere. Scattered and separated by considerable physical distances, they previously had been unable to coordinate actions, but the opportunity to communicate across the breadth of the country via the Net meant more effective resistance to government's anti-opposition measures. Even Indonesians abroad could participate in the country's political scene. One person who did this, Abigail Abrash working at the Robert F. Kennedy Memorial Center for Human Rights in Washington, D.C., watched events unfold through the Internet. During the turmoil in Jakarta she relayed U.S. news media reporting of events in Indonesia and skimmed reports flooding back from correspondents on the scene in Indonesia. Abrash, who described amazement on her discovery that "even remote towns in Indonesian Borneo [Kalimantan] were 'wired,'" observed that "in a country that's as far-flung as Indonesia, the Net has meant that people have been able to communicate at a time like this." The strength of numbers provided by the Internet, together with its anonymity, gave the opposition greater leverage. As one respondent who used the Net alias Asia Son wrote on a chat group, "one or two people saying [they are opposed to Suharto] are easily dragged away and silenced. One or two million it is not so easy" (Marcus, 1998).

Numerous antigovernment campaigns were launched via the Internet. One such example was an appeal by George Aditjondro, a prominent Indonesian academic, seeking a boycott of companies associated with Suharto's family. Aditjondro, who served as a lecturer at University of Newcastle in Australia, was a frequent critic of Indonesia's "New Order" government. He left Indonesia in 1995 after issuing strong criticisms of East Timorese policies. Aditjondro's boycott aimed to punish U.S., European, and Australian firms that had business arrangements with Suharto's children (Aisbett, 1996). Not only did activists promote their political positions, but in a few instances opposition-inspired hackers attacked government Web pages, disabling them or leaving behind resistance slogans. At one point in early in 1996, engineers at the Agency for Assessment and Application of Technology (BPPT) admitted that their Web home page had been attacked by politically motivated hackers who left behind graffiti for "Free East Timor." At the time, Suharto supporter and later interim president B. J. Habibie headed BPPT. According to one engineer, the hacker had been traced to Portugal, the country that had ruled East Timor until Indonesia annexed the territory in 1976 (Jacob, 1996).

Many questioned the accuracy of reports bouncing around the Net—and with good reason. Stories were often distorted through the perceptions of untrained overzealous observers, and some were sheer fabrications. Pictures of violent unrest, often portraying the most grisly scenes imaginable, were a common feature of Internet reports from the Indonesia in the weeks leading up to the end of the Suharto government. But some images of victims that were distributed widely on the Internet were identified as hoaxes. One picture showing a woman being viciously beaten was displayed on an Indonesian news Web site but was later found to be a stock photo from a site specializing in gory photographs (Kwok, 1998).

It was not merely the activists who wanted information from the Net. Confusion in Indonesia during 1998 produced among many residents an enormous swell of interest in reliable, up-to-date information. Popular news sites such as the BBC and CNN reported increases in readership. The *Straits Times* in Singapore was one of the leading newspapers in the region, and it provided extensive coverage of events in neighboring countries through its popular on-line edition. The *Straits Times* reported a 40 percent increase in hits during 1998 from the preceding year, mostly attributable to an increase of 25 percent in hits from overseas browsers. Indeed, the newspaper reported that the rise appeared to be largely due to more accesses from overseas readers, probably for coverage of the troubles in Indonesia and the dismissal and subsequent trial of Malaysia's Deputy Prime Minister Anwar Ibrahim. One journalist at the on-line edition, Raoul Le Blond, reported that he received e-mail from witnesses to street violence and from observers in threatening situations. Some Chinese Indonesians sent their reports on Indonesian events to the on-line edition of the Singapore newspaper because "access to their local media was blocked to them" ("ST Interactive," 1998). Popularity of the on-line edition seems to have been at least partly a result of expanded readership for online newspapers. A survey in 2000 found that 26 percent of Internet users had read an electronic newspaper ("Internet and cable," 2000).

INDOCHINA'S INTERNET PRESENCE

Few areas of the world held as little apparent promise for Internet utilization as did the former Indochina. The three countries of Vietnam, Cambodia, and Laos maintain different forms of post-Soviet socialism and have fundamentally agrarian societies, even though industrialization is gradually building. From the creaky government center in Vientiane to the rapidly modernizing Hanoi, however, there is a big contrast in development. And, as suggested earlier, Cambodia is still reeling from one of the most brutal and destructive regimes in modern history. In barely more than three years, over the period of 1975–1979, the entire educated class was eliminated, and the country's economy was turned back to little better than Stone Age conditions. Laos' economy is particularly underdeveloped, and the slow-moving and hesitant government has had little to show for its development investments. Vietnam, on the other hand, after mismanaging its economy for a decade following the end of the war, introduced liberalization in the form of *doi moi*—or restructuring—beginning in 1987. This, coupled with changes in party leadership and the further liberalization of the Seventh Party Congress of 1991, produced a turnaround in the national economy. For a time in the early and middle 1990s economic expansion in Vietnam was among the highest in the world, nearly 10 percent annual growth in gross domestic product. Even so, because Vietnam has the second largest population in Southeast Asia, economic growth has produced only moderate improvements on a per capita basis.

Vietnam had little access to the Internet until the late 1990s. Up to then, there were only experimental services available, including one e-mail pilot project initiated by an Australian university. This project revealed that pent-up demand was high; from its start in 1994, the service reported a doubling of traffic every five months (Marr, 1998). The government was put under more and more pressure to answer demands for access to the Net, but it was only in 1997 that authorities licensed three state corporations to operate as Internet service providers. Those three were the Vietnam Data Communications Company (VDC), the Saigon Postal Company, and the Military Telecommunications Company. Under official rules, access was not generous. On-line fees at VDC came to USD $1.80 per hour, and at this price level it was far too expensive for personal usage for any but the wealthiest Vietnamese. Beyond this, subscribers were required to pay an installation fee of USD $40 and a monthly service charge of USD $4 ("Vietnam switches," 1997).

Internet consciousness grew quickly in spite of costs. Within a matter of months, well before the end of 1997, a number of newspapers had begun online editions: *Electronic Times, Trade, Labor, Vietnam Investment Review, Que Huong* and *Nhan Dan* as well as the Vietnam News Agency. *Que Huong* was placed on the Internet specifically to serve overseas Vietnamese readers. It proved to be well received; in its first months of operation it experienced about 50,000 hits per month ("Four Vietnamese," 1997). Given the price structure in place, commercial applications were predominant. The marketing manager for a textile company in Vietnam claimed to prefer selling his products on the Internet. He said, "looking for customers on the Internet is faster than grabbing a suitcase and going all over the world. Even then you can't expect to find the sort of customers you want" (Mehta, 1998). In fact, the Internet's commercial possibilities are the main reasons for party tolerance of the troublesome Network. In November 2000 the newspaper *Labor* reported that Vietnam's own mini-Silicon Valley, the Saigon Software Park, had been connected with a 2Mb Internet line "to promote e-commerce with organizations abroad" ("Software park," 2000).

The Mekong Project Development Facility (MPDF) offers itself as a model organization for commercial utilization of the Internet. This MPDF was formed in 1997 with World Bank funding to support private small and medium-sized enterprises in Indochina. From its headquarters in Hanoi, the organization provides assistance to private entrepreneurs through local business services and through links to foreign and domestic financial institutions. In a report released in August 2000, the MPDF urged small and medium-sized enterprises to set up their own Web sites. An official at the organization explained that "we want to get Vietnamese sellers and foreign buyers closer together" (Son, 2000). Its Web site (www.mpdf.org) was inaugurated in 1999 and offers multilingual resources (English, Vietnamese, Lao, and Khmer) for small business operators. The purpose of the Web site is to link with private companies and encourage entrepreneurship and to aid privatization in Indochina. It also serves to demonstrate how to go about projecting an organization through the Network. The Web site has a pleasant design, but it is very simple. Uncomplicated designs are necessary to keep access times low in areas where Internet speeds are slow, as they are likely to be in Indochina.

From the beginning, the Vietnamese government clearly had misgivings about Internet. When users sign up with an ISP, they receive a brochure explaining the strict regulations they must follow, and they are warned that the Culture and Information Ministry will monitor their use of the Internet. As late as 1998, organizations that implemented Internet access had to give the Culture and Information Ministry a complete list of staff members, including their career histories. If that were not enough, officials have taken steps to block access to sites considered dangerous. Even with all these precautions there are signs that the government is not happy with the way the Internet has been used. The official newspaper *Labor* reported dismay over e-mails flowing into Vietnam. In its April 9, 1999, edition, it reported, "It is noteworthy that the exiled reactionaries and hostile forces have sent many bad and reactionary documents via the Internet to Vietnam. Some people inside the country have encrypted their documents before sending them overseas. Many of our secret documents have been exposed on the Internet. This has not been discovered and prevented properly." The report concluded that adequate measures taken to enforce regulations had not been taken ("Vietnam report," 1999).

Another country that has had qualms about public use of the Internet is Laos—more formally known as the Lao People's Democratic Republic. Reportedly, use of the Internet was banned, and some people were prosecuted for secretly logging on to the Net. It definitely was the last country in Southeast Asia to set up an infrastructure for connections to the Internet. The establishment of a state-operated ISP was finally made official in late April 2000 when Prime Minister Sisavat Keobounphanh signed a decree to create the National Internet Company. This service would be organized by the prime minister's office to provide "very important" communication links with the world ("Laos to set up," 2000). A committee of senior ministry officials was appointed to administer the company that serves as the sole state agency to manage Internet and its uses. Actual implementation of the government ISP was scheduled for December 2000. More than two years before this launch, Laos Telecommunications Company had announced plans to set up an ISP, but it apparently never came into operation. It had formed a partnership with Thailand's Shinawatra International, but service startup was postponed because, so it was said, of delays in receiving equipment. Another report indicates that an Australian firm, PlaNet Online, had been granted a license for operation (Uimonen, 2000). This does not mean Laos had no Internet access at all. Those with sufficient means could subscribe to an ISP in Thailand (Vientiane sits on the Eastern bank of the Mekong river dividing Thailand from Laos) and dial into it via telephone. I tried this technique in early 2000 but found it too expensive for regular use.

Like so many features of life in Cambodia, the Net's influences have ranged from sublime to ridiculous, and its development has exposed the country's best and worst features. Measures to capitalize on or to restrict the Internet seem to have been perfunctory; the nation's political unsteadiness since the 1991 signing of the Agreement on Comprehensive Political Settlement of the Cambodia Conflict kept officials' attention elsewhere. When working there in 1997, I found few options available for Internet access. By far the most popular alternative among expatriates was offered by a nongovernmental organization (NGO), Open Forum. Through the NGO, Cambodians could get an e-mail and newsgroup account for USD $8 (for foreigners the fee was USD $25). In theory users could also access the Web, but in practice connections to the Net were too slow to permit any serious browsing. Users could also access a collection of public documents stored electronically. At the time, Open Forum also produced a weekly English-language summary of the major Khmer-language news publications offered on a subscription basis to the country's large international community. Demand for Internet services was not particularly great; in early 1998, Open Forum had only 450 subscribers.

Even though the Internet had hardly begun to emerge as a force in Cambodia, a few were concerned about it. For example, a 1998 article published in the *Business News Review* (Cambodia) described the Indochina countries as "already facing an information downpour in the form of the Internet" ("Cambodia ASEAN," 1997). Most likely, that kind of thinking was simply an instinctive reaction against any channel of communication lacking an easy means of control. In modern times, Cambodia has never experienced anything less than a threatening political environment, and its political leaders have all restricted the media ruthlessly. Mehta (1997) explained the situation in this way: "newspapers' lives were short; they tended to vanish from the scene for a variety of reasons, chief among which was closure by the government, censorship, and imprisonment of an editor or director" (p. 15). More than 60 newspapers have been licensed in Cambodia, most producing editions irregularly. But the small number of readers and the even smaller number of advertisers made it impossible for more than a few to meet their expenses. To survive, most newspapers turned to political parties for financial support. This, in turn, has resulted in newspapers becoming subservient to the political agendas of their benefactors. Media coverage of political events invariably tends to be one-sided and often vitriolic. Because of this and because newspapers and broadcasting stations are known to have patrons and hidden agendas, there is little public trust of Cambodian media.

These conditions should ensure a high degree of interest in the kind of open information available on the Internet, and yet growth in the Net's adoption has been slow. The number of computers is not great; residents of the capital city of Phnom Penh probably own something on the order of 10,000 computers, many of them not really up-to-date. One estimate placed the number of Internet accounts in 1999 at only 2,500, and among these a large proportion belong to foreigners (Leslie, 1999). This figure is misleading, however. A common practice in the less-developed countries of Asia is for groups of persons to share one Internet account. This reduces subscription costs substantially, although naturally it means a loss of privacy because e-mail messages are open for all to read.

Although computers have not penetrated deeply into the society, they have played an important role in the political process since United Nations–monitored elections took place in 1993. Sam Rainsy, one of the key opposition leaders in Cambodia, made extensive use of e-mails in political campaigns and in sustaining his fractured movement. His followers have employed the Internet as a channel to persuade and to reach out to an international constituency, particularly the half-million expatriates still living abroad. In Sam Rainsy's view, the visibility provided by the Internet prevents heavy-handed tactics by his political opponents. As he noted, "sometimes [the Internet] can save lives. If someone is arrested, the world knows they have disappeared. If the world knows, there is hesitation from the authorities" (Dupont and Pape, 1999). Reportedly, Sam Rainsy hired an American with technical skills as his communication officer during his election campaign in 1998 (Leslie, 1999). The fact that he finished a fading third may indicate that although the Internet may be a useful tool for global communication, in underdeveloped Cambodia traditional personal campaigns (and the power of military force) are much more effective. One conduit through which e-mail flowed freely was the "camnet" list server. Although it seems to have been discontinued in late 2000, it had served up a daily digest of news items on Cambodia for years. Readers could contribute to the collection of reports that were distributed without subscription fees. Camnet kept scholars, researchers, activists, students—and most of all— the overseas Cambodian community linked together. Inflammatory reports are often relayed through channels such as camnet, but little official effort has been made to suppress them, although there is not much likelihood anything could be done to stop them in any case. In this respect, the Net reflects the bitterly conflictive yet wild and barely controlled character of political life in Cambodia. Misuses of the network do not seem to be matters that greatly trouble the country's authorities.

The untamed character of the Internet in Cambodia is reflected in many ways, some frankly repellant. Government officials reacted casually when a report was published about a pornography Web site established in Phnom Penh. The site promoted themes such as "Asian sex slaves" and portrayed naked Vietnamese women performing sex acts while blindfolded or tied up. The Web site was administered by an American who reportedly shrugged off objections to its content saying "it might promote violence against women in the United

States, but I say 'good' … " ("Cambodia up," 1999). Phnom Penh's Svay Park, more commonly known as "11 kilometers" is the sprawling center of the city's sex trade. It was lauded via the Internet's World Sex Guide, where it was claimed to offer even the availability of child prostitutes. A note on one Web site once claimed that in Phnom Penh "a six-year-old is available for $3" ("Virgin," 1996). Prostitution engages an estimated 15,000 in the capital city alone, even though some reports indicate that about one-third is HIV positive. Finally, Cambodia has found itself subject to a range of other Internet abuses such as a scam reported in 1999. The Khmer Web Internet cafe was accused of undercutting its competitors by dropping access fees to just USD $4 per hour, substantially less than other operators. But it developed that the cafe was covering its cash flow shortfall by using stolen passwords to charge on-line time to other user's accounts. A university professor reported this to authorities after getting a USD $2,500 bill from his ISP for one month's usage of 500 hours of on-line time ("Cambodian cyber," 1999).

INTERNET ACTIVISM IN MYANMAR

Although the Internet provides powerful new tools for communicating political messages, for many opposition groups it functions merely as an augmentation of existing communication networks. As has been described in Indonesia and Indochina, government opponents have employed the Internet extensively. However, the use of new technologies by dissidents has been known for quite a long time. Their efforts to wrest power from established political regimes always seemed to profit from use of the latest technologies, possibly because their entrenched opponents tended to be less proficient in their use. In the Beijing Tiananmen Square uprising in 1989, fax machines were used to disseminate opposition reports. In 1992, Thais received alternative descriptions of events in the military uprising through satellite reception of CNN. The same kinds of reporting via new media were factors in the collapse of communist governments in East and Central Europe, the abortive Russian coup in 1991, and dozens of attempted revolutions around the globe. The Internet's unique contribution to political activism is its reach and pervasiveness. A message originated in one point can travel anywhere in the world within seconds, leaping across borders and bypassing the complex screening processes that control the flow of information in conventional channels.

A war of political influence and power is being waged through the Internet over politics and ideology in Myanmar (formerly Burma). After the long-awaited resignation of Ne Win brought massive public demonstrations against the socialist government, a military junta seized power in 1988. In place of a constitutional government, the State Law and Order Restoration Council (SLORC) was installed. General Saw Maung, leader of the junta, became chairman of the SLORC and prime minister. Promising a speedy return to civilian rule, multiparty elections—the first in 30 years—were held in 1990. In that election, the main parties were the National Unity Party (successor to the Ne Win Socialist Party and supported by SLORC) and the National League for Democracy (NLD). The NLD won the vote in a landslide, apparently much to the surprise of the SLORC leadership. Refusing to accept their defeat, the SLORC forbade immediate convening of the Constituent Assembly, thereby preventing the elected government from taking power. For more than a decade, NLD has tried to force SLORC to resign and provide a transition of power to legitimate civilian rule. Worldwide attention was directed to Myanmar's political situation when Aung San Suu Kyi was awarded the Nobel Peace Prize in 1991. But intense global condemnation of the military government in Yangon (formerly Rangoon) seemed to make little difference to SLORC leadership. Instead, SLORC has focused its attention on NLD leader Aung San Suu Kyi, daughter of the nationalist leader Aung San. Under house arrest and constant surveillance, she has continued to agitate for political change. Political discord in the wake of these developments, and a long-running independence insurgency mounted by ethnic Karen, drove tens of thousands out of the country. Large refugee camps sprang up along the border in Thailand to accommodate people driven from their places of residence. These camps became semi-permanent homes to displaced peoples, especially for dispossessed Karen.

All of this became a recipe for conflict, and the political debate began to be played out on the Internet where political activists established a host of Web sites, Internet radio services, mail lists, and other informational initiatives to drive home their claim of the Yangon government's illegitimacy. Refugee camps serve as the contact points for opposition informational activities. Because internal communication channels are strictly controlled by the government, and to facilitate communication with the expatriate community, the Internet has become the preferred medium for antigovernment activists. An opposition newspaper, *New Era Journal,* produces about 15,000 copies each month on the Thai-Burmese border. Reportedly, about 85 percent of the output is distributed within Myanmar, despite the threat of a seven-year jail term for possessing the newspaper (Kurlantzick, 1998). The newspaper has its limitations—its reach is largely confined to areas along the border and distribution is slow. The Internet provides faster dissemination and messages travel globally with few impediments.

An important vehicle for communicating among Burma activists is BurmaNet, a mail list that offers regular information on practically all subjects concerning Burma, including human rights abuses, economic sanctions, and ethnic minorities. The editor of BurmaNet, known by the pseudonym "Strider," laid out the following explanation of the list:

We know that the SLORC monitors traffic on BurmaNet and has assigned intelligence personnel in Bangkok and Washington to subscribe and report on what gets said on the net. According to one fairly reliable source, Lt. Gen. Khin Nyunt [Secretary Number 1] is even a regular reader. Rather than seeing this as a threat, we welcome the chance to put a broad range of information and opinions before the gentlemen in Burma who hold the guns. They may in time see that there is little they can, or should want to do, to stop people from sharing uncensored news about Burma. In the meantime, they are helpless to stop us, so let them watch (Post from Strider, editor of BurmaNet, 21 July 1996, cited in Brooten, 1998).

The BurmaNet was founded in 1993 with funding from the Soros's Open Society Institute at Chulalongkorn University in Bangkok. It serves as the preeminent Internet channel of discourse on Burma-related issues. It carries news releases from a variety of sources, including the major international news services, as well as firsthand accounts and opinion. Brooten (1998) studied exchanges posted on the BurmaNet and discovered an effort by contributors to present themselves as spokespersons for larger causes to cloak themselves with legitimacy. She found that antigovernment activists framed their rhetoric as part of an all-embracing global struggle for democracy and human rights, not merely a localized clash of political forces. In reply, pro-government posting claimed to speak for "the people of Myanmar" not just as members of the military regime.

A story picked up from the *Myanmar Times and Business Review* carried on BurmaNet included an explanation of thinking in Yangon on the Internet. The articles praised the wealth of information sources available on the Net but cautioned that "much of it is what can best be described as junk." The article offered a description of a bright new world in which scholars, professionals in fields such as health care, and businesses would gain from the new possibilities. The technical director of CE Technology, Dr. Aung Maw, was quoted as explaining that "It is technically possible to just let through some sites. ... It would not be an intra-net, it would be the on-line use of the Internet with a firewall blocking the sites we do not need" ("Small steps to the Net," 2001). The need for improvement in the infrastructure to support Internet was acknowledged in the article, mainly in the area of improved telephone lines.

Aside from text-based Web sites, there are at least seven radio broadcasters streaming Burmese programs to an international listenership outside Myanmar. Among the most influential is the Democratic Voice of Burma (DVB), an opposition service based in Norway, at the address www.communique. no/dvb. In early 2001, its Web site explained its purpose as "an alternate news source informing about the progress of the Burmese democracy movement in liberated areas of Burma, and provid[ing] the various groups opposing the

Rangoon regime with a voice through which they can freely and openly express their views in a democratic manner." Another station is Radio Free Burma at www.fast.net.au/rfb. This Web site also provides text stories, a photo gallery, and a small collection of documents.

Although the Web gave activists a grand opportunity to spread their viewpoints worldwide, they had no ability to communicate with residents of Myanmar itself. Although lip service is given to the value and function of the Internet in Myanmar, access to it is severely restricted. The best example of this contradictory stand is the presence of a cyber cafe in Yangon which, according to the BBC, in early 2000 had neither computers nor access to the Internet (BBC, 2000). One informant indicated later that computers had, in fact, been installed at the cafe, but no Internet connections made. Until 1999 no official local Internet service was allowed to operate. Indeed, a 1996 law made it illegal merely to own a computer modem. When finally, near the end of 1999, the creation of a Burma-based ISP was announced, it was the government's own Myanma Posts and Telecommunications (MPT) that offered Web connections. Previously, an e-mail only service for a small number of users had operated for a few years ("Myanmar to provide," 1999). Five servers had been operating without government approval, but these were shut down and their equipment seized when the government ISP started functioning (Pennington, 2000). The government service was made available in Yangon and in Mandalay, and it was believed to be reaching about six hundred subscribers. The ISP was seen as a significant development by Burma watchers because it was yet another sign that the country was trying to move away from its international isolation. This isolation was occasioned both by the insular tendencies of the government itself and by opposition groups that hoped to pressure the regime by cutting it off from sources of international financing and global markets.

Not long after introduction of the Internet, and in a clear move against antigovernment activists groups at home and abroad, Myanmar enacted a decree banning Internet use for political purposes in January 2000. Included in the prohibitions were any "writings detrimental to the interests of the Union of Myanmar" and any "writings directly or indirectly detrimental to the current policies and secret security affairs of the government of the Union of Burma" ("Regulations for," 2000). Presumably, Burma-related mail lists such as BurmaNet are banned under these regulations. The ruling junta's ability to put this policy into practice was largely unchallenged, because of the government's monopoly on Internet service. In Myanmar, most observers believe that officials closely monitor the content of messages sent and received by users within the country. This seems to have been the means used to identify six persons, including one senior Burmese military officer, who were accused by authorities of downloading antigovernment material. They were charged with violating Myanmar's Official Secrets Act. There can be no doubt that authorities are prepared to exercise the full extent of their power to stop any technology that might be used against the regime. James Nichols, an honorary consul for several European countries and Aung San Suu Kyi supporter, died in prison in 1996. He had served six weeks of a three-year sentence for the crime of using a fax machine (Bardacke, 1996).

Government paranoia over the Internet is not limited to opposition activists' use of the Net. One senior official, Lt. General Khin Nyunt, told an information technology symposium in Yangon that Western nations were using the Internet to "destabilize" developing countries. He also mentioned the need for these countries to prevent the penetration of "decadent culture" ("Burmese leader," 1998). To aid their control over Internet, officials have established a "Cyber Warfare Center" in Yangon, with facilities developed by a Singaporean firm. The sophistication of this system is presumed to be great enough to intercept messages transmitted through the system. As a consequence of the Myanmar government's focus on the Internet, Burmese opposition groups based outside Myanmar—for instance, ones in Thailand—are believed to employ encryption routinely in their messages. The government also is fighting back by its own determined use of the Internet. A sophisticated Web page hosted by the Myanmar government operates from a server in the Washington, D.C., area. On this Web site visitors can get the latest explanations and official spin on events. In 1998, authorities used the official Internet site to counteract international reaction when the military government detained hundreds of pro-democracy opponents. The site carried photos that claimed to portray detainees relaxing at "government guesthouses." The shots were titled "NLD members who have been invited by the government to ask for their cooperation to help maintain the current peace, stability and development of the nation" ("Myanmar junta," 1998).

INTERNET VERSUS NON-WEB MEDIA

The impact of the Internet on other media remains an open question. Concerns expressed so far seem to focus on outlets that governments employ as channels to disseminate official announcements and campaigns. In most Southeast Asian countries, these consisted of the government broadcasting organizations and the semi-official newspapers. By the end of the 1990s, alterations in media habits had already begun to appear as a result of Internet online editions. A report by ACNielsen Media Index in October 2000 showed that in Singapore, cable television's weekly reach jumped from 20 percent to 28 percent in one year, while adults using the Internet grew from 30 percent to 37 percent during the same period of time. The total number of adults using the Internet at least once weekly totaled 1.1 million at the end of 2000. That increase was attributed to gains among professionals, managers, executives, and business people ("Internet and cable," 2000). This estimate meant that nearly 40 percent of the total population was tapping into Internet resources weekly. Cable television subscriptions in Singapore had risen sharply over the preceding year, from 19 percent to 27 percent, or about 820,000 homes. Meanwhile, newspapers' reach dropped slightly from 98 percent to 97 percent. News and information content was especially important in attracting media audiences. Although most television channels' reach showed a drop as the availability of channels grew, ACNielsen reported Channel NewsAsia went against the trend, with its audience rising by 4 percent over the year. One sign of the dramatic shift toward the Internet was an upsurge in advertising on Singapore Internet portals. According to ACNielsen, the total grew from USD $6 million in all of 1999 to USD $38 million in the first half of 2000 (Teh, 2000).

One of the Internet's most interesting features is its ability to consolidate existing media within its range of functions. Internet radio has blossomed, as have on-line newspapers, and even Internet television has begun to seem a real possibility. On-line newspapers have become especially important, and today no major newspaper would want to be without its own on-line edition. Southeast Asian on-line editions are considered vital to reach out to millions of expatriates living away from their homelands. A few such as *Malaysiakini* are uniquely on-line and have no printed versions. This interesting example is examined in detail in Chapter 8. On-line editions potentially offer a number of advantages over their print counterparts, but there is little evidence that publishers in Southeast Asia are exploiting them. Massey and Levy (1999) studied Asian on-line newspapers' attempts to achieve interactivity and found that "scant use was made generally of the Net's capacity for immediacy and for allowing readers to add their own content to the newspapers' sites" (p. 147).

At the time of this writing, most of Asia's leading newspapers officially viewed their futures optimistically, expressing no sense of threat from the Internet. At a conference on the subject sponsored by ING Barings Asia in October 2000, optimism reigned. Denis Tay, deputy president of Singapore Press Holdings (SPH), publisher of the Singapore's *Straits Times*, argued that rather than on-line readership depressing circulation, "readership on the Internet is driving readership on the print side. ... Print and the Internet complement one another." He admitted that his organization had started several new publications to compete against the growth in news sources available on the Internet and had undergone a "branding exercise" that led to promotions such as a charity duck race and reader's forum on favorite writers and stories. At the same meeting, Thaddeus Beczak, vice president of Hong Kong's *South China Morning Post*, predicted little impact on the advertising side of his newspaper.

He stressed the news value provided by his newspaper: "our business is content. Our competitive advantage is writing about China. ... That's our focus—we don't have to be all things to all people" (Tan, 2000).

Languages utilized by on-line newspapers, and on the Internet generally, raise some important questions. As things have evolved, English is the principal language of the Internet. Thus, to gain maximum benefit from it, users must be proficient in the language. Other languages can be used, but because the Internet has international coverage and because so much of the traffic on it originates from, or is intended for, the United States, English does tend to predominate. Obviously, the use of this language restricts the Internet's utility in certain areas of Southeast Asia, but English has become the main link language throughout the region. In the Philippines, Singapore, Brunei, and Malaysia, study of English is compulsory in schools, and hence educated residents can use the language. In Indonesia and Thailand, it is used mainly in cities with varying levels of facility. Even in the former French Indochina, English is replacing French as the most important link language. In Vietnam the author found that French tended to be spoken only by the educated who were more than 50 years of age. Some Southeast Asian languages have special problems on the Internet because of the scripts they require. To properly display languages such as Thai, Khmer, Burmese, and Lao (among others), specific software is required. This is also true of *Jawi* script Malay, but its use is fading in favor of roman script *rumi*. Vietnamese, too, is based on roman script, with diacritical marking. Throughout the region, English fluency is commonly considered an essential requirement for success in the commercial world. To answer the need for instruction, proprietary training schools have proliferated in major cities. The Internet provides a further incentive to learn the language, and for those just learning English, the Net offers a fine opportunity to practice reading and writing skills.

REFERENCES

Aisbett, N. (1996, August 20). Academic uses Net to call for boycotts. *The West Australian.*

Ang, P. (1996, July 27). Man-in-the-street to get access to Internet. *Straits Times.*

Bardacke, T. (1996, October 5). Burmese risk stiff jail sentences for surfing the Internet. *Financial Times* (London).

BBC. (2000, January 20). *East Asia Today* broadcast.

Beware dangers of the Internet. (1996, January 19). *Straits Times.*

Brooten, L. (1998, November). Burma spiders, the Web, and other metaphors of identity in the global age. Paper presented at the National Communication Association 1998 meeting, New York.

Burmese leader warns West using Internet to "destabilize" countries. (1998, July 1). *BBC World Monitoring.*

Cambodia ASEAN must initiate a more pro-active media policy in the context of globalisation of the industry. (1997, December 1). *Business News Review* (Cambodia).

Cambodian cyber cafe funded by stolen accounts. (1999, October 25). *Deutsche Presse-Agentur.*

Cambodia up in arms over bondage pornography Internet site. (1999, October 14). *Deutsche Presse-Agentur.*

Dupont K., and Pape E. (1999). E-mail is a real revolution. NGO Forum [cam-news.v001.n875.7}.

Fadzil G. (1996, September 20). Acquire info knowhow, businessmen urged. *New Straits Times.*

Fluendy, S. (1997, March 13). Mail call: It's time to turn to the power of e-mail. *Far Eastern Economic Review.*

Foo, F. (1996, July 30). Thumbs up for new Mimos rates. *The Star.*

Four Vietnamese newspapers now available on Internet. (1997, April 10). *Asia Pulse.*

Frankenstein, J. (1997, August 7). Managing in Asia-Special report: The Internet. *Far Eastern Economic Review.*

Gordon, J. (1996, September 26). Cyber-censorship grows in East Asia. *Los Angeles Times.*

Indonesia awakes to the post-Suharto era. (1998, May 23). *The Economist.*

Internet and cable TV luring away Singapore audiences. (2000, October 3). *Deutsche Presse-Agentur.*

Jacob, P. (1996, February 9). Hackers leave E. Timor graffiti on Indonesia's electronic pages. *Straits Times.*

Kaur, K. (1996, July 14). National Internet Advisory Committee to be set up soon. *Straits Times.*

Khine, M. S. (1994). Development and status of educational technology in Brunei Darussalam. Educational Resources Information Center accession number ED378951.

Kurlantzick, J. (1998, September 20). Burmese media—You can't put down a good newspaper. *Bangkok Post.*

Kwok, Y. (1998, August 21). Internet campaigns. *Asiaweek.*

Laos to set up its first government-run Internet company. (2000, May 1). *Deutsche Presse-Agentur.*

Lee S. L. (1996, July 18). Business over the Net by next year, says Mimos head. *New Straits Times.*

Leiner, B. M., Cerf, V. G., Clark, D. D., Kahn, R. E., Kleinrock, L., Lynch, J. P., Roberts, L. G., and Wolff, S. (2000). A brief history of the Internet. *All about the Internet.* Retrieved January 11, 2001 from the World Wide Web: http://www.isoc.org/internet-history/brief.html.

Leslie, J. (1999, November). Operation Phnom.com. *Wired.*

Lim, E. (1999). Southeast Asian subject gateways: Examination of the classification practices. Paper presented at 65th IFLA Council and General Conference, Bangkok.

Marcus, D. L. (1998, May 23). Indonesia revolt was Net drive. *The Boston Globe.*

Marr, D. (1998). Introduction. In D. Marr (Ed.), *The mass media in Vietnam* (pp. 1–26). Canberra: Australian National University.

Massey, B. L., and Levy, M. R. (1999). Interactivity, online journalism, and English-language Web newspapers in Asia. *Journalism and Mass Communication Quarterly, 76,* 138–151.

Mehta, H. (1997). *Cambodia silenced: The press under six regimes.* Bankok: White Lotus Press.

Mehta, H. (1998, December 30). Indochina jumps into cyperspace. *Business Times* (Singapore).

Myanmar junta launches Internet offensive on NLD arrest accusations. (1998, September 10). *Agence France Presse.*

Myanmar to provide Internet service. (1999, December 24). *Xinhua General News Service.*

Pabico, A. (1999, January 14). South-East Asia: The Internet, a handy political weapon. *Inter Press Service.*

Pennington, M. (2000, April 23). Fearing Pandora's box, Myanmar's rules block Internet. *Associated Press.*

Rashidah B., and Wong, S. J. (1999). Internet use in libraries in South East Asia with special reference to the Universiti Sains Malaysia library in promoting the use of the Internet for teaching and learning. Paper presented at 65th IFLA Council and General Conference, Bangkok.

Regulations for Internet users issued. (2000, January 21). *BBC Summary of World Broadcasts.*

SCV's Internet TV trial starts on Friday. (2000, August 17). *Channel NewsAsia.*

September launch for Internet service (1996, August 15). *New Straits Times.*

Small steps to the Net. (2001, February 5-11). *Myanmar Times and Business Review* [carried on BurmaNet News, issue 1728, February 6, 2001].

Software park gets 2Mb Internet line. (2000, November 30). *Saigon Times Daily.*

Son, X. (2000, September 11). "Get yourselves Webpages and management info systems," small companies. *Vietnam Investment Review.*

ST Interactive sees big jump in hits. (1998, September 14). *Straits Times.*

Taking it to the streets, online. (1998, January 23). *Asiaweek.*

Tan, L. (2000, October 20). Top Asian papers see Internet as no threat. *Straits Times.*

Teh H. L. (2000, October 3). More people surfing Internet, watching cable TV: Survey. *Straits Times.*

Telekom Malaysia should follow suit. (1996, July 30). *The Star.*

Uimonen, P. (2000, March 7). Net cafe society puts Laos on-line. ABIX: *Australian Business Intelligence.*

Vietnam report says system for regulating Internet not yet established. (1999, April 16). *BBC Summary of World Broadcasts.*

Vietnam switches to Internet but warns it would censor. (1997, November 12). *Bernama.*

Virgin territory. (1996, March 2). *The Economist.*

Wireless Internet to benefit 120,000 rural folk. (2000, October 26). *New Straits Times.*

Chapter Seven

Media Content and Audiences

Audiences are just as much a part of systems of mass communication as are   135
media organizations, policy makers, regulators, and government agencies—
subjects of previous chapters. Media audiences in Southeast Asia underwent a
tremendous transformation over the final decades of the twentieth century.
Technology advances offered new opportunities—a degree of interactivity,
worldwide reach, and technical convergence. Occurring simultaneously were
large shifts in demography and social geography—people were migrating,
changing their work habits, moving to cities, moving from cities to suburbs,
moving away from family villages, reading more, becoming more educated,
adopting consumer behaviors, buying more industrial goods—and the
changes seemed to have no end. The following describes how these things led
to a significant departure in habits and in the character of media consumers.

AUDIENCE RESEARCH

Advertisers require reliable audience information to plan advertising campaigns and to determine the reach of their messages. Growing wealth in Southeast Asia produced a sudden increase in advertising, and this in turn generated
greater demand for research on mass media consumption patterns. Historically
speaking, audience research in Southeast Asia has been dominated by the Survey Research Group (SRG), the regional corporation whose subsidiaries included Survey Research Indonesia, Survey Research Singapore, and Survey
Research Malaysia among others. The Survey Research Group was acquired by

ACNielsen in the late 1990s, and this boosted even further the firm's technical expertise and experience. ACNielsen is one of the largest audience research organizations in the world and is one of the most important in U.S. television ratings. ACNielsen had been active in Asia in places such as Singapore for a number of years, so the acquisition of SRG was a logical step in its business activities. Much of the analysis in this chapter draws heavily on data supplied by SRG and by ACNielsen.

In Southeast Asia, television ratings are measured by two means: peoplemeters and diaries. Diaries were the preferred method of collecting data until the 1990s. Diaries are booklets into which viewers enter a written record of the programs they watch, the times viewed, and other related details. This method has several known defects, most importantly the tendency for viewers to record their media use from memory long after seeing programs. Any lapse of time in entering diary information introduces errors. Viewers also tend to exaggerate the number and extent of programs they watch that are considered socially meritorious such as ones with high intellectual content or high culture. Peoplemeters, on the other hand, are devices that attach to the television set and automatically record times and channels viewed. In addition to greater measurement accuracy, peoplemeters permit overnight tabulation of television viewing in a sample of homes. Most peoplemeter systems also track which individual family members are watching programs. By the mid-1990s, peoplemeters had been implemented in Malaysia (sample of 660 households in the peninsular region), Philippines (sample of 300 homes in Metro Manila), Singapore (sample of 340 homes), and Thailand (Bangkok and Central Thailand sample of 340 households). Diaries were still used in Indonesia (Jakarta and four other major cities total sample of 850 homes) and in Vietnam (Hanoi and Ho Chi Minh City sample of 600 homes). In developing countries, a difficult issue is sampling. Advertisers are less interested in figuring exact audience sizes than in determining which programs have appeal to more affluent viewers. Julie Petersen, director of research services at Star TV, once proposed that upper-income homes be added to all sample panels to provide a better sense of consumer preferences. As she explained, "It may not be democratic, but oversampling among wealthier households would render a panel more useful" ("The rate," 1996). Notwithstanding the advantages for advertisers, such samples obviously are not helpful to programmers attempting to design schedules to reach less-affluent portions of the population.

RADIO LISTENING

From the 1930s onward, radio had been the most important mass medium across all of Asia. Illiteracy, which remained high in most countries until after World War II, restricted newspaper readership. Radio served as the primary mass medium for rural segments of society throughout the 1960s, 1970s, and well into the 1980s. When it began to be supplanted as the principal means for governments to communicate with their citizens, radio underwent a transformation. Paradoxically, the dwindling importance attached to the radio medium coincided with an increase in the number of stations and networks operating in a number of countries. Privatization was a major factor in the growth in numbers of stations in Singapore and Malaysia. In Indonesia, there had been many private stations since the establishment of the "New Order" in the 1960s, and in that country expansion of the private sector depended on a strong economy. In other countries, different issues influenced radio's status. As an example, in Vietnam, where no private stations are allowed, many stations were on the air by the end of the century. A complex system emerged there, seemingly because of political interests embedded in its highly decentralized governmental structure. At the national level, two channels of Radio The Voice of Vietnam are transmitted nationwide. These are the main services of national government. In addition, by the 1990s every province had its own radio transmission service, and an additional 266 district stations were reported on the air as well. Beyond these were hundreds, perhaps thousands of wired speaker systems installed in villages and cities. Vietnam reported that about eighteen thousand of its citizens were employed in broadcasting, mostly in radio, not counting staff of wired speaker networks.

Radio's transition from an official voice of the government to something less important acted as a catalyst for adjustments in broadcasters' programming strategies. Traditionally, radio services had used block programming, in which programs from 15 minutes to a few hours in length were tailored for specific audience segments—perhaps a long newscast at 7:00 A.M. followed by a discussion show, then a short music interlude, followed by a current affairs feature, and so on. This kind of programming permitted all members of the audience to be served by a single channel in the course of a day's transmission, and it worked well when there was little competition. But as the number of stations grew, specialization began to occur. Some stations carried nothing but music of a particular type, another carried mostly news and information. By operating on this basis, a specific segment of the audience could be carved out and claimed by each radio station, assuring a consistent and predictable audience throughout the broadcast day. Programming like this of course was based on the use of format programming instead of block programming, and it produced great fragmentation of audiences all across the region. The adoption of format programming generally meant smaller audiences for each service, yet one that potentially was more attractive to advertisers because commercial messages could be more accurately targeted to desired audience segments.

Even though more and more time has been allocated to television viewing by Southeast Asia residents, radio remains important. In Malaysia for instance, roughly 90 percent of the population now tunes into radio at least once each week and the number of listeners continues to edge upward. The overall audience size rose by 0.6 percent between 1998 and 1999, according to Survey Research Malaysia research. The growth occurred particularly among twenty- to twenty-nine-year-old listeners, a demographic segment radio programmers eagerly seek because of its importance to advertisers. (Advertisers place a premium on this age group because personal buying habits are formed in these years.) Other groups accounting for the audience expansion were young professionals and housewives. On average, according to the 1999 study, each adult spent a sizeable 4.28 hours each day listening to their radios (Eirmalasare, 2000). In other countries of Southeast Asia the general outline is similar, with minor variations. An exception is the Philippines, where radio listening has not increased. Substantial declines have occurred among children, probably due to displacement by television viewing. Among boys aged ten to fourteen years, daily listening dropped from 54 to 34 percent between 1995 and 1999 ("Cable TV," 2000).

Among Southeast Asian countries having pluralistic populations, personal habits and access to media usually differs by ethnic affiliation. These demographic characteristics were not only of interest to advertisers but to programmers and policy makers. Differences in media use might counteract national efforts to shrink social divisions separating ethnic groups. The most important determinant of audience sizes in different ethnic groups is the access each has to media. For example, by the 1980s in Malaysia most homes could receive not only radio broadcasts but television as well. Malaysia's Department of Statistics reported in 1991 that 74 percent of Bumiputra (Malay) homes reported that they owned a radio and 75 percent said they had a television set. Among Chinese households, 81 percent owned radios and 88 percent owned televisions. Indian Malaysians reported ownership of both about the same, radio at 85 percent and television at 86 percent (WhiteKnight Communications, 1996). But radio listening showed a pattern opposite to set ownership. In 1995, ACNielsen figures show that even though more Chinese families had radio receivers, they were not so likely to use them. In that year, surveys found that 78 percent of Chinese listened to a radio at least once in the preceding week whereas 89 percent of Malays had tuned into a radio station. Indian Malaysian radio listeners were almost as large a proportion at 87 percent (ACNielsen, 1996a).

A key factor in further audience fragmentation has been diversity in languages. All countries in Southeast Asia have multiple language groups, and the media must somehow reach out to each one. In Malaysia, the most important responsibility of the government broadcaster is to "foster national unity in our multi-racial society through the extensive use of Bahasa Malaysia" (Ministry of Information, 1989). Judging from audience research, radio has not had much success in encouraging unification. Listeners for Radio Television Malaysia's Radio 1, broadcasting only in Bahasa Malaysia (Malay), have been predominantly from the Malay community. A 1991 survey of radio listening in Peninsular Malaysia by Survey Research Malaysia (SRM) indicated that 92 percent of Radio 1's weekly audience consisted of ethnic Malay listeners, while just 4 percent were Indian and 4 percent were Chinese listeners. There was little evidence of Malaysians listening to radio programs in another group's language. Indians made up 89 percent of the audience for Tamil language Radio 6, and of the remainder 7 percent were Malays and 4 percent Chinese. The same pattern held true for the Chinese radio channel, Radio 5. Of its audience, 96 percent were Chinese, while Indian and Malay listeners came to only 2 percent each. True to its role as a link language, English programs drew listeners roughly in proportion to each ethnic group's population. The English network, Radio 4, had a weekly audience of 43 percent Malays, 43 percent Chinese, and 15 percent Indian listeners. Of course, the total English audience was smaller than the audience for Malay radio, at slightly less than 900,000 cumulative listeners each week. This compared with 3.25 million listeners for Radio 1, 980,000 for the Chinese network, and 660,000 for the Indian network (Survey Research Malaysia, 1991). Malays are the largest group in the radio audience as they are in the population, totaling 67 percent of all radio listeners. Chinese and Indians account for about 17 percent and 11 percent respectively (Survey Research Malaysia, 1990a). The same trend was also evident in audiences for local radio stations in Malaysia. A 1991 radio diary survey found that local radio stations offering programs in Bahasa Malaysia in Kuala Lumpur, Alor Star, Ipoh, Kuantan, Kuala Terengganu, Johore Baru, Shah Alam, and Seremban each had audiences composed of 92 percent or more Malays (Survey Research Malaysia, 1991).

MOVIE VIEWING

Shrinking movie audiences can be attributed to a number of factors. The availability of movies on video CD (VCD) for a cost less than the price of two adult tickets was one of the most important. As described in Chapter 3, pirated VCDs were sold on street corners or shops in many Southeast Asian cities for just slightly more than USD $2. The fact that these were produced without copyright permission mattered little to the typical shopper. In discussing this issue, many informants described the Hollywood and Chinese film producers as rich and undeserving, and it was in this manner that most people justified the purchase of pirated movies. The fact that police made only infrequent and desultory enforcement efforts seemed to send a signal that even though technically illegal, such purchases were not really wrong. The influence of VCDs and other factors can be clearly observed in Malaysia. In 2000, only 3 percent of peninsular residents surveyed said they had seen a movie in a theater in the preceding week (ACNielsen, 2001a). This figure compares with 6 percent in 1998 and 8 percent in 1995 (ACNielsen, 1996a, 1999a).

The loss of audiences affected all movies, not just ones from Western sources. In Thailand during the late 1990s, the number of Chinese films imported into Thailand experienced a drop ("Chinese productions," 2001). In 2001, only about fifteen Chinese films were screened in Thailand, compared with about four times that number a decade earlier. Explanations for the decline focused on changed habits that became evident after the economic hard times of 1997–1998 and a greater preference among younger viewers for Western movies. Domestic producers saw the waning interest in foreign films as an opening for locally produced titles. Estimates placed the total number of locally produced Thai films in 2001 at about twenty movies having an aggregate budget of USD $30 million. In the preceding year, the seven Thai movies that were released had a combined budget of USD $7 million. By 2001, domestically produced films accounted for about 20 percent of the market. The sudden increase in local films actually caused an increase in the total number of titles screened in the country during 2001 despite sagging attendance ("Thai movies," 2001). Thai theaters screened about 180 movies in 2000. For comparison, about 140 films were screened in Indonesia in the same year.

Cinema attendance in Singapore fell in the same period as well, dropping from 18.1 million admissions in 1995 to 14.7 million in 2000. Singapore claims to have the highest per capita ratio of movie theaters in the world, so the figures were surprising. The highest grossing movie of 2000 was *Mission Impossible-2*, which earned Singapore $2.99 million. This was a significant drop from the preceding year when three movies exceeded $3 million in earnings, including the locally produced film *Liang Po Po*. According to Singapore thinking, success of these blockbuster movies was not only attributable to strong appeals, but also to their high production standards. Flora Goh, Singapore marketing manager for film distributor UIP, explained that

> Chinese movies have a tougher time competing with English ones because they often don't have the sleek production values of Hollywood. The reason a Chinese movie like *Crouching Tiger, Hidden Dragon* did so well is because it was made in Hollywood (cited in Helmi, 2001).

Falling attendance prompted Singapore theater owners to experiment with reduced ticket prices in early 2000, but when the decline continued, fees were raised again. Another possible factor in slipping cinema attendance was the availability of sexually explicit materials on the Internet. In Singapore, films rated Restricted (Artistic) by censors are the most daring seen in movie theaters. These are films deemed to have artistic merit even though containing strong sexual themes. In truth, most are soft porn. Audiences for these movies suffered a gradual loss over the 1990s. According to theater firm Overseas Movies manager Teo Choong Nan, "Art buffs think R(A) movies are sleazy, while those out for sleaze think the shows too arty" (cited in Cheong, 2000). The same trend held in other countries of Southeast Asia. Even Vietnam found movie attendance skidding. There were only one hundred theaters believed to be operating in 1997, but many of these were on the verge of closing. Except for Ho Chi Minh City, audiences were down across Vietnam in the late 1990s, yet entrepreneurs planned to introduce modern multiplex theaters and expand the range of films screened to draw more attendees. One new multiscreen theater in Hanoi combined the films with a karaoke lounge, a bar, and a gymnasium ("Vietnam: Cinemas," 1997).

TELEVISION

Across Southeast Asia, television's rising popularity was sustained through the 1980s and 1990s. An important explanation of its popularization was a large increase in access to the medium in rural areas because of the further activation of television transmitter and satellite relays. In addition, as wealth trickled into rural areas, ownership of television receivers became more common. The trend toward increased viewership was noted in all countries except Singapore and Brunei, where by the early 1980s national coverage was available and television sets had become an essential home appliance. Perhaps the viewing trend was most obvious in Indonesia. Here population density combined with a populace dispersed on thousands of islands magnified the progressive effect of climbing audience figures. During the 1980s, every few months a jump in Televisi Republik Indonesia audience would occur as it opened transmitters on one more island. Marching across the archipelago island by island, television swept viewers up in a national experience unlike anything that preceded it. The same took place all across Asia. In just a few years India and China became home to the world's largest television audiences. An enthusiasm for the medium's possibilities became contagious. Viewers, advertisers, and television professionals alike each aimed to make the most of the new medium.

A 1998 Survey Research Indonesia report revealed how much television audiences had changed as a result of the wider coverage. By that date the total number of homes with television had reached 49 million, well over 90 percent of all homes in the country. Across the archipelago, there were estimated to be about 3.5 million homes equipped for reception of satellite television, and in Sumatra cities, penetration of satellite television reached 18 percent. The youth audience in Indonesia became surprisingly large, pushed upward perhaps by the popularity of MTV, which was second in popularity as a satellite channel only to Malaysian channel TV3. Daily cumulative audience figures for MTV, which was transmitted on terrestrial channel AnTeve as well as satellite, reached as high as 16 million homes. Young adults in the range of fifteen to twenty-four years of age were estimated to watch more than twenty-six hours weekly, and even those not living in homes with a television still found ways of watching an estimated twelve hours weekly (Tungate, 1998).

In several countries of the region, television viewing, like radio listening, had an important ethnic dimension. Perhaps Malaysia exemplifies this best. The Survey Research Malaysia audience summary for October 1990 shows peak viewing at about the time of the main newscast in Malay at 8:00 P.M. At that time, all channels including the private channel TV3 were required to carry news in the national language. According to data collected at the time, 56 percent of Malay homes were watching, compared with only 8 percent of Chinese households. Although SRM did not tabulate figures for ethnic Indian viewers because of their small size, other evidence indicates that only a small portion of that segment of the population was watching. Later that week a Malay language drama *Meski Arapun* aired at 10:00 P.M. on TV1. Among Malay viewers this was a popular show, and 31 percent of Malay homes were watching. The proportion of Chinese homes viewing the program was too small to measure. At the same time on TV3 a Chinese film titled *Crocodile Evil* was scheduled. This drew 51 percent of the Chinese homes but only 11 percent of Malay households (Survey Research Malaysia, 1990b). In 1990, SRM classified approximately 72 percent of Malays as either heavy or medium television users, but among Chinese only 61 percent were placed in this category. Heavy and medium viewers among other groups, including mainly Indians, totaled 65 percent (Survey Research Malaysia, 1990c).

Another way of looking at ethnic contrasts is to compare audience ratings. Table 7.1 presents a summary of ratings for all adults in Peninsular Malaysia, broken down by ethnic group and by date. This table shows an overall growth in viewing over the five years included in this analysis, with the increase among Chinese greatest. The table also shows that the margin of difference between Malays and other groups decreased over the sample period. This is a bit deceptive because the presentation of overall ratings for all ninety-six quarter hours each day somewhat masks interethnic differences. For example, television viewing reaches its peak between 9:00 P.M. and 10:00 P.M. each evening. Looking only at this time period in the year 2000, the rating among Malays

Table 7.1 Malaysian Television Viewing by Ethnic Groups, Average Ratings All Dayparts

Ethnic group	1995	1998	2000
Malay	12	13	12
Chinese	6	8	9
Indian/Other	7	9	10

Note: Compiled from ACNielsen. (2001b). *TV quarter-hour summary reports, 1995 through 2000.*

was 38, while among Chinese the rating was 25, and Indian/Other 25. The predominance of the Malay audience was a by-product of the enlarged coverage areas of television stations and the shift in programming to more locally produced Malay-language dramatic programs and soap operas that tend to be scheduled at the heart of prime time (ACNielsen, 1996b, 1999b, 2001b).

The penetration of emerging media technologies differed from country to country depending on the circumstances in each. Even though Indonesia's per capita annual income was less than one-fourth that of Malaysia in 1996, the penetration of cable and satellite television was almost twice as great (5 percent compared with 3 percent in Malaysia). This statistic, although it might seem small, shows cable and satellite television had gained a greater adoption than most other electronic technologies. For example, in Indonesia only 2 percent of homes had telephones at the time ("Late entrants," 1996). Within Southeast Asia, only the Philippines and Singapore have seen much success in cable television. In Singapore, the slow rollout of the cable system kept cable audiences from growing as swiftly as it might otherwise have done. Apparently, installation of the wired infrastructure proved more challenging than first expected. Even so, its adoption crept upward steadily. Between July 1999 and the same month one year later, a jump of 8 percent in cable users was recorded in the republic, up to 28 percent weekly reach. Penetration in the same period grew from 19 percent to 27 percent. Even on a typical day, according to ACNielsen, about 24 percent tuned into cable television, up greatly over the 16 percent estimated in the previous year. The change in media habits seems not only to have been a consequence of better access but also of a preference for international channels. Singapore viewers for satellite service Channel NewsAsia rose by 4 percent between 1999 and 2000, during a time when most popular channels were losing audiences as a result of audience fragmentation (Teh, 2000).

In Indonesia, one of the important engines of audience expansion was the program type known locally as the *sinetron*—melodramatic television series produced on the fly in Jakarta studios. The programs leave much to be desired from an artistic point of view. These shows, similar to U.S. soap operas or Latin American *Telenovelas,* are based on formulaic stories and fantastic plot turns and rely on large doses of emotion to sustain viewer interest. Programs tend to be hastily prepared; generally fifty pages of weepy dialogue are shot on a tight schedule. The resulting shows suffer from weak production values. As Bella Saphira, the leading actress in the series *Dewi Fortuna,* complained,

> How can I be free from stress as the shooting schedule must be completed as fast as possible in order to be able to meet the broadcast schedule? For example, the shooting of an episode must be completed on Tuesday, notwithstanding the availability of time, because it must be aired on Thursday ("Style comes," 2000).

The series tend to be populated by the new icons of Southeast Asian popular culture—upward-bound young suburbanites. Capitalizing on characters displaying the stresses—and the rich benefits—of life in the city, *sinetron* have created new media stereotypes such as the feckless unfaithful husband or the forgiving and long-suffering mother. Stories built on these stock types are manufactured for mass audiences, most members of which will never achieve the "good life" depicted in the series. Stories allow people from homes with small incomes to share vicariously in the lives of wealthy and glamorous characters while simultaneously taking pleasure in the contrasting moral and spiritual superiority of their own lives.

Indonesian rules require that broadcasters must program at least 70 percent of their schedule with locally produced programs. This goal is not easy to meet, and so it is that many of the *sinetron* are of marginal quality. Starting with Rajawali Citra Televisi (RCTI) in 1989, followed by Surya Citra Televisi (SCTV) a year later, the number of private stations continued to grow, including Televisi Pendidikan Indonesia (TPI), Andalas Televisi (ANteve), and Indosiar Visual Mandiri. Additional private stations have been authorized to begin transmissions in 2001. To feed the program schedules of all these stations, a tremendous production industry has taken shape. One report placed the number of production houses at 600, including 317 officially registered corporations, mostly firms concentrating on serials and other kinds of television programs. From these houses an estimated three thousand television programs were produced in 1997 (Widiadana and Ramani, 1997).

Another boost to television viewing was the availability of good-quality sports programming. The broad appeal of this type of programming is especially advantageous for state television channels because it tends to attract viewers who otherwise are not heavy users of television. Audience fragmentation produced by the inauguration of new channels makes it difficult for the state broadcaster to maintain competitiveness. Unlike other channels that may rely chiefly on entertainment programs, as noted before the state stations must reflect a national perspective and must present a diet of socially worthwhile shows. Sports programming is always acceptable on government television because it provides opportunities to communicate unifying nationalistic messages while sustaining large audience ratings. Among the new generation of viewers, sports broadcasts are very popular. The 1998 Commonwealth Games, staged in Kuala Lumpur, was one of the year's most popular television offerings in Malaysia. According to Zenith Media, 94 percent of all Malaysians watched some portion of the sports broadcast. The largest audiences were the opening and closing ceremonies, with the opening garnering audiences of more than one in three of all adults in Peninsular Malaysia ("Games one of biggest," 1998). Large audiences are also reported for football (soccer) matches and Formula 1 auto racing.

Still another factor driving the amount of television watching upward was an unexpected strength of local production houses in making children's programs. This was an area in which foreign products had long held sway. Cartoons from Japan and the United States were the staple fare for children's shows in most countries, although for a while good-quality children's programs were imported from the former socialist countries, especially in Indochina. One example of the locally created children's show was Indonesia's *Keluarga Cemara* [Cemara's Family]. Sometimes compared with the U.S. show *Little House on the Prairie,* it concerned a wholesome but comparatively realistic view of life in Indonesia. The program began airing in 1996 and was broadcast daily on weekdays. Other programs for young Indonesians mostly concerned superheroes, a robot boy, or similar fantastic themes.

Generational differences undoubtedly account for some shifts in Southeast Asian media use. Youngsters entering adulthood at the turn of the century had a totally different life experience than that of their parents. In Vietnam, young adults had no memory of the wars that had deeply imprinted the previous generation. In this country, a baby boom at the end of war led to a doubling of the population from 1975 to 2000. The balance of population was affected so much that half of the population was under 20 years of age by the 1990s. Many younger Vietnamese grew weary of the heavy ideological programming that predominated on state-run media. Alternatives such as videos and satellite television were preferable, and so official stations began to program more locally produced entertainment and music shows, copying some of the more popular international programs, including several MTV knockoffs. Thai and Malaysian television began offering imaginative local programs for younger audiences similar to the Indonesian *sinetrons.* Dramas of this sort were built around the stresses of life in cities and the cultural tug-of-war between traditional values and the new "modern" social values. Although constrained by rules imposed by censors, the shows treated sexual themes in a slightly more open and constructive way than those aimed at earlier generations and matter-of-factly dealt with serious social issues such as drug use and corruption.

Television music programming for Asian youths suddenly became a crowded field in the mid-1990s. Two international channels were aimed at the region—MTV Networks Asia, majority owned by U.S.-based MTV Networks, and Channel V! owned by Rupert Murdoch's News Corp. The two built programming based on their highly successful international formula, but tailored for Asian viewers. The ability of these channels to fashion audiences of eighteen- to twenty-five-year-olds led many Asian producers to attempt copying their formats. A significant departure in their programming was that all of the music channels presented lifestyle-based services rather than simply presenting music for entertainment. A Thai music channel known as Smile TV was launched in 1993, but it closed four years later. At its peak there were as many as fifteen music television channels based in Asia, and others were in planning stages in the Philippines and Malaysia. But after the economic shake-out of 1997–1998, only four main services remained—in Korea, m-net and KMTV; in Taiwan, Hwa Hwei; and in China the Hong Kong–based Youth Music Channel ("Music television," 1999).

Youthful adults in Indonesia and Malaysia were gradually moving away from a village psychology that had dominanted throughout history. Samsudin and Latiffah (1999) reported on a national survey they conducted in Malaysia in which they examined media use among young adults. The media habits reported in the study show a distinct departure from findings in earlier research. For example, nearly one-third of those between thirteen and twenty-five years of age had access to video game players, and individuals in their study devoted slightly more than six hours per week to their use. As these young adults grew older, they tended to use more electronic media and less print media. Respondents between thirteen and fifteen years of age spent a combined total of 23.1 hours reading comics, short stories, novels, newspapers, and magazines while those aged twenty-one to twenty-five years only spent 18.1 hours reading. Conversely, twenty-one- to twenty-five-year-olds devoted 30.4 hours each week to satellite and terrestrial television, whereas the thirteen- to fifteen-year-old respondents spent 21.1 hours watching TV. One of the surprising findings of their study concerned youngsters' leisure and recreational preferences. Although not as common as visits to cinemas or karaoke lounges, about half of those sampled reported visiting a video center or cyber café within the preceding month. The popularity of these centers grew enormously in the 1990s, particularly among teenagers. The authors pointed to the apparent contradiction between parental objections to these places—on the theory that they supposedly lead to "truancy"—while the centers "are in line with the government policies to encourage computer literacy and creating an IT culture among the young" (Samsudin and Latiffah, p. 11).

PRINT MEDIA

By the end of the century, Southeast Asian consumption of print media had risen to levels that rivaled those in developed countries of Europe and North America. In fact, newspaper readership levels were among the highest in the world. The highest in all of Asia was in Singapore, where 85 percent of adult residents read a newspaper each day. Close behind were China with 79 percent readership and Taiwan with 77 percent. Elsewhere in Southeast Asia, Thailand and Indonesia had readerships of 37 percent and 46 percent respectively. Vietnam's readership was only 23 percent. Choices among newspapers were least restricted in Singapore, where there were only 204,000 people per newspaper

title. Only fourteen newspapers are produced in Singapore. Vietnam and
Thailand had the fewest choices at 1.7 million persons for each newspaper title. There are forty-three daily newspapers published in Vietnam and thirty-
five newspapers in Thailand. Magazine readership was similar. Singapore's consumption was the highest among countries sampled at 58 percent readership.
Indonesia, Thailand, and Vietnam's readerships were 41 percent, 30 percent,
and 22 percent respectively (Kerk, 1994).

As a result of economic problems and the popularity of electronic media,
newspapers in some countries suffered setbacks in the 1990s. Readership of
certain dailies in Malaysia, including some prestigious newspapers, began declining about the time of the 1997 fall in the economy. Even after the economy rebounded, readership for some dailies continued to drop. This was especially the case for the once leading daily newspaper the *New Straits Times*. I
was told by a number of Malaysians that the declines in Malaysia were not
only attributable to the financial crisis, but to a loss of faith in the journalism
practiced by the government-aligned print media. One study found that
Malaysia's leading Malay language daily *Berita Harian* suffered an 11-percent
decline in readership between 1998 and 1999. Similar losses were reported for
Indonesia's *Pos Kota* and Thailand's *Thai Rath,* each losing 12 percent readership in the same year. Singapore alone in Southeast Asia showed growth at a
modest 4 percent (Clark, 2000).

Competition in print media escalated in a number of places as well. After
Suharto left office in 1998, many Indonesian newspapers resumed production
after bans on their publication were lifted. Indeed, many new newspapers were
launched in the giddy atmosphere of the immediate post-Suharto period. By
1999, the total number of newspapers authorized for publication topped two
hundred, and there were seventy-nine dailies and eighty-eight nondaily newspapers actually being published. Circulation of dailies between 1997 and 1998
jumped an estimated 49 percent, according to a study by MindShare (Clark,
2000). In Singapore, a strictly regulated market, two tabloids were introduced
at the end of the century. *Streats* and *Today* were launched as free newspapers
targeted at commuters. Initially, their impact was marginal. Only *Streats* fig-
ured as a leading publication; it rated fourth among newspapers with a readership of 16 percent of those sampled in a 2000 survey. Singapore's newspaper
market is dominated by the *Straits Times* with a daily readership of 47 percent.
Two Chinese newspapers follow in popularity, *Lianhe Zaobao* and *Lianhe
Wanbao,* with readerships of 23 and 17 percent respectively ("Sectionised,"
2000). At the same time, the progressive erosion of readership in Singapore
seems to be a long-term trend, though not at the same steep rate seen in
Malaysia. ACNielsen reported in late 2000 that newspaper's reach had dipped
to 93 percent, 1 percent less than at the same time in the preceding year (Teh,
2000).

MEDIA ADVERTISING

The success of all types of local television productions owed a great deal to the rising emphasis on television advertising. Commercial rates soared as demand for advertising exceeded availabilities in the highest rated shows. Although none of the Southeast Asian nations could be considered a huge advertising market when compared with other countries of the Pacific Rim, they were among the fastest growing in the 1990s. Advertising revenues reported by Zenith Media show increases of more than 13 percent just between 1995 and 1996 in each of the countries of Indonesia, Vietnam, Malaysia, and the Philippines. Vietnam's advertising growth rate of 60.4 percent was by far the highest in the entire Asia-Pacific region ("Ad and subtract," 1996). As increased sums of money flowed into broadcaster's accounts, many plowed additional resources into development of local productions. Advertising possibilities in Vietnam, Southeast Asia's second most populous country, inspired a number of proposed partnerships between foreign companies and various domestic broadcasters. News Limited, the Australian subsidiary of Rupert Murdoch's News Corp, once worked out a deal for nationwide broadcast of Twentieth Century Fox Film of the Week, only to watch the arrangement fall apart. The programs would have been transmitted with commercials intact as marketed by News Limited, via a national hookup through Vietnam Television (VTV). The problem—a common one in this country—was that Ho Chi Minh City TV (HTV) refused to participate, and then other provincial stations balked, too. At the same time HTV was busy rebroadcasting Australian Channel Nine programs under an arrangement worked out by entrepreneur Kerry Packer. In Vietnam, the lack of central coordination is a chronic problem, making large-scale development of advertising in the country difficult (Aarts, 1996).

As an example of trends in Southeast Asia, a snapshot of advertising in Malaysia is provided in Table 7.2. It shows how allocations of advertising funds changed among media over the period between 1995 and 2000. As can be seen, the total advertising market grew at a steep rate, roughly 54 percent in the five years between 1995 and 2000. Most of the expansion in ad allocations occurred between 1998 and 2000. The economic downturn of 1998 undoubtedly depressed advertising figures in that year. The biggest winner in the period was radio, with advertising on this medium increasing by about 72 percent. Growth in radio advertising clearly was influenced by the addition of a number of private stations and by increasing sophistication in programming on all stations. As suggested earlier, a shift to format radio programming made the medium much easier for advertisers to target their ad messages to selected audiences. Advertising on videocassettes dropped as a result of the takeover of the video market by pirate VCDs. Possibly for the same reason, cinema advertising was flat during the period included in the survey. Newspaper advertis-

Table 7.2 Malaysian Advertising Expenditures (Millions of Ringgit)

Medium	1995	1998	2000
Television	654	700	936
Radio	59	66	102
Newspaper	1,129	1,262	1,866
Magazines	118	111	131
Rediffusion	9*	...	...
Video	11	10	9
Cinema	7	11	10
Direct mail	14	21	24
TOTAL	2,001	2,181	3,078

Note: Compiled from ACNielsen. (2001c). *Summary of yearly advertising expenditure (ADEX), 1995 through 2000.*
*Rediffusion's wired radio service was discontinued before 1998.

ing revenues showed strength, increasing by 65 percent despite large drops in circulation among several of the largest dailies. Other studies bore out the same finding; according to Bani (2000), in the first nine months of 2000, overall newspaper ad revenues topped USD $41 million, an increase of 36 percent over the same period in the preceding year. Finally, television grew by 43 percent, a respectable result but less than the increases reported by radio and newspapers (ACNielsen, 1996a, 1999a, 2001a).

Newspapers in other parts of Southeast Asia generally experienced continued strength in their ad revenues. A study by MindShare found a whopping growth of 37 percent in advertising allocations in Indonesia during 1999. The growth in Thailand was nearly as great at 32 percent in that year, while figures in the Philippines grew at slightly more than 15 percent. This nation's newspapers compete in a rough-and-tumble market populated by numerous newspapers but ruled by a few strong dailies. Like Indonesia, Philippine print media tend to have readerships restricted somewhat to cities because of costs and problems of distribution in remote areas and scattered islands. The 1997–1998 recession had a devastating effect on Philippine newspapers. Between 1995 and 1997 no less than twenty dailies and regional nondaily newspapers ceased publication (Clark, 2000).

THE NEW SOUTHEAST ASIAN AUDIENCE

If there is one overarching pattern, it is that audiences have been split into such tiny fragments that no single channel commands anything approaching dominance. In 1970, the main divisions within audiences were based on language, but today there are many more factors splitting media users, such as age, gen-der, and geographic location. Government stations were the big losers in the fight for viewers and listeners. When private stations entered the competition, they focused on the segments of the audience that advertisers wanted most— young city adults, mainly 18 to 35 years of age. Government programmers also wanted to reach this audience, not only for its commercial appeal, but also build support for government policies. But government stations, unlike private broadcasters, could not concentrate on this segment. They had an obligation to maintain services to segments of less interest to advertisers such as the less affluent, children, and older residents. In meeting their responsibilities as national broadcasters, they lost ground to the private stations. In some cases, audience losses and revenue drops were so great that the very viability of the government stations began to be questioned.

Audiences have many more options today than they had forty years ago. Film and television have been joined by VCRs, VCDs, DVDs, satellite, and cable television. News is no longer available only from print or broadcast media but now can be received via the Web in various formats. Although many of these options are expensive, improved personal income in every country of the region brought the new media within the reach of large portions of the population. The result is that even though television viewing has crept up slowly, its growth has not been as great as might be expected. Radio survives, but it has changed from being the principal entertainment medium to playing only a supporting role. It has assumed more of a companionship function in the region, much as it has in other parts of the globe. Other media also have had to find their place in the emerging hectic lifestyles of people in the region.

The addition of rural viewers to television audiences during the final two decades of the twentieth century altered programming equations for broadcasters in Southeast Asia. Programs in national languages, set in local settings and dealing with themes familiar to people living in the countryside, did so well that local production industries truly blossomed. Hundreds of independent production houses now spin out thousands of hours in Indonesia, Malaysia, Thailand, and the Philippines every year. Even though domestic film production has slumped against foreign competition, the vitality of local television ensures that the overall cultural content of Southeast Asian media remains Eastern, not Western.

There is little doubt that audience segmentation will become increasingly pronounced as additional over-the-air channels crowd into Asian markets and as new satellite channels attract small numbers of viewers to narrow "niche" program channels. In Indonesian radio, where the number of private stations nationwide is in the hundreds, including dozens operating in the vicinity of Jakarta, fragmented audiences have been a fact of life for decades. Even in Singapore and Malaysia, segmentation of radio audiences has been growing since the late 1980s when private local stations began to appear. However, television audience fragmentation in these countries did not start until almost a decade later when the growth of private television finally began to divide viewership among more stations. In satellite television, audiences for any channel are likely to be small compared with terrestrial stations, and satellite channels' content will be devoted mostly to narrowly defined interests within sports, music, and movie classifications. If the experience of North America and Europe can be used as a guide, the specialization of satellite channels is likely to tighten as time passes. For example, by the end of the 1990s in the United States, movie channels had evolved into a variety of extremely narrow specialties, including recent releases, comedy, science fiction, classics, art films, and so on.

Languages remain another significant factor in defining audiences. Indeed, link languages have been pivotal to success of most international television channels, even though in most countries link languages cannot yet reach genuinely mass audiences. In India, less than 10 percent of the population is conversant in English, and there still remain perhaps 30 percent who are unable to use Hindi. Likewise, in Southeast Asia, no single language can encompass more than a subsection of the whole population. At the moment, the Asian practice is to target regional audiences in regional languages, for example, STAR focuses on Hindi and English across the Indian subcontinent while using Mandarin and English for East and Southeast Asia. Here again, specialized language services boost audience segmentation. The same is true even in the United States, where one can tune in by satellite an array of services for American ethnic groups—Chinese, Korean, Spanish-speaking, and so on—available by cable-delivered satellite television.

REFERENCES

Aarts, M. (1996, January). Channel surfing. *Manager.*
ACNielsen. (1996a). *Media index 1995.* Kuala Lumpur: Author.
ACNielsen. (1996b). *TV quarter hour summary reports 1995.* Kuala Lumpur: Author.
ACNielsen. (1999a). *Media Index 1998.* Kuala Lumpur: ACNielsen.
ACNielsen. (1999b). *TV quarter hour summary reports 1998.* Kuala Lumpur: Author.
ACNielsen. (2001a). *Media Index 2000.* Kuala Lumpur: ACNielsen.
ACNielsen. (2001b). *TV quarter hour summary reports 2000.* Kuala Lumpur: Author.
ACNielsen. (2001c). *Summary of yearly advertising expenditure (ADEX), 1995 through 2000.* Kuala Lumpur: Author.
Ad and subtract. (1996, November). *Cable and Satellite Asia.*
Bani, E. (2000, December 6). Major newspapers set to adjust ad rates. *Business Times* (Malaysia).
Cable TV, Internet expands marketing options. (2000, November 21). *Business World* (Philippines).

Cheong S. W. (2000, September 3). R(A) no more a turn-on? *Straits Times.*

Chinese productions lose the plot and Thai viewers. (2001, January 29). *Bangkok Post.*

Clark, K. (2000, April 21). Asia: Print prospects. *Campaign.*

Eirmalasare, B. (2000, March 29). 9 out of 10 Malaysians listen to radio: Survey. *Business Times* (Malaysia).

Games one of biggest TV draws in 1998. (1998, December 30). *Business Times* (Malaysia).

Helmi Yusof. (2001, January 3). Ticket sales drop. *Straits Times.*

Kerk, C. (1994, October 14). Asian newspaper readership on the rise. *Business Times* (Singapore),

Late entrants post strong growth. (1996, May). *Cable and Satellite Asia.*

Ministry of Information. (1989). *Radio Television Malaysia.* Kuala Lumpur: Department of Broadcasting.

Music television channels struggle to convert viewers into profits in Asia. (1999, July 28). *Music and Copyright.*

Samsudin A. R., and Latiffah P. (1999). *The emerging generation: Media penetration and the construction of identity among young adults in Malaysia.* Unpublished paper, Universiti Kebangsaan Malaysia.

Sectionised ST a faster read, say readers. (2000, December 21). *Straits Times.*

Style comes first in local TV series. (2000, October 29). *The Jakarta Post.*

Survey Research Malaysia. (1990a). *A review of the Malaysian radio audience.* Kuala Lumpur: SRM.

Survey Research Malaysia. (1990b). *SRM weekly TV diary report Peninsular Malaysia, week 42 1990.* Kuala Lumpur: SRM.

Survey Research Malaysia. (1990c). *SRM 1990 establishment survey presentation.* Kuala Lumpur: SRM.

Survey Research Malaysia. (1991). *Media Index Presentation 1991.* Kuala Lumpur: SRM.

Teh H. L. (2000, October 3). More people surfing Internet, watching cable TV: survey. *Business Times* (Singapore).

Thai movies are on a winning roll. (2001, January 29). *Bangkok Post.*

The rate stuff. (1996, September). *Cable and Satellite Asia.*

Tungate, M. (1998, May). Indonesian research. *Media International.*

Vietnam: Cinemas widen their scope. (1997, October 30). *The Saigon Times Daily.*

WhiteKnight Communications. (1996). *Media guide: Media and advertising guide book.* Kuala Lumpur: WhiteKnight Communications.

Widiadana, R. A., and Ramani, Y. T. (1997, November 30). Will teleserials' glory days last? *Jakarta Post.*

Chapter Eight

Censorship and the Asian Values Debate

Media censorship has been the subject of persistent controversy in Southeast   153
Asia. Criticism of censorship frequently originates from outside the region,
and for this reason political observers and scholars have identified the issue as
one that divides East and West. This judgment has some merit, but complaints
have been regularly voiced from within Asia as well. The following discussion
examines the practice of censorship within Southeast Asia, as well as its criticisms and justifications. The question here is not whether censorship is inherently undesirable—every society develops its own rules defining the boundaries of acceptable discourse—but whether motivations and logic advanced to
support the systems of censorship are reasonable and whether the goal of social good is actually served by the censoring policies.

Western media scholars have authored many publications on censorship.
Their writings have tended to place the censoring within a "press freedom"
frame, in which restrictions or other government interventions in the media
are considered contrary to democratic principles. According to this view,
greater media openness provides the public with exposure to a full spectrum of
political viewpoints. A contest for the minds of citizens naturally ensues when
ideologies clash; individuals sample the philosophies offered by different parties, eventually selecting the most agreeable from the "free market of ideas."
More than merely a philosophical issue, Western authors commonly believe
the principles of press freedom to be a foundation for democratic political systems. They argue that in modern mass societies, political leaders cannot present themselves to the voting public in the traditional face-to-face manner but

must rely on mass media's communication networks. For media to function in this way, however, information passing through their channels must not be filtered. If it is—generally by censoring—then the public will not be afforded a full range of viewpoints on issues, and the political system will tend to be controlled by whomever has control over media content.

ASIAN VALUES—HUMAN RIGHTS

In Asia, mainly in Southeast Asia, government defenders recently began to offer a counter-argument to the anticensorship, press freedom concept. Their contention has been that press freedom is an idea that Westerners advanced with the intention of molding the rest of world in their image and in ways that really serve the political and economic aims of Western elites. Government officials explain that unique and worthwhile Asian values are vulnerable to displacement or degradation by foreign cultural content. To prevent socially destructive values from creeping into Asian cultures, it is argued, there is no alternative to censoring. Furthermore, proponents argue that restrictions on Asian media are merely extrapolated from the region's cultures and therefore are more appropriate than rules employed in Western media. They also counter that a lack of controls on Western media has been a cause of social conflict and confusion in Western countries.

The application of censorship as a protection against the globalization of cultures and against foreign influences enjoys substantial support in Southeast Asia, and some Western scholars have been sympathetic, too. As Harper (1997, p. 507) noted, "A new Zeitgeist has arisen: 'Asian values.' The idea has been given wide international exposure, especially by intellectuals in the United States. It has formed the basis of a grand historical narrative." The origin of the "Asian values" construct can be found in the post–World War II renaissance of East Asia. Experts judged Japanese reemergence as an industrial dynamo after the devastation of defeat and occupation a "miracle." In the 1980s, Western management consultants encouraged the kinds of behaviors that supposedly produced Japan's rapid economic expansion. Management and economics scholars who studied Japan's industrial and corporate practices claimed to have discovered cultural traits that were the basis of the national rebirth. Quite a number of Asian countries attempted to model themselves after Japan, not least among them Malaysia, which adopted the "Look East" slogan in the 1980s. Asian cultural qualities of hard work, discipline, acceptance of leadership, and social cohesiveness—among others—were attributes suggested as sources of vitality in economies of East Asia, especially in the "tiger economies." Chen (1977) was one of the first Asian scholars to study Asian values as a source of the region's economic successes. He attempted to spell out the exact cultural characteristics that have been positive factors in Asian development. He identified five: (1) group spirit and paternalistic employer-employee relationship; (2) mutual assistance and community life; (3) parent-child relationship and cohesive family life; (4) friendship patterns; and (5) normative ideology and value concept. Chen admitted, however, that his analysis was limited to "only those [values] of the East Asian culture, mainly Chinese and Japanese cultures, which are familiar to me" (p. 20).

Finally, in the 1990s, advocates began asserting that Asian cultures fostered different and superior qualities not only in the commercial realm but also in mass communication. One of the leading spokesmen for the validity of "Asian values" as a justification for media controls was Malaysia Prime Minister Dr. Mahathir Mohamad. The subjects of Asian values and Eastern differences from the West were consistent themes in his speeches during the 1990s, and he frequently urged other national leaders in Southeast Asia to resist Western intrusion in local cultures. Possibly his most complete analysis on the subject was contained in an address to the Pacific Basic Economic Council (PBEC) meeting in 1996. The PBEC is a regional organization devoted to stimulating regional economic cooperation and development. Conference attendees, representing more than 1,200 multinational corporations in nineteen countries, witnessed the prime minister's speech. His remarks began by brushing aside claims of universal values, although acknowledging the existence of "common values which we all share; arising out of the fact that we are human." But he went on, "just as European values are more universal than American values, Asian values are more universal than both." He complained strongly about pressures from Western sources to modify what he considered culturally based policies in economics and the media. "The countries of the West have a right to their preferences. But they have no right to ram their preferences down everyone's throats." He then revealed a provocative outlook on Western media.

> There are some democracies where political leaders are afraid to do what they know is right, for one reason or another. And the people and their leaders live in fear—fear of the free media which they so loudly proclaim as inviolable. Indeed, they are quite literally oppressed by their own media, the way people in feudal societies were oppressed by their rulers—knowing their unfortunate situation but not daring to raise their voices against an established institution, so as to curb its excesses. (Mahathir, 1997, p. 11)

But surprisingly the prime minister ended his speech with an upbeat admonition: "Let us deliberately prepare for and enthusiastically partake of a feast of civilizations, where we each take the best that all of us have to offer—and together build for the first time a single global civilization such as the world has never seen" (Mahathir, 1997, p. 12—13).

This speech was given extensive coverage in major Asian newspapers such as the Singapore *Straits Times* and Hong Kong's *South China Morning Post,* thus advancing Dr. Mahathir's views and prompting a round of discussion among Asian intellectuals and businesspeople.

Mahathir carried his argument even further at the 1997 meeting of Association of Southeast Asian Nations (ASEAN) where he asserted that no universal understanding of human rights exists, and he defended internationally criticized human rights practices in Southeast Asia as consistent with Asian values. He suggested that the United Nations "review" its Universal Declaration of Human Rights, saying that the document was "forced on the world by superpowers at the end of World War II" and might now be outdated and unsuited to the needs of developing countries. His recommendation received an endorsement from Indonesian Foreign Minister Ali Alatas, who commented that "everybody knows that human rights does not consist of individual political and civil rights. People are now much more aware that economic rights, cultural rights, social rights are just as important" (cited in Richburg, 1997). The proposal caused a furor, producing an especially strong reaction among Western diplomats. U.S. Secretary of State Madeleine Albright vowed to maintain "relentless" opposition to any weakening of the charter.

And so "Asian values" were offered not only as an explanation for economic success and as a justification for a style of governance that critics called authoritarian and paternalistic, but also as an argument for a different approach to human rights. As a corollary, this thesis asserted that the global values promulgated by international organizations dominated by the Western powers amounted to a new form of colonialism—a way of subjugating the developing world to the dictates of industrialized European and North American nations. Because the tiger economies were so successful, the claims of cultural superiority, or at least distinctness, had a degree of plausibility. This rationale began to lose its persuasive power when the economies of East Asia went into a tailspin in mid-1997. As economic good times began evaporating, weaknesses in the "Asian" way of doing business surfaced. As Linda Lim (1998) asked in a commentary published in the Singapore *Straits Times,* "the regional tigers have gone bust. Should they abandon the 'Asian values' model for the Western ideal of free-markets-with-democracy?" She answered that "the Asian economic crisis is cause for rethinking the long-established consensus about the region's 'miracle' economic growth."

Critics in Southeast Asia, many of whom had questioned the motives of Asian values advocates from the beginning, began to speak out. As early as 1975, the Asian values thesis had been refuted by Ho Wing Meng (1976). Speaking at a faculty seminar of the University of Singapore, he referred to the idea as stereotypical. In his opinion,

> the argument that the tradition of philosophic, religious and moral contemplation make Asians more tolerant, non-aggressive, non-violent and non-militant in their internal and external relations with people is simply false. Non-violence is hardly a national trait of any nation in Asia when its interests are at stake (p. 11)

He also rejected the notion that Asians are less acquisitive on the grounds that wars fought over "cattle, spices, tea, gold, silver, silk, land or beautiful women . . . would indicate ... that Asians were no less materialistic in their outlook than Westerners." Well-known Malaysian opposition intellectual Chandra Muzaffar (1997) offered a strong critique of the Asian values argument in a commentary published in the *New Straits Times* in 1997. First, he noted that Asian values often cited as the source of regional strength, hard work and family commitments, "are by no means unique to Asia. They can be found in other continents and other cultures too." He also argued against the idea that a single set of values characterizes the Asian region. According to his analysis, "Asian values are as diverse and complex as Asia itself." He rejected Asian cultural values as a basis for the political systems found in the region. He observed that although "authoritarianism and autocratic rule ... violate the moral core, the spiritual foundation of [Asian] religion ... most Asian societies for most of history have been authoritarian."

The assertion that a uniform set of cultural values could characterize 2.7 billion persons in a region stretching from Turkey to Japan drew fire from many. Paul Krugman (1998) not only contended that Asian values were not the basis of economic success, but that they were behind the financial meltdown experienced in 1997–1998. In his view, the tendency toward excessive loyalty to family or clan led to nepotism, crony capitalism, and corruption. He cited as examples the Philippines, Indonesia, and Thailand, countries where these had been chronic issues. Researchers pointed to large differences in measured cultural orientations among Asian nations and to the fact that the values that are most familiar in Asia are also similar to cultural values found in other parts of the globe. Charles Wolf (1999) of the Rand Corporation, and a fellow at the Hoover Institution, reported on his study of these cultural questions. He noted that "on only two of nine value dimensions did Asians significantly differ from Westerners. ... Moreover, variances within the Asian and Western groups' responses was quite similar," with two exceptions. "Asian respondents vary more widely among themselves in the importance they assign to good relations with 'others,' as distinct from families, and in the importance they assign to leisure activity than did their Western counterparts." Wolf's analysis was based on data collected by the Japanese Dentsu Institute for Human Studies in 1997 and 1998.

I also studied cultural values in Asia. In a series of training courses for senior broadcasting managers beginning in 1990, I presented participants with a questionnaire asking each person to rank eighteen values such as familism, religion, education, and so on. More than a dozen countries, most in South and Southeast Asia, were included in the survey. This study was loosely based on the work of Hofstede (1980, 1984). The findings revealed little consistency among countries, and even on the value of "family and close kinship ties"— which Asian values proponents often cited as a prevailing theme within the region—sharp differences were evident. This value was ranked first by broadcast managers in the Philippines, but by participants from Indonesia it was ranked seventeenth. Among the most consistently ranked values was "knowledge, wisdom, understanding of nature" which ranked first or second among participants in all countries surveyed except one (the Philippines). But this value has tended to rank highly in practically all countries, Asian and Western alike, in studies conducted by a number of authors (see, for instance, Hickson, 1993).

Objections to Western journalists' advocacy of fewer media restrictions and their lack of cultural sensitivity have some merit; their writings often suffered from a narrow vision. For many years journalism students in the United States were trained using a model that divided media systems into just four categories: authoritarian, Soviet Communist (later just Communistic), libertarian, and social responsibility (Siebert, Peterson, and Schramm, 1956; Merrill, 1974). This simplistic conceptualization was ideologically naïve, but its use as an analytic tool persisted into the 1990s. Other approaches were often equally flawed. In the early 1980s, one popular American text published on world media summarized the situation this way:

> North America has a great amount of press freedom. Latin America has very little. Europe is highly polarized, with the nations of Western Europe largely enjoying very free press systems and the countries of eastern Europe going to the other extreme. … Many of the emerging nations of Africa and Asia are in a state of flux, generally gravitating toward more control (Merrill, 1983, pp. 43–44).

Seen from the perspective of Asian media scholars and professionals, such limited analyses, lacking in nuance or depth, demand rebuttal.

The Asian Mass Information and Communication Centre in Singapore hosted a conference in 1995 to consider the Asian values argument in the journalistic realm, and proceedings were published not long afterward (Masterton, 1996). No consensus was produced by the conference. Numerous viewpoints were offered on the debate, but it was Eric Loo who attempted to present a less polemic position and a synthesis of opinion. He suggested that the terms of discussion should be revised from Asian values in journalism to Asian-centered journalism, in which "Asian media must avoid an antagonistic relationship with the West and its media industries, since this would sabotage any bid for fairer representation" (p. 117). He then offered a definition of "Asian-centred" journalism as contrasted with the "Western liberal tradition." In his view, "Asian centred journalism claims to be guarded when contentious, constructive when adversarial, and supportive when critical. It also believes that it is, and should be, development oriented" (p. 119). The majority of speakers at the meeting expressed grievance with Western press coverage that they described as too often ill-informed, motivated by the sensational and commercial, and lacking in an appreciation of Asian cultural sensitivities.

For media that have physical properties, that is, books and other printed matter or films and videotapes, censoring need not be too complicated. Materials can be required to pass through screening processes that check content by blocking or editing items that fail to meet standards. For any item to be blocked, the censors' best pressure point is the production center, the place where multiple copies are to be made. In the case of books and magazines, regulators have a good chance of suppressing undesired content because the facilities required for production are comparatively expensive and thus tend to be few in number. As long as the means of production is not broadly available and the skills needed to produce media content remain high, the number of sources will not be great. The small number of sources makes it easy to identify and to stop production of undesirable materials at their sources.

Southeast Asian practice usually depends on censoring materials at their sources. Even so, in this region—and perhaps everywhere—such regulatory systems are at best imperfect. Materials can filter throughout societies clandestinely, passing from hand to hand instead of moving through commercial channels. Pornography can be found everywhere, provided one has sufficient interest and the proper contacts. Oppositional materials are just as broadly disseminated, although the penalties for their distribution are so much greater that secrecy tends to be higher. Another way of controlling information at the production source is through licensing arrangements or simply by closing troublesome media sources. In Indonesia the major news weeklies *Tempo* and *Editor* as well as *DeTik* were shut down by the Suharto government in its final years. Numerous other publications were banned by authorities there in the mid-1990s, including newsletters such as *Kabar Dari Pijar,* whose editor was charged with fomenting hatred against the government and *Mitra Media,* published by the Kalyanamitra Foundation, a women's advocacy organization. Another Indonesian tactic in management of information was to discipline reporters through the state-controlled Association of Indonesian Journalists. Under laws dating from the 1960s, journalists were required to be members, but those who ran afoul of government often found themselves expelled (McBeth, 1995). As a measure of the controls exercised by the Indonesian government, the number of licensed publications surged upward from just 285 to 1,138 just a year after Suharto's resignation (Kafil, 1999).

One of technology development's chief aims has been to make production of materials simpler and less expensive. Yet as this happens, suppression of unwanted content becomes immensely more difficult, forcing regulators to resort to ever more Draconian measures to stop its spread. Ithiel de Sola Pool (1983) proposed that government crackdowns on producers is "most likely not before a technology … comes along, but only afterward when the powers that be are challenged by the beginnings of change" (p. 14). He offered as an example the tightening of censorship and publication controls that were enacted by the

Roman Catholic Church "in reaction to the heresies that flowed from the print shops." A good illustration of how this works is provided by the photocopy machine, a technology that enabled small-scale production of printed materials from the 1960s onward. In the Soviet Union, photocopy machines could not be privately owned. Access to the machines was tightly controlled in an effort to prevent their use in mass production of banned literature, something that had become a problem for the regime immediately upon the introduction of photocopying. In particular, machines replaced hand copying as a means of automating reproduction of *samizdat,* informal newsletters that circulated secretly throughout the USSR. Shane (1994) explained that the technological backwardness of the Soviet Union was not merely a result of the inefficient and bureaucratic state of the country, but was a matter of policy aimed at restricting tools that might be used to subvert the state. In the end, the policy failed as even the comparatively few copiers in use were heavily engaged in the dissemination of publications that ultimately undermined the center's political legitimacy.

The single factor that most brought censorship into the foreground at the end of the twentieth century was that technologies introduced since the 1970s had all advanced one key feature: they shifted control from media centers and national officials to individual consumers of information. Governments, often with the backing of religious groups and civic organizations, struck against the materials that spread throughout Southeast Asia via new media. But even the most imaginative schemes for blocking access to videos, satellites, and the Internet failed. A primary reason for the failures is that the classical model of mass communication—one source to many receivers—no longer applied. Today, a vast multitude of sources exist. Before the 1970s, few could electronically produce and distribute mass content. Costs were prohibitive for all but the largest commercial or publicly funded organizations. Furthermore, the skills demanded to create products were limiting; not many knew how to produce radio or television programs or to publish newspapers. But new production technologies greatly simplified the making of mass materials and drove down costs, enabling anyone who could point and shoot a video camera or who could operate a personal computer to become a content producer. With numbers of sources rendered uncontrollable, censoring bodies could not hope to clamp down on every producer of unwanted content.

Within Southeast Asia, material subject to censorship generally can be grouped within two broad categories. In the first classification are topics deemed socially unwholesome, typically because of the treatment of sexual themes, but sometimes because of other social taboos. Presentations of violent, threatening, or dangerous behavior are subject to censorship in many countries and receive condemnation practically everywhere. Tolerance of depictions of nudity, sexual acts, and the like varies greatly from country to country, even among groups of countries that are culturally similar. Variations among countries can arise from different regulatory frameworks as well as cultural or social differences. In the wake of Suharto's retirement from government, Indonesia has again taken up the definition of what is acceptable in a modern era. A number of the dozens of newly licensed publications pushed the boundaries of Indonesian modesty, so much so that at least five editors of tabloids that specialized in saucy photos and titilating stories were issued summons in 1999 under a provision of the Criminal Code pertaining to "indecency." Religious leaders resisted looser definitions of publication codes. A statement issued by the Indonesian Ulema Council in the same year stated that "pornography in any form is an evil, and those who participate in the making, distributing and publishing of it are devils." One editor responded "give me a clear idea of what pornography is. ... If people's sexual desire is stimulated by our artistic pictures, then the problem is in their minds." But a female Indonesian lawmaker rejected such arguments, saying, "Let's make it simple. Those who defend pornography in the media are those who get advantage from the exploitation of women's bodies" (Kafil, 1999).

Censoring on grounds of decency in Southeast Asia presents an especially thorny set of problems because of the region's pluralistic societies. Content rules that satisfy one cultural group may seem inappropriate to another. In Malaysia, for instance, strict interpretations of Islamic standards are demanded by conservative groups and by the political party PAS (Parti Islam) but are resisted by others such as intellectual groups. Disagreement on matters governed by religious interpretations are routine, spanning a wide range of behaviors such as dress, consumption of alcohol and products containing alcohol, and physical contact such as touching and handshaking. These tensions are played out in the censoring of media content, resulting in standards that are continually in flux as various parties contest practices. In the early 1970s standards were extremely restrictive, and kissing of any type was prohibited, leading to what was called the "Malaysian kiss" in films—characters lean toward each others, then suddenly jump apart (caused by cutting the film to remove the kiss). But by the late 1980s, standards had been loosened. Once during that time I saw a film on Malaysian television late at night that had a scene containing full frontal nudity. Then, as complaints mounted and Islamic groups began to exercise their leverage on political fronts, officials reinstituted tougher standards. In addition, they created a new system of ratings to alert viewers to program contents. The rating guidelines present warnings for programs that might offend some parts of the audience. However, in practice few broadcast programs fail to gain the "U" (for *Umum,* Malay for "general") rating that indicates content "suitable for all levels of society." Malaysian rules for censoring are seldom made public, but one source reported that in 1995 guidelines for censors prohibited mouth-to-mouth kissing in Asian films or passionate kissing in any film, kissing on parts of the body other than the face, kissing that shows passion or lust, or any embrace under sheets while sitting or lying down (Keenan, 1995a).

Violent content can be a cause for censoring, but the standards for violence seem to vary from place to place even more than those for sexual themes. Practically all countries have standards concerning violence on the screen, but how the standards are applied is another question. Throughout Asia, the extremely violent Hong Kong action films, including ones from the so-called Kung Fu genre, are highly popular, yet their physical excesses seldom get censored. Similarly, it is not unusual to see news footage showing mangled bodies in terrible highway accidents or the bloody victims of stabbings and shootings. Usually considered offensive by Western news producers, such portrayals by Asian producers tend to be explained away as a good lesson for viewers who drive recklessly or who might be tempted to break the law. Although it might appear that Asian audiences are less distressed by scenes of gore and death, violence does remain a matter of concern. As Malaysian Information Minister Mohamed Rahmat explained, "If it's too violent, we'll still censor." One interesting provision of Malaysian censoring rules on crime and violence is the ban on "detailed instructions on how to prepare and operate explosives and other weapons" (Keenan, 1995a).

The second category of censorship is made up of political or ideological content considered dangerous, subversive, or even impertinent or impious. It is in this category that the most heated disagreement occurs. As suggested previously, generally accepted democratic principles require an open dialogue on politics. According to conventional logic, any restriction in the "free market of ideas" jeopardizes the quality of resulting dialectic. Yet it would be difficult to identify any country where there is a total absence of limits. Western countries that consider themselves thoroughly open societies have enacted laws that clearly circumscribe public discussion. In the United States, laws remain in place that were enacted when political leaders such as Senator Joseph McCarthy mercilessly hounded the political left, and in Germany, materials promoting or reflecting Nazi ideology are still prohibited, to mention just two examples. One frequent justification for restrictions in political discourse is that inflammatory materials could undermine governments, leading to political instability. This reasoning was often offered in Southeast Asia until the end of the 1980s, but after this time it was largely abandoned. By then, governments seemed very firmly established in countries such as Malaysia, Brunei, and Singapore where no serious threats to stability had arisen in decades. Moreover, the economic strength of the tiger countries suggested anything but unsteadiness.

Of course, censoring in the ideological realm presents abundant opportunities for political mischief. Many examples could be cited, but one of the most thoroughly researched incidents occurred in Thailand during student clashes with the army in 1992. As briefly described in previous chapters, a military junta seized power from the civilian Chatichai government in February 1991. It was a government that was considered rampantly corrupt. When the junta named army chief Suchinda Kraprayoon prime minister in April of the following year, opponents of military rule were outraged and took to the streets with demonstrations and civil disobedience. Within a month events began to spin out of control as demonstrations spread. Military efforts to quash the demonstrations turned into bloody confrontations that received extensive coverage on international channels. Military leaders, on the other hand, responded as authoritarian governments had done for decades when confronted with events it did not like to see reported: it censored coverage. A large portion of the nation's broadcasting stations were owned and operated by the military, and other media outlets were heavily censored by the military government, so accounts of the ugly suppression of demonstrators were mostly deleted on domestic channels. This produced an anomalous situation in which people outside Thailand knew more about the events in Bangkok than people within the country.

But some in Thailand did have access to international satellite coverage. In the southern part of the country, along the border with Malaysia, Radio Television Malaysia (RTM) could be viewed. RTM carried a daily digest of CNN news and during the unrest in Bangkok included most of the footage available from Thailand. They saw a stark contrast in the interpretation of events by heavily censored military controlled channels and uninhibited satellite television broadcasters. The military government's tactic of suppressing reports of demonstrations backfired, because people who had access to international television—including most of the political elites—saw that the military government had no other apparent motive than to cover its own excesses. This not only caused a loss of confidence in the military regime, it convinced a large portion of the Thai public that political censorship was dangerous and should be curtailed. Many observers credit coverage by CNN International and BBC World Service Television with motivating the much respected and revered King Bhumibol Adulyadej to intervene, leading to the resignation of military head Suchinda as prime minister. An election later that year brought parties opposed to military rule into power and provided the impetus for rewriting Thai laws to forestall news censoring of the sort adopted by the military government.

The reaction of Southeast Asian countries to the events in Thailand provide a revealing picture of how censoring strategies have been modified under force of changing technology. In a commentary on the Thai political crisis, the *Far Eastern Economic Review* included this perceptive observation.

> The borderless information world created by the satellite TV services of CNN and BBC made any attempt to restrict the flow of news coverage a futile exercise. Even those governments which have reason to fear the contagion of such a popular movement showed sophistication

by taking a low-key approach. A notable exception was Burma, a regime widely condemned for its violent suppression of democratic aspirations ("Going with," 1992).

The lack of censorship applied to the Thai student uprising story in neighboring countries does indeed reveal a shift in thinking. But the shift was to reduce censorship efforts not only because technology made it too difficult, but also because public resistance to censoring—which now was much easier to detect through new technologies—had risen sharply. Naturally, this generalization excludes Burma (officially known as Myanmar), which in 1992 was in a precarious political state because of SLORC's rejection of the 1990 election balloting results and whose residents had very little access to new electronic technologies.

Strategies of media content management vary from country to country. In the Philippines where the press is often considered one of the least tightly controlled, Corazon Aquino and other political figures used the courts to pressure journalists when stories displeased them. In the post-Marcos era there was an explosion in newspaper circulation, with the number of dailies growing from eleven to twenty-six in just a few years. This corresponded with a much more competitive environment and hence political coverage that was much more critical of authorities. Unaccustomed to tough investigative reporting after years of Marcos's suppression of the media, political elites found the newly liberated media difficult to accept. Aquino lodged a libel suit against the well-known columnist Luis Beltran and the *Philippine Star*, claiming the Philippine press to be "abusive and sometimes licentious." Her attitude toward the press was determinedly negative. At one point she seethed, "not only is [the press] contentious; it is at best critical—of organized government, of history, of humanity itself" (Tiglao, 1991). Additional libel suits include ones brought by Juan Ponce Enrile's son, Philippine senator Heherson Alvarez, and Aquino's sister-in-law among others.

CENSORING VIDEO AND SATELLITE CONTENT

Movie censorship in Southeast Asia regularly spawns controversies. The resulting debates probably help professionals in the media work out a clearer idea of what is acceptable and what is not. Always there is a tension between those who censor and those who disagree with the basis for a particular cut or who disagree with the whole idea of censorship. An instance occurred when the blockbuster movie *Titanic* appeared in Singapore theaters in 1998. A furor erupted when viewers discovered that fourteen seconds of the film had been cut in local showings—the piece snipped out showed Kate Winslet's bare breasts. The Board of Film Censors (BFC) is responsible for clearing all films distributed for theaters and must recommend edits or ban movies when it believes standards are not met. It explained that the shot was eliminated from *Titanic*'s Singapore showings because by cutting the film, it could be rated PG and therefore could be seen by a larger audience (Kuzmanovic, 1998). The *Straits Times* published a number of letters submitted to the editor on the subject. Most writers who complained about the censor's decision argued that cutting the shot eliminated an important story element, not that censoring was bad or that nudity should not be a subject of censorship.

Singapore's regulations covering movie and video content are arguably the most strict in Southeast Asia. In the same year of the *Titanic* censoring flap, rules for video program contents were tightened even further. In February, the Ministry of Information and the Arts announced that officers had seized eleven thousand uncensored videos in raids on seven shops. Apparently a thousand of the videos were considered pornographic, but the remainder were not characterized by the ministry, suggesting that they were screened out on political grounds. In the same public statement announcing the seizures, the ministry announced that it was amending the Films Act to raise penalties for infractions involving porn videos. Just before this the Singapore parliament enacted new legislation called the "Undesirable Publications Act," which also increased fines for trafficking in banned materials. This act also redefined the term "publication" to include computer-generated materials such as video CDs, CD ROMs, and computer graphics. ("Singapore authorities," 1998). Among the approximately 170 publications banned by authorities in Singapore are ones such as *Playboy, Penthouse,* and even *Cosmopolitan.* All but a small number on the list of forbidden publications are deemed pornography, officially defined as "explicit sex-related magazines or those which promote a promiscuous lifestyle." Other items that have been outlawed are periodicals from the People's Republic of China and ones from Jehovah's Witness and a few other religious groups ("Singapore authorities," 1998).

The popularity of the video CD as a medium for film distribution contributed to significant changes in the process of censoring. Unlike videocassettes, which had to be individually recorded from master tapes, video CDs could be produced in massive quantities once stamping masters had been made. The result was both an unprecedented quantity of copies and much lower costs. For video CDs sold in Southeast Asia that were manufactured without legal authority, there were no copyright fees to be paid either. In Indonesia, Thailand, and Malaysia sales of video CDs had two forms. Copies made under copyright by movie studios, their subsidiaries, or designates were sold through regular retail outlets. Shops like these offered both audio and video CDs. Because these were produced under copyright license, these movies were priced in the range of USD $5 to $15, most in the upper portion of the range. The second sales channel marketed pirate copies of videos and sales were through vendors who set up on the street. Card-table collections of a few hundred could be packed quickly in case police took an interest in their offerings. Most of these illegally produced titles could be purchased for less than USD $2. Hundreds of little sales kiosks scattered across a city like Kuala Lumpur made copyright enforcement impossible. However, only the "legitimate" videos carried censoring certification. The pirated films hardly ever were edited; versions were sold with violence, nudity, sexual scenes, and coarse language fully intact. In the year 2000 it was even easy to find films that had become infamous as a consequence of being banned—*Schindler's List* for instances in Malaysia.

Satellite television originating from offshore sites present censors with a special challenge because relayed materials can easily bypass screening procedures. This happens when viewers employ their own parabolic dish receiving equipment. The usual way around this problem is to require that foreign programs pass through domestic channels that can be regulated while simultaneously banning use of home satellite receiving equipment. This tactic works well in conjunction with cable systems. Singapore has adopted this approach, and for a time Malaysia experimented with it also. In the latter country, Mega TV was licensed to provide a few satellite channels via its "wireless" cable system in the mid-1990s. The technology employed was known as multipoint microwave distribution system (MMDS). Systems of this type use frequencies above the UHF band to transmit the programs. MMDS systems have the advantage of quick startup because no cables need be installed but have the disadvantage of limited channel capacity, usually less than ten channels. The extremely high frequencies used by MMDS systems can present coverage problems as well. As a Mega TV subscriber living in a distant suburb of Kuala Lumpur, I had frequent reception problems, and I had little success in getting technical assistance from the company. Despite these drawbacks, policy makers encouraged the censored cable as a way of lessening the appeal of illegal uncensored parabolic reception and pirate videos. In 1997, following complaints voiced in Malaysia's Parliament about Mega TV's programs, the Information Ministry examined the cable system's censoring practices. Although no serious deficiencies were found, stringent rules were laid down by the government for cable program services. Included in these was the requirement that all CNN transmissions be delayed 5 minutes so that censors could screen its programs (Rahmad A. Kadir, personal communication, 24 April 1997).

An arrangement like this may be workable with Mega TV's five channels but censoring on Malaysia's ASTRO—which carries about two dozen channels—is more difficult. The mushrooming number of programs to be censored soon overwhelmed the capacity of state censoring boards, and government threw up its hands, turning screening responsibilities over to organizations like Mega TV and ASTRO that redistribute satellite programs. Malaysian Prime Minister Mahathir Mohamad observed that although the government had provided this service earlier, "now we have thousands of titles … how can we do censorship?" ("TV stations," 1996). But government officials across the region retain the right to "guide" censoring practices. For instance, in Indonesia, not long before facing the information deluge that ultimately drove him from office, President Suharto cautioned against reports on internal unrest, suggesting that "inaccurate data, especially on sensitive issues, could have large implications inside or outside of the country" ("Suharto warns," 1996).

CENSORING THE INTERNET

Censorship of the Internet became a critical issue as the number of on-line browsers exploded in the mid-1990s. Pornography is abundantly available on the Web, not to mention plenty of other materials many find offensive. Operators of portals such as Yahoo report that sexual and scatological terms tend to be among the most frequently used search keywords used on the Internet, and sites featuring practically every known sexual preference can be found there. Across the world, condemnation of excesses on the Internet grew more insistent as time passed, and so regulatory options to restrict pornographic Web sites were studied nearly everywhere. To the dismay of lawmakers and regulators, managing content on the Internet proved to be much more complicated than any technology they had previously encountered.

Internet's technical attributes, that is to say the way that messages are exchanged, seriously impede any effort to filter its content. First, a person "browsing" a Web site employs software that calls for and receives a set of small files. These files are displayed in the receiving computer according to instructions provided in the form of hypertext markup language (HTML). To censor undesirable Web sites, it is necessary either to block access to the site or to filter out the offending files. Of the two, blocking the Web site is a more practical solution; filtering files would involve complex procedures to check each and every one. Because a single Web page might contain dozens of tiny files, and given the difficulty of automating testing procedures for the files, file checking has never been used as the basis for censoring. To block Web sites requires that users relay their file requests through a central computer that checks for calls to prohibited sites. Technically, this is known as the use of a proxy server. The central computer acts as a proxy, sending calls onward to requested sites then returning files and other responses to the receiving computer. This process demands very powerful computing capacity of the proxy server to avoid delaying the file transfers unacceptably. In any case, proxy servers inevitably add to the time required to access Web sites.

The problem in using proxy servers is that they must have a way of identifying sites that should be blocked. Several different strategies can be employed. The most common approach is to develop a list of offending words that can be matched against search engine summaries of web content. Web sites that contain keyword matches are added to the list of Internet addresses to be blocked by the proxy server. But simply using search engines in this way turns up many innocent sites that are identified as offenders. For instance, medical Web sites often score keyword matches on pornography content because of terms they use are relevant to sexual function, obstetrics, and gynecology. Even among Web sites that contain verifiably nasty material, it is a trivial matter to obtain and use a new domain name, abandoning a Web site name that triggers blocking. There are other considerations in operations such as these, of course, but detailed technical issues need not be explored here. The ultimate ability of these techniques is not known as this is being written; research and experimentation is still underway, a good deal of which is ongoing in Singapore where several companies are acknowledged to be global pacesetters.

As described in an earlier chapter, Singapore's policy on Internet content was strict, the toughest in the region. In this country, the use of proxy servers is compulsory so that public access to objectionable Web sites can be prevented. The rules governing Internet and other network communications took effect on July 15, 1996. Each Internet service provider (ISP) is defined as a "broadcaster" and thus must be licensed by the Singapore Broadcasting Authority (SBA). All license holders are responsible for the content each relays and must put in place procedures that observe rules forbidding certain kinds of content such as gambling, fortune telling, and pornography. As for ideological censoring, any information that jeopardizes public security or national defense, disturbs racial and religious harmony, or denigrates public morals is prohibited as well (Wang, 1999). Furthermore, ISPs are obligated to aid the SBA in investigating any suspected infractions of the rules. Revisions to the rules were issued in 1997, but the intent was merely to clarify, not to modify goals or standards.

There is some evidence that a tremendous Internet filtering effort is being expended to correct a very small problem in Singapore. In 1994, an ISP conducted a scan of user accounts searching for files with the extension .GIF. GIF files contain photographs, drawings, or other kinds of graphic materials. Such files are typically used to provide illustrations or decorative figures for Web sites. Of the 80,000 files scanned, only five were judged pornographic. Although the incident was termed an "accident" (Ang and Nadarajan, 1996), it aroused a storm of anger. Many subscribers felt their privacy had been violated by the ISP's intrusion. Rodan (1998) suggests that the incident was not unintentional. According to him the search "by design [would] have a suitably chilling effect" (p. 77).

As Ang and Nadarajan (1996) explained, the Singapore government accepts the validity of "anecdotal evidence" that consumers can be harmed by exposure to depraved or subversive media contents and thus it is "wiser to err on the side of caution through censorship." They offered as examples the communal clashes in 1950, 1964, and 1969, which they blamed on "uninhibited reporting" by the media. Finally, Ang and Nadarajan reported that censoring is not only favored by political leaders, it is also supported by public opinion. They described a survey on the subject they conducted that asked respondents to rate their views of censoring on a scale of 1 to 7, with 1 representing the most negative opinion and 7 the most positive. Censoring of "materials for the young" (5.44), "news leading to racial conflict" (5.33), and "offensive public expression" (5.25) were the most acceptable to the public. These researchers report that the overall mean rating was 4.15, which they interpreted as a slightly positive view on censoring of all kinds. There is another possible interpretation, however. Because the overall average rating fell at roughly the midpoint of the scale, it must mean that about half of those surveyed had a negative view of censoring. Although these findings indicate that official censorship enjoys grudging acceptance, overall figures only slightly above midscale do not seem to suggest much public enthusiasm. At any rate, in Singapore public discussion of issues such as this are highly weighted toward government policy through state-managed mass media. In the absence of a balanced discourse, it is not surprising that public opinion tilts toward the government's position. All of this ignores the difficulty of accurately measuring public opinion on controversial subjects in a society such as Singapore, where openly expressing views against government policies is awkward at best.

There is further evidence of lukewarm acceptance of Internet censoring in Singapore. The government stipulates that each ISP must make available a special "family-friendly" service that blocks access to an even larger number of sites than conventional proxies. The additional sites are identified from databases maintained in the United States, producing a result similar to those delivered by commercial blocking products such as Net Nanny and Cyber Patrol. These services reportedly have been flops. The largest ISP SingNet reported only about a thousand had signed up by the end of 1998, even though the surcharge for the additional filtering was less than USD $2.50 per month. As one user was quoted as saying about the service, "personally, I think all this talk that parents are the ones pushing for control over the Internet is just a handy excuse for the government to go in and do it" (cited in Hamilton, 1998).

It isn't likely that public opinion was the main consideration in weighing Singapore's policy alternatives. The republic's drive to build its information technology industry requires the participation of major multinational corporations. These firms ordinarily regard censoring as an anathema, on the grounds that suppressing content will dampen use of computer technology for communicating, storing information, and carrying out normal business activities. Singapore has tried to present its censoring strategy in a light that would be acceptable to global information technology industries and to modulate its policy so as to arouse the fewest complaints among potential investors.

Singapore's Internet censoring strategy was first laid out in a document published by the Ministry of Information and the Arts (1992) containing a set of guidelines developed by the Censorship Review Committee. It outlined the way that censoring is nuanced through the application of "differentiation," that is, "varying the degree of censorship according to the type of medium" (p. 20). In addition, the plan recommended that five factors should be weighed in making censoring decisions. Materials intended for youngsters and materials intended for public rather than private consumption should be more conservatively censored; the artistic and educational value of materials should be considered in making censoring decisions; and lastly, national interests dictated that materials "inimical to Singapore national interests should continue to be disallowed" (p. 21). Included in materials fitting the last category were any that might erode the moral values of society, subvert national security, lead to racial or religious misunderstanding or conflict, or denigrate any religion or race. Ang and Nadarajan (1996) concluded from the report that "materials going into the home are more heavily censored than those going into the corporate world," which they explained as arising because information for the home is "less critical" and that censorship would not have such a "deleterious" result. Alternatively, one might suppose that, unlike home users, corporate users have the power to respond to censorship in ways that censoring agencies might not like.

Malaysia's policy on Internet censoring has been quite different from Singapore's. For the same reasons as Singapore, this country found itself in a quandary—it was inclined to make an effort to censor the Web, perhaps to satisfy political and religious conservatives within the ruling coalition, yet this collided with its effort to attract high-tech firms to the Multimedia Super Corridor. Initially, Malaysia seemed headed toward Internet censoring practices similar to ones that were evolving in Singapore. When complaints about the Internet grew louder during the mid-1990s, the government began investigating ways of controlling its content. Even though officials had spent years in a frustrating attempt to control the content of other new media such as videos, they were undaunted. Deputy Information Minister Datuk Suleiman Mohamad announced in 1996 that his ministry was "looking into the possibility of wiping out unwanted information on the Internet by censoring them." Apparently referring to mechanisms Singapore had already put into place, Datuk Suleiman suggested that his ministry would examine possible remedies and would learn from the experiences of other countries. He concluded with a mixed message: "What we want the public to know is that the government encourages the use of the Internet but one must be selective and avoid anything that has a negative impact on the society" ("KL looking," 1996). Comments such as this had an immediate chilling effect. Talk of firms choosing not to participate in the Multimedia Super Corridor (MSC) because of Malaysian information policies grew. Southeast Asian scholar Bruce Gale described one large international bank that changed its plans to base its operations in Singapore "out of concern that Malaysia might try to regulate Internet access" (cited in Omestad, 2000).

Although never disclosed publicly, it appears that experimentation with censoring took place at about this time. In early 1997 I received instructions from my Malaysian ISP, Jaring, on setting up my computer to make use of a proxy server that it hinted would be obligatory soon. Improbably, Jaring explained this as a "benefit" and as something that would make access to international sites easier and quicker. I did not follow these instructions and never had a problem using the Internet. After this initial message, no further communication followed on the subject. Reportedly, at the time Jaring was blocking access to *Playboy, Penthouse,* and *Hustler* Web sites while filtering pornography-related Usenet lists (Ang and Nadarajan, 1996).

It seems clear that censoring the Internet was a topic of debate within the Malaysian government and that there were sharp differences in opinion. Mixed signals continued to be issued by different government officials during the period 1995 through 1997. For example, in 1996, Deputy Prime Minister Datuk Seri Anwar Ibrahim spoke on the subject, promising that the government had no plans to control or to prevent access to "pornographic materials available on the information superhighway." At the time, Anwar was the second most powerful government figure. Although in his remarks he called attention to the preponderance of Western values on the Internet, he noted that "the Internet can be regarded as a powerful tool to project our own culture and values to the global community as well as to expand our business reach" (Yeow, 1996). Anwar also pledged to ensure the growth in the use of Internet and to expand inexpensive and unfiltered access to the Internet. These comments appeared to reflect a consistent position on censoring. As early as 1994, he advised against "hysteria" over cultural domination via satellites or the Net, explaining that "the threat is real enough, but censorship and closing the sky are not the answer in this late 20th century" (cited in Menon, 1994). Anwar's words contrast with the more apprehensive views expressed by the prime minister. In retrospect, this might have been symptomatic of the growing divide between them, a divide that eventually resulted in Anwar's dismissal and jailing. In January 1997 Information Minister Datuk Mohamed Rahmat announced that his ministry had been given responsibility for "monitoring" the Internet and that "some measures have to be taken to ensure materials are suitable. ... Even in a cyber environment, elements of violence, horror, and sex would still be curbed" ("Tok Mat," 1997).

In April 1997, only four months after his previous declaration, Information Minister Mohamed Rahmat announced the decision that, in the end, the Malaysian government chose to not censor the Internet in the MSC. Apparently limited to activities within MSC boundaries only, the step was almost certainly taken because foreign technology firms were reluctant to join in the project without the assurance of open and free access to the Net. The minister explained "our philosophy is that we will accept what is good from outside and reject what is bad. So, basically what we want to do is to develop 'self-censorship' within our population" ("No censorship," 1997). Adding that campaigns were being planned to educate Malaysians on intelligent use of multimedia, he argued that "Malaysians are educated enough to decide what is good and bad." Michael Lim, an executive on the staff of the MSC, later offered a policy clarification that was more to the point, "Net-savvy people strongly prefer no censorship. ... We see guaranteeing that their preferences are respected as giving us a competitive advantage" (Gordon, 1998).

Government officials found it necessary to restate the government policy again and again to dispel skepticism among potential foreign investors. This proved necessary after four Malaysians were arrested and charged with using the Internet to spread rumors in 1998. Minister of Energy, Telecommunications and Posts Datuk Leo Moggie reaffirmed that the government was not blocking Internet sites in the wake of the incident. But MIMOS CEO Tengku Mohd Azzman Shariffadeen subsequently revealed that his agency traces the sources of rumors "upon the request of the police where there is suspicion of a crime" (Banoo, 1998). Tengku Azzman also warned that "more than 50 percent to 80 percent of the time, what you read is not true. Think of the Internet as a new media for information [sic] but at the same time be careful of what you read."

ON-LINE JOURNALISM

Malaysia's decision to eschew Internet censoring not only provided foreign technology companies free access to the Web and other network resources while operating in the country, it also created an opening for domestic groups to reap the same benefits. This frequently forced the government into clumsy measures as it attempted to limit opposition uses of the Internet. In particular, the newspaper *Harakah,* published by the Islamic party PAS, found itself in a series of skirmishes brought by the government to reduce its influence. This newspaper grew enormously in popularity following the jailing of Anwar, when it began to emphasize investigative coverage of government issues. Many stories it covered, other newspapers dared not touch. *Harakah* for the first time attempted to reach out beyond its traditional Malay readership, even adding a section in English. A study by Universiti Kebangsaan Malaysia scholar Rozhan in 1998 showed that among e-mail users he surveyed, *Harakah* had become the predominant choice, read by 70 percent of those sampled while no other newspaper had more than a 25 percent readership ("A preliminary analysis," 1999). At its peak of popularity, *Harakah* had a readership of more than three hundred thousand, a figure that compares well with circulation figures of the major English dailies ranging from one hundred thousand to two hundred thousand and with those of Malay newspapers that have circulations of one hundred thousand or more.

The government's answer to *Harakah*'s rising readership was a ruling issued by the government in early 2000 that because the newspaper was a party publication, its circulation should be limited exclusively to party members and sold from party offices. It had previously been available on newsstands across the country. Police staged raids in several cities around the country to enforce the directive. Even this was not sufficient; soon thereafter the publication's editor Zulkifli Sulong and the newspaper's printer Chea Lim Thye were arrested and charged with sedition. Charges were based on an article in *Harakah* that quoted Keadilan deputy president Chandra Muzaffar's claim in reference to the Anwar case that there was a "major conspiracy by the prime minister and his cohorts" (Sprague and Oorjitham, 2000). (Keadilan is the opposition party formed following the former deputy prime minister's jailing. It is headed by Anwar's wife.) In reaction to the suppression of the newspaper's printed version, *Harakah* staff began to beef up its on-line version. The on-line newspaper even began offering a WebTV newscast, but the slow server made it difficult to watch. This led to another government action—it ruled that party newspapers could not publish more than two editions monthly. The ruling must have been aimed directly at *Harakah,* which had been producing editions every Monday and Friday. The ruling from the home ministry was explained by the new Deputy Prime Minister Abdullah Ahmad Badawi as a move to "standardize" the frequency of publications for all political parties and therefore "was not extraordinary" ("Home Ministry allows," 2000).

Every newspaper in Malaysia must hold a license from the Home Ministry in order to publish. *Harakah*'s license term expired in the middle its struggle with the government. When the license was finally renewed in March 2000, Deputy Prime Minister Abdullah Ahamad Badawi said the frequency of the on-line version had to be the same as the printed version. Of course, on-line newspapers do not have publication dates like print versions, and the ruling seems to have been ignored. Nevertheless, government's successive application of further strictures effectively brought to an end the influence and reach of the party newspaper. The on-line newspaper is still accessible at *www.harakah-daily.com,* but in early 2001 English pages were no longer maintained, and even the Malay version did not appear to be updated regularly.

Still, the Internet presented an opportunity for all on-line newspapers. Every major Malaysian publication opened on-line versions by the end of 1999, but one of the most interesting of these had no print version. *Malaysi-akini* [Malaysia Now] emerged as the leading on-line newspaper in the aftermath of the Anwar trials and the fuss over *Harakah*. This newspaper was not affiliated with any party but specialized in reports from its own journalists as well as e-mail letters from readers. *Malaysiakini* (www.malaysiakini.com) projected a professional and enterprising approach to news stories, although it frequently covered stories unflattering to the government. The Web site offered bilingual text, with Malay and English items intermixed throughout. As an exclusively on-line newspaper, it did not attempt to provide a complete account of each day's news. Instead, it emphasized stories that it considered were underreported in the mainstream press or stories in which its reporters could present an alternative "take" on events.

Malaysiakini received a grant of USD $100,000 in November 1999 from the Southeast Asian Press Alliance to fund the newspaper's startup. The newspaper's editorial offices are maintained in Bangsar, a trendy cosmopolitan district of the capital city, but the Internet server is based in the United States. According to the newspaper, "the site was created by journalists unhappy with one-sided news coverage and the lack of press freedom in the country." The newspaper also "hopes to test and push the boundaries of free speech and press freedom in Malaysia by providing credible and up-to-date news and analysis through unbiased reporting, regular updates, editorials and opinion pieces" ("About *Malaysiakini*," 2001). Detractors have accused *Malaysiakini* of serving as a mouthpiece for Anwar Ibrahim, a charge denied vigorously by the newspaper. Editor Steven Gan countered that the newspaper merely reports on stories that "are of public interest" and had often covered stories that "the opposition is not very happy about" ("New online," 2000).

Malaysiakini is a small operation compared with the larger print publications and cannot be considered a major journalistic force. Only thirteen persons comprise the entire staff. Still, at the end of 2000 the Web site claimed daily hits of more than 120,000, a remarkable achievement for a country where only a fraction of homes have a computer with Internet access. Perhaps more significantly, *Malaysiakini* has earned the admiration of influential international organizations. Editor Steven Gan became the first Malaysian journalist to receive the International Press Freedom Award in 2000. Gene Roberts, chairman of the Committee to Protect Journalists, the organization that selects winners, cited Gan and other winners "for their great courage in the face of enormous risks." Gan, who was the first on-line journalist to receive the recognition, had earlier been declared a prisoner of conscience by Amnesty International when he was jailed over his effort to cover a nongovernmental organization meeting on East Timor in 1996. *Malaysiakini* itself was the winner of the Free Media Pioneer Award in 2001. This recognition came from the International Press Institute and was co-sponsored by the U.S.-based Freedom Forum.

SELF-CENSORSHIP

Aside from technology changes, media privatization also became a factor in Southeast Asian censorship. Tools for government management of content on the privately owned stations were rather more limited than those for government outlets. In addition, the number of stations increased so rapidly in some countries, Malaysia and Singapore for example, that it outgrew the capacity of censoring agencies. The tidal wave of media content generated by new stations, Internet channels, satellites, and video CDs made censoring of each and every source utterly impossible. The reduction in control over content forced government authorities to reevaluate their censoring strategies. In the end, officials increasingly have been forced to depend upon professionals working in the media to practice self-censorship, that is, to avoid voluntarily topics or content that might displease the government. This is really nothing new, as it has been a practice in Southeast Asia from the early days of newspapers and radio.

For self-censorship to work, there must be a compelling reason for compliance. The carrot-and-stick approach seems to work effectively in the region. In countries like Vietnam, Brunei, Malaysia, or Laos where organizations tied directly or indirectly to the government conduct all broadcasting, staff members who stray from officially accepted practices or viewpoints face harsh penalties. But for those who toe the line, there are rewards. Longtime Malaysian news anchor Mahadzir Lokman is owner-manager of a public relations firm that he operates as a sideline to his work in broadcasting. In 1995 he served as producer of an English-language television talk show, *Global*, at a time when a number of its episodes annoyed authorities. In one broadcast, a telephone caller called Malaysia an "overwhelmingly authoritarian state." Embarrassments such as this led to production changes which, in addition to eliminating call-in participation, ensured topics were more carefully screened to reduce the possibility of upsetting comments. As Mahadzir, whose PR firm depends on the government as a client, explained, "I wouldn't do anything to jeopardize my self, my company or my station. Malaysia is a small society. One small wrong thing you do—it will affect you forever" (cited in Keenan, 1995b).

Indeed, the evidence suggests that worries about the consequences of unintentional offenses are so great that workers tend to act with excessive caution. Feeling that potential controversies are not worth the risk, journalists and producers tend to avoid troublesome topics, even when the resulting coverage is likely to be within bounds of acceptability. When this level of compliance is achieved, the result is even more conservative and lacking in diverse perspectives than would be imposed by censors. It is easy to understand the reluctance of media professionals to take even small chances; benefits for pushing the envelope are simply outweighed by the possibility of negative consequences. In Southeast Asia, this problem is well understood by professionals who often agonize over content choices they must make in producing programs. As an indication of the problem's seriousness, *Malaysiakini*'s Web site proclaims as one of its aims "to counter the culture of self-censorship in the mainstream media" ("About *Malaysiakini*," 2001).

REFERENCES

A preliminary analysis of the UKM survey. (1999, August 15). Unpublished paper circulated via Internet e-mail lists.

About *Malaysiakini*. *Malaysiakini*. Retrieved January 20, 2001 from the World Wide Web: http://www.malaysiakini.com/leftbar/aboutus.html.

Ang, P. H., and Nadarajan, B. (1996). Censorship and the Internet: A Singapore perspective. *Communication of the ACM, 39*(6), pp. 72–78.

Banoo, S. (1998, September 29). Sites on the Internet not being censored or blocked. *New Straits Times.*

Chandra M. (1997, June 23). View Asian values in right perspective. *New Straits Times.*

Chen, P. S. J. (1977). Asian values and modernization: A sociological perspective. In Seah, C. M. (Ed.), *Asian values and modernization.* Singapore: Singapore University Press.

de Sola Pool, I. (1983). *Technologies of freedom.* Cambridge, MA: Harvard University Press.

Going with the flow. (1992, June 11). *Far Eastern Economic Review.*

Gordon, J. (1998, November 30). East Asia too, is giving up on censorship. *International Herald Tribune.*

Hamilton, A. (1998, November 20). See no evil, surf no evil. *Asiaweek.*

Harper, T. N. (1997). "Asian values" and Southeast Asian histories. *Historical Journal* [Great Britain], *40*, 507–517.

Hickson, D. J. (Ed.). (1993). *Management in Western Europe: society, culture and organization in twelve nations.* New York: Walter de Gruyter

Ho W. M. (1976). *Asian values and modernisation—A critical interpretation.* Singapore: University of Singapore.

Hofstede, G. (1980, Summer). Motivation, leadership, and organization: Do American theories apply abroad? *Organizational Dynamics,* 42–63.

Hofstede, G. (1984). *Culture's consequences, international differences in work-related values.* Beverly Hills, CA: Sage.

Home ministry allows *Harakah* to be published twice a month. (2000, March 2). *New Straits Times.*

Kafil Y. (1999, July 29). Politics, sex are staples in "Reformasi" era. *Media-Indonesia.*

Keenan, F. (1995a, November 16). Some don't like it hot. *Far Eastern Economic Review.*

Keenan, F. (1995b, November 16). Stage fright: Malaysia takes a more moderate line on censorship. *Far Eastern Economic Review.*

KL looking into ways to censor Internet. (1996, September 26). *New Straits Times.*

Krugman, P. (1998). *The accidental theorist: And other dispatches from the dismal science.* New York: Norton.

Kuzmanovic, J. (1998, February 25). Cut or spare: Censors' snip at "Titanic" divides Singapore. *AAP Newsfeed.*

Lim, L. (1998, March 29). "Asian values" idea: Is it out? *Straits Times.*

Mahathir M. (1997). *The Asian values debate.* Kuala Lumpur: ISIS Malaysia.

Masterton, M. (1996). Introduction. In M. Masterson (Ed.), *Asian values in journalism* (pp. 1–5). AMIC: Singapore.

McBeth, J. (1995, April 6). Troublesome types. *Far Eastern Economic Review.*

Menon, V. (1994, June 25). Economics alone not enough, says Anwar. *New Straits Times.*

Merrill, J. C. (1974). *The imperative of freedom: A philosophy of journalistic autonomy.* New York: Hastings House.

Merrill, J. C. (1983). *Global journalism: A survey of the worlds's mass media.* New York: Longman.

Ministry of Information and the Arts. (1992). *Censorship review committee report 1992.* Singapore: Author.

New online paper tests KL press limits. (2000, January 22). *Straits Times.*

No censorship within Malaysia's Multimedia Super Corridor. (1997, April 15). *Asia Pulse.*

Omestad, T. (2000, September 25). Building a high-tech magnet. *U.S. News and World Report.*

Richburg, K. B. (1997, July 30). Asians, West clash over human rights; few at ASEAN see U.S. concerns as valid. *Washington Post.*

Rodan, G. (1998). The Internet and political control in Singapore. *Political Science Quarterly, 113,* pp. 63–89.

Shane, S. (1994). *Dismantling utopia: How information ended the Soviet Union.* Chicago: Ivan R. Dee.

Siebert, F. S., Peterson, T., and Schramm, W. (1963). *Four theories of the press.* Urbana: University of Illinois Press.

Singapore authorities seize 11,000 videos in censorship crusade. (1998, February 25). *Deutsche Presse-Agentur.*

Sprague, J., and Oorjitham, S. (2000, January 28). No more Mr. nice guy. *Asiaweek.*

Suharto warns media on unrest reporting. (1996, September 21). *New Straits Times.*

Tiglao, R. (1991, February 28). Manila's press: Who owns the truth? *Far Eastern Economic Review.*

Tok Mat: We'll monitor materials on MSC. (1997, January 27). *The Sun.*

TV stations told to do own vetting. (1996, October 23). *New Straits Times.*

Wang, G. (1999). Regulating network communication in Asia: A different balancing act? *Telecommunications Policy, 23,* 277–287.

Wolf, C. (1999, November 7). Are "Asian values" really that unique? *Los Angeles Times.*

Yeow, J. (1996, March 8). No plans to censor Internet info: Anwar. *New Straits Times.*

Chapter Nine

Concluding Thoughts

Financial uproar rolled across the economic tigers of Southeast Asia in 1997   179
when currency exchange rates began to falter. With optimism buoyed up by
the region's history of strong financial growth, entrepreneurs had set up overly
ambitious development and industrial schemes. The innate risk in some of
these plans eventually led to a loss of investor confidence. Southeast Asians
who had become accustomed to sustained economic growth and the resulting
improvements in living standards were surprised and unprepared for the
downturn. Political stability that countries had enjoyed through the 1980s and
1990s was partially attributable to strong economies; people could see their
circumstances improving year by year, hence they were loathe to raise objections even when they disagreed with government policies. But when
economies started to flounder, their reluctance to express themselves began to
vanish. Media, of course, were not responsible for the economic crisis, although their reports certainly gave little encouragement to those trying to arrest the financial slide. But the media had become a different kind of catalyst
for political affairs because of their changing technology. Technical advancement had been a touchstone for Southeast Asian development, especially in
the field of electronics. Electronic media's newly acquired capacity to circumvent traditional information gatekeepers was an unexpected problem for policy makers, many of whom had spent years promoting precisely those technological developments that took information control from them. As the
economic downturn cut into support of established political regimes, new alternative media became important in advancing the agendas of opponents
who were clever enough to exploit them.

Perhaps electronic media became politicized through their use in nation-building. Colonial administrators and post-independence political leaders assigned media a central role in national integration everywhere in Southeast Asia. Radio was favored because it could reach people who could not gain access to print media—notably residents in outlying districts and illiterate persons. Applying broadcasting to problems of newly independent countries was by no means a bad thing; radio created "imagined communities," inspiring a sense of nationhood that served as the foundation of national unification. Early broadcasts created a tradition of programming heavy with nationalistic themes. Because of the need to heal social and ethnic divisions, broadcasting was expected to promote a sense of belonging and a commitment to shared ideals. Ideals were formulated in easily understood sets of principles such as *Pancasila* in Indonesia and *Rukunegara* in Malaysia and then promulgated through radio and television. To some extent, radio broadcasts went beyond this to awaken regional awareness. In the 1920s and 1930s social and political leaders as well as intellectuals and hobbyists often listened to stations from across Southeast Asia. The popularity of radio outlets in Saigon, Manila, and Jakarta contributed in a small way to a regional identity that still exists.

Explicitly and implicitly the messages transmitted via state-owned broadcasting organizations encouraged stability, a stability to be achieved through acceptance of existing political structures. The nations of Southeast Asia emerged from colonialism as somewhat fragile entities; separatist movements and insurgencies were present in every country, so the need for political stability was genuine. But stability also provided security even for corrupt or incompetent politicians. The Marcos and Suharto governments were certainly stable, lasting decades and providing continuity and consistent political conditions. But both leaders' families grew rich while their countries' economies stumbled. In both Indonesia and the Philippines, media aided stability though unification campaigns that protected the interests of national figures, justified in the name of political stability.

Power elites in a number of countries were implicated in the failings of political leadership. They provided financial rewards and resources needed to support a system that had its base not at the grassroots level, but in the economic and social aristocracies. Only after Marcos's and Suharto's departure did investigations reveal full details of the complex networks of cronies that grew up around their governments. Powerful associates in the narrow cliques around political leadership naturally had a hand in the media. When the bureaucratic and stodgy state broadcasting system came under fierce competition from new types of entertainment, media privatization seemed a good solution to maintain control of information. Wealthy associates surrounding national political figures became logical choices as operators of the new private stations—they would provide the capital and the government would offer its indulgence. This was a transparent bargain in Indonesia where it was understood that no private television broadcaster could be licensed unless a member of the Suharto family was made a partner in the corporation. Privatization that might have brought greater diversity of perspective and political opinion to the airwaves instead turned out to be little more than an extension of existing government-based media systems.

COMMUNICATION AND NATIONAL DEVELOPMENT

Nation-building involved more than just unification. Programs on state media, and on the state sanctioned private media, maintained a constant flow of optimistic information about national achievements and aspirations. Negative stories were downplayed or dismissed. When there were problems that needed attention, media presented corrective news reports filled with instructions and lectures to "the people." This paternalistic style of communicating was identified as an outmoded approach long ago in the UNESCO MacBride Commission report *Many Voices, One World.*

> The developmental models of the past mainly utilized communications to disseminate information to make people aware of the "benefits" to come from and "sacrifices" required for development and to instill a readiness to follow leaders (UNESCO, 1980, p. 204–205).

Even though discredited, this "top-down" strategy of motivating citizens toward development goals tended to be maintained.

Grassroots strategies are favored over paternal models by developmental theorists, international agencies, and nongovernmental organizations because they permit people whose lives are affected by development to define their own needs. This also is viewed as more democratic than externally determined development planning. But political leaders sometimes counter that the "top-down" approach fits the traditional way of development better because it relies on the initiatives of community and national leaders—in keeping with "Asian values." It is undeniable that history offers many examples of charismatic Southeast Asian leaders who inspire masses to follow their notions of social and political development. Sukarno's "Guided Democracy" comes to mind here. A problem with such leadership is that it invites abuses of power and gives rewards to the influential. As the MacBride Commission report (UNESCO, 1980) noted,

> Today it is acknowledged that these theories [of "guided" development] in developing countries have produced greater benefits for the more advanced sectors of the community than to its more marginal sectors and that the gulf between rich and poor is not decreasing (p. 205).

Indeed, analyses of development projects in the Philippines under Marcos reveal that the lowest economic levels became more impoverished, even while overall economic measures showed gains. The greatest economic benefits, it appears, were enjoyed by those with the best political and financial connections.

Through the 1970s and 1980s, media grew in importance as means of motivating mass participation in development activities. In those years, Southeast Asia was in a prolonged phase of energetic industrial and trade expansion that led the most rapidly developing countries to become known as the tiger economies. The media played a central role in shaping national visions to match the economic ambitions of political leaders. Because governments were able to manage the content either directly or indirectly, mobilization campaigns usually proved effective. The state information machinery of countries such as Singapore perfected the recipe of nationalism, patriotism, and calls to efficiency and industriousness. These were offered as shields against economic challenges posed by giant Asian neighbors.

All of this was done in the interest of national development. But there was rarely any effort to study the effectiveness of messages conveyed in this way; officials seemed to operate under the assumption that messages transmitted would be messages received and acted upon. Anecdotally, there was plenty of evidence that at least some messages were not having the desired effect. In Malaysia and several other countries, antidrug campaigns were a staple in the media. Malaysian anti-*dadah* [drug] messages were routinely broadcast in prime time from the early 1980s onward. Rumors of widespread addiction and drug use were largely ignored by news media, whose reporting stressed tough enforcement of drug laws by police. But by the end of the 1990s police officials acknowledged that reliable estimates placed the number of Malaysian drug users in the many hundreds of thousands. Years of information and education campaigns had failed to prevent the occurrence of drug problems commonly experienced in other countries.

INFORMATION POLICIES AND POLITICAL LEADERSHIP

As discussed in preceding chapters, the transformation in media and information technologies witnessed by Southeast Asia produced a change in the region's political dynamics. One important effect was a greater openness in the media. But power elites generally resisted openness because it threatened the status quo and therefore their hold on influence. Of course, technology is only one of the forces shaping Southeast Asian politics. Growing integration of global economies makes it much more difficult for political events in one country to remain isolated. Moreover, the slow drift of power to regional and international regimes such as the International Court of Justice in the Hague, the United Nations and all of its specialized agencies, NATO, ASEAN, and so on makes the world more interdependent and the actions of individual nations less capricious.

This work's premise is that political reconstruction in Southeast Asia occurred partly because new channels of information gave citizens greater awareness of political conditions, enabled them to communicate more openly, and empowered them to become more engaged in political processes. Through new technologies, large numbers of Southeast Asia residents gained access to information less affected by censorship and other forms of information management. New technologies also offered information from a broader range of sources. Diversity in information sources brought about greater sophistication about political, economic, and social realities, and with more complete information, citizens were motivated to take control of their own politics in places like Jakarta and Manila.

When the Suharto government resigned in 1998, the country was in the midst of a financial crisis. In the days leading up to his resignation, gasoline prices were raised 70 percent, and plans to push up electricity rates by 60 percent were announced. A decade earlier, government resistors could have been kept isolated because protesters would have been unable to communicate easily. But with the Internet, they were not only able to communicate, but to coordinate actions and to create a sense of community within their movement. Satellite news channels transmitted appalling details of the Indonesian army's clashes with protesters, especially deadly ones involving student demonstrators. Perhaps seeking not to be perceived as shielding the public from such information, government authorities became uncharacteristically passive and stood by as terrestrial stations offered up unusually candid reportage of events. Information Minister Alwi Dahlan referred to the coverage as "too dramatic" but suggested that "we try to be calm about it" (cited in Cohen, 1998). Former director general of Televisi Republik Indonesia and broadcast entrepreneur Ishadi studied this episode, reporting that the private stations in Jakarta all carried graphic reports on the army's tough response to student demonstrations. His view was that the private stations acting independently chose to present balanced reporting of incidents leading up to Suharto's resignation (personal communication, February 12, 1999). Indonesian media regulators were possibly aware of repercussions that had flowed from officials' censorship of news reports in other countries facing such unrest and, conscious of an ending era, began to make way for a political transition.

INFORMATION MANAGEMENT

Most Southeast Asian countries tried to regulate new technologies because they sensed a danger in them. Yet, despite the threat of large fines, illegal earth stations appeared in East Malaysia by the thousands. Although every conceivable control mechanism was set in place by Singapore Internet service providers, users still could access prohibited sites. Frustrated by this, a few governments decided to halt access altogether. As shown in previous chapters, this hardly ever worked out satisfactorily. Attempts to outlaw technology produced only delays and incompletely effective restrictions. Technology cannot easily be held in check—unless, of course, a country seals itself off from the world as Myanmar has attempted to do for much of its recent history. But even Myanmar does not want, nor can it achieve, total isolation. In Cambodia and Vietnam the Internet is increasingly becoming an adjunct to everyday business, and the same will occur in Myanmar if it succeeds in expanding its industrial sector and enlarging foreign investment. In Laos, Vietnam, and even hesitantly in Myanmar, barriers to the use of Internet are quietly being lowered.

Censorship continues to be an instrument for managing information, even though technology has made it less and less effective. Setting aside censoring of political content, it is questionable whether censoring is any longer the answer to questions of programs' cultural validity, given greater ease of access to content from international sources. The Internet and satellite services present so many pathways from source to receiver that no government agency can hope to monitor them all. The current situation can be traced to the adoption of technologies that reduced costs of producing content and made its distribution easy, even for the novice. Government authorities too often have behaved as though nothing has changed and have attempted to impose regulations where such rules cannot possibly succeed. When this happened, officials were made to appear impotent, and a backlash against censoring often followed. Once again, Thailand military's ill-advised censoring of news about quashing of 1992 student demonstrations stands as an example of how such misjudgments can rebound against government officials. In that case, the military was forced to withdraw from government ignominiously, and laws were enacted making censoring more difficult. At the margins are Asian countries such as Singapore, Myanmar, and China that have kept their tough censoring practices. A great deal has been made of public acceptance of censorship in Singapore, but informants have often expressed dismay to me over various aspects of official information policy. Even formal studies in that country show that a large portion of the public is not satisfied with government censoring practices.

Officials sometimes explain that their censoring practices were simply inherited from policies in place under colonial rule. This claim is factually true; colonial authorities rigorously managed content of the media, especially publications opposed to colonial governments. It is an irony that many of Southeast Asia's laws prompting the greatest international condemnation are ones based on legislation enacted during colonial times. The notorious Internal Security Act (ISA) laws are another example. Many former British colonies kept ISA laws that colonial administrators had used to combat anticolonial movements, as in Malaysia's communist insurgency of the Emergency. Under provisions of ISA, governments can, without publicly announced cause, arrest and detain any person, and individuals are basically powerless to intervene. South Africa's government used this law, and ones like it, to detain and punish apartheid resisters. Whatever the logic, colonial precedents cannot be a good basis for continuing a policy three decades and more after independence.

For many in the West, especially for those who do not follow events in Southeast Asia closely, news coverage controversies have tended to create a vague impression of countries there as confined and rigid. When these cases are reported in Western press, as regularly happens, their political and legal systems too frequently emerge as mean-spirited and vindictive—or simply foolish. Asian leaders often unwittingly contribute to the overly negative image with their own approach to the media. The Murray Hiebert trial and jailing in Malaysia is a case in point. The story began in 1997 when Hiebert, a correspondent for the *Far Eastern Economic Review,* authored a story called "See you in court." It concerned an increase in the number of lawsuits seeking large settlements that had been passing through the Malaysian courts. Hiebert chose to illustrate the trend with a story about a suit that had been lodged by the son of a Court of Appeal judge against a school that dismissed him from the debating team. It was a minor story, but Hiebert's account was judged to have "scandalized the court," and the journalist was charged with contempt of court. The magazine admitted that the published story did contain a factual error that had occurred through an editor's mistake at the news office in Hong Kong, but the publication stood behind Hiebert's reporting. Despite this, the journalist was found guilty and given a six-week sentence. Predictably, the conviction caused a furor in the foreign press. As it happened, Malaysian Prime Minister Mahathir Mohamad had been scheduled to address the United Nations in New York during the period when Hiebert served his sentence. The journalist's case threw a shadow over the official visit, and the Prime Minister had to face indignation in the United States over the incident. Mahathir seemed to have been caught off guard by the reaction. He complained that "I find that in America, the Americans are obsessed with the jailing of the journalist. They kept repeating this questions over and over and over again. Wherever I went, this was the question." His response was to lecture the media about how journalists should behave. He reported instructing that "we have to get our priorities right. There are lots of people who are being slaughtered, massacred, killed all over the world. Their fate deserves greater attention … than the fate of one single journalist jailed for only six weeks" (cited in Chanda, 1999). Malaysia and Singapore seem to be particular targets of Western complaints on treatment of journalists and censoring, even though nearby Brunei, Vietnam, and Myanmar are much more strict. Perhaps expectations for those two countries are different because they are economically better developed and maintain close commercial relationships with the West.

A justification of censoring in Southeast Asia is that it conforms to the region's cultural values. Much has been written about the "Asian values" argument, and it would be pointless to fully recount that debate here. Little credible evidence has been brought forward to support the position that all Asian cultures share unique values that distinguish them from Western societies. Despite this fact, more than a few scholars have argued that Asian values do provide a reasonable rationale for censoring. But just as many have criticized the Asian values justification. As Masterton (1996, p. 1) acknowledged, "there is no consensus within Asia, nor perhaps in any region within the world's largest continent, about what Asian Values are, in journalism or in anything else." Nonetheless, in Asia the basic premise of the Asian values argument is commonly accepted. The most outspoken proponents of Asian values have been political leaders, not scholars or social commentators. This is troubling because it is reasonable to suppose political leaders' motives might be political. Indeed, unpopular acts of governments are often justified because they are based on "Asian values." In cases such as these, officials respond to international criticism by asserting that their actions are perfectly acceptable when placed within an Asian cultural context. At first glance, this argument seems to have some validity; quite a few Asian countries have a tradition of paternalistic governance. But countries across the globe have the same tendency, so it cannot be a uniquely Asian trait. As a consequence, unfortunately, some Western critics have interpreted the Asian values argument as cynical and self-serving.

Everyone agrees that there are differences between East and West, but then again there are huge differences among societies within both East and West. Kharel (p. 29) argued that "it is our individual national and regional values, as far as they can be identified, that are under threat and must be preserved from outside influences, even from within Asia." There is no consensus on censoring in the region, however. In every country there are debates about what should be censored and why. Most countries in the region are pluralistic, and definitions of their national values are continually being contested. Certainly preservation of cultures is a worthwhile goal, and responsible scholars could hardly argue against it, but there have been instances in which this aim has collided with the rights of free access to information and freedom to speak openly that are internationally recognized. Only the most extreme advocates of Asian values would wish to revise or eliminate the principles embodied in, say, the United Nations' Universal Declaration of Human Rights.

THE STATUS OF "OLD" ELECTRONIC MEDIA

On the whole, radio's importance as a medium for national communication is on the wane, and it is being converted from a primary channel for entertainment and information to background music and companionship functions. Within Laos, Myanmar, and in certain districts of other countries, the changeover lags because radio is still the only medium available to the masses. In fact, Laotian radio is still in a growth phase. In Vientiane, FM radio is a recent innovation, and it still covers only the capital city and nearby areas. Elsewhere, the number of stations continues to climb because of new licenses still being granted to private firms. The new private stations' programs differ from old programming, consisting of DJ shows interspersed with call-in talk shows. In spite of it all, listenership for the medium remains large.

In a few countries, radio call-in talk shows have widened the range of political discourse. Opinions expressed on these programs have a way of straying outside normal limits. In the Philippines and Thailand, call-in radio became one of most popular formats, but in other nations program managers thought it too hazardous. An executive of Malaysia's Time Highway Radio was quoted as saying "we don't really want to get into call-in programmes. ... There would have to be some serious self-censorship. You must remember you can't easily control talk radio" (Elegant, 1996). The large number of radio stations in the Philippines and Indonesia works in favor of greater diversity of opinion in all sorts of programs. One study found that women's issues were gaining more attention via radio than on more advanced media in the Philippines. Hughes (2000) mentioned a count of thirty-two radio programs aimed specifically at female listeners.

Video recording became the first technology to liberate audience members from controls on their personal viewing choices when professional recorders were redesigned as small portable units for use in homes in the 1970s. Video played an important role in forcing reform and restructuring of Southeast Asian broadcasting. The central issue was that video could not be managed by government officials in the same way preexisting media were handled. Because authorities in countries such as Thailand, Singapore, and Malaysia could not control video's uses—including uses of which they did not approve—they were compelled to alter broadcast programming to curtail the decline in television viewing. But major concessions in programming philosophies were necessary to draw audiences back to sanctioned messages on government media.

Before video, television viewers in countries such as Malaysia were faced with a "take it or leave it" situation; government programmers did not have to worry about competitors, therefore they had little motivation to accommodate audiences preferences. This attitude is evident in that fact that even in the late 1980s, Malaysian audience rating information was available only to Radio Television Malaysia's department heads and not to general programming staff. The resulting offerings were often criticized for drabness and poor production quality. It took a number of years before the nature of this situation was completely understood and an effective response formulated. The introduction of private television was the first in a series of new policies that produced profound changes in the content of broadcasting. Privatization caused consequences that few policy makers anticipated. Even though the new Malaysian channels were strictly controlled by government rules, their commercial orientation assured substantially greater entertainment values in programming, something that cheered viewers and inflated audiences, especially among nonurban and Malay residents. The much more competitive atmosphere in broadcasting that followed was not only a bonanza for audiences, but media professionals who found it produced a more stimulating and creative work environment.

Television's growth includes new terrestrial channels that continue to sign on the air in a number of cities. Five new television stations licensed for sign-on by 2001 in Indonesia and the new FTA TV Channel 8 in Malaysia all hope to carve out their own share of viewing audiences. Whether this can be accomplished soon enough to avoid financial trouble is a question asked by many in the broadcasting field. Malaysia's fourth channel, Metrovision, had suspended its operations by 1999, presumably because of an inability to cover operational costs with advertising revenues. The new channels are being issued licenses just at a time when the growing number of other pastimes is beginning to have a significant impact on potential audiences. As competition rises, the biggest loser tends to be the state broadcasters, simply because they have more difficulty in responding to newcomers—state channels tend to be constrained by regulations requiring programs that do not attract large numbers of viewers. The size of Southeast Asia TV audiences is still growing, particularly in Indonesia, Cambodia, Laos, Vietnam, and Myanmar. If the consumer economy keeps growing in these countries, advertising revenues should be able to sustain additional television channels. In general more fragmentation in television audiences is likely to occur across the whole region, not merely because of added terrestrial channels but also as a result of increased numbers of satellite television channels.

The future of satellites in the mass media mix depends upon two factors: demand for new channels and demand for information unavailable through terrestrial systems. In Europe, broad adoption of satellite-delivered radio and television was driven by a hunger for more entertainment choices. State broadcasters dominated European land-based television. These broadcasters had to provide, either by law (as in the Netherlands or the United Kingdom) or by rules of the marketplace, a menu of programs for an undifferentiated audience. In contrast, satellites offered all sports, all news, all music, all movie, and many, many even more specialized channels. In the United States, the progress of satellite television was not so quick, probably because cable and terrestrial stations already presented enough alternatives to satisfy a majority of viewers. But in Southeast Asia, the lack of entertainment choices and the sometimes low credibility and appeal of terrestrial channels gave satellite television a boost. Malaysia's ASTRO satellite system experienced slow growth until the perception of unbalanced reporting in the Anwar case eroded confidence in official media. After this, ASTRO's subscriptions rose more quickly, spreading access to CNN and other international channels to a greater number of Malaysians.

Some countries saw the new technologies as opportunities. Thailand, Singapore, Malaysia, and to a lesser extent Indonesia and the Philippines aimed to establish initiatives that would launch each as the regional pacesetter in satellite communications. Obviously, not every country on the Pacific Rim can be a leader in this field. It is interesting that Malaysia, Singapore, and Thailand each adopted policies in which their country was projected as an information and entertainment hub for the region. Again, there might be room for more than one nation to be a major player in media and telecommunications, but there cannot be three separate hubs.

TECHNOLOGIES OF THE FUTURE

Most readers probably consider cable broadcasting an old technology. In the United States, cable television grew in the 1950s from the need to relay television signals into isolated towns having poor reception. Only in the 1970s when the technology was harnessed to satellite relays did cable begin to have a big influence on national television. In Southeast Asia, introduction of this technology is a recent phenomenon. In Malaysia, Indonesia, Cambodia, Thailand, and Singapore cable systems built during the 1990s offered alternatives to terrestrial broadcasts, but in most cases failed to develop into major players. Singapore is as yet the only country in which cable has earned an important role. In 2000, the local cable operator, Singapore Cable Vision (SCV), had about nine hundred thousand subscriber homes, with numbers still rising as the last uncabled neighborhoods were being wired. The popularity of cable in Singapore was probably due to an absence of other opportunities to obtain satellite channels (home satellite dishes are banned in the island republic) and SCV's strong menu of choices delivered at a reasonable cost. For about twenty channels, a subscriber must pay S$34 each month, or about USD $19. There are very few areas in the country that do not have access, in comparison to the spotty coverage afforded by cable systems in other Southeast Asian countries. Costs in other places are much less affordable as well; monthly fees for the same tier of service amounting to USD $20 in Malaysia and Thailand and USD $16 in Indonesia are high compared with each country's middle-class incomes ("Cable TV," 1999).

All of this is on a small scale compared with India, the unrivaled leader in Asia where 37 million of the 67 million television households are connected to a cable system. The situation in India is unique, however. Many of the ninety thousand cable systems in the country are tiny, serving a neighborhood or perhaps as few as a hundred households. Siti Cable is India's largest operator with 4.5 million homes in forty-three cities (Leung, 2001). Prospects for cable in most countries depend on the competition of satellite television and on the degree of urbanization. In countries where satellite is outlawed, as in

Singapore, or where urban concentration of populations makes cable more cost-effective than satellites, as in India, cable should do well. But in Malaysia, satellite broadcaster ASTRO is surging ahead of Mega TV in the race to sign up subscribers. The capital-intensive cable technology has not done particularly well in Indonesia either, where availability of cheap legal satellite receivers makes cable a less attractive proposition.

Evolution in information technology continues with fascinating possibilities looming on the horizon as this is being written. Some technologies might send Asian media in unexpected directions. The video compact disk (VCD) has certainly had this kind of effect. Practically unknown in 1995, it became the principal delivery format for video recordings in Southeast Asia within just a few years, effectively pushing prerecorded videocassettes out of the marketplace. The driving force for VCDs was the availability of inexpensive pirated movies. This, plus players costing less than USD $50, brought the format within the reach of even those who could not afford VCRs. In fact, VCDs were so affordable that video CDs found their way even into villages and squatter's settlements. In other regions of the world, this format was little used, being overtaken by DVDs. Although DVDs look like VCDs, they offer much improved audio and video quality, and DVDs can contain lengthy video recordings with less digital compression. But DVDs cost many times more per film, and players are more expensive as well. It appears that the DVD will not supplant VCDs until costs can be reduced, because high technical quality seems not such a big attraction for Southeast Asian viewers. Many of the pirate VCDs are produced from video recordings surreptitiously made with camcorders slipped into movie theaters. The resulting video and audio quality is miserable, but this has not seemed to detract from VCDs' salability.

The time may not be ripe for another rising technology—time-shifting devices known by various names but usually marketed under the rubric of personal television recorders. The best known of these products were marketed under the brand names Tivo and ReplayTV. These units allow home users to record television programs at predetermined times for playback at viewers' convenience. Introduced in 1999, they began moving into retail outlets across the United States in the following year. The difference between these devices and conventional VCRs is that they record on large computer hard drives that afford users random access to any part of a show—no fast forward or rewinding necessary. A great advantage of random access technology is that on playback viewers can easily and instantly skip commercials. Additionally, these recorders can duplicate slow-motion and instant playback functions. Even though sales are gradually picking up momentum in North American markets, at this writing they have not yet found their way into Southeast Asia to any significant degree.

One technology that is certain to have an impact in Southeast Asia is digital television. Digital television employs video and audio signals that have been converted to digital formats before transmission, greatly improving picture and sound quality. In the United States, Europe, and Japan this type of television transmission is slowly being implemented. Conversion of radio broadcasts to digital transmission seems likely, too, but interests working toward its introduction are not so well coordinated, and digital television may be fully realized before digital radio gains much headway. Adoption of digital television technology is occurring very slowly because television receivers are much more costly than analog sets, typically in the range of USD $2,000 to $5,000. At these prices, introduction of digital television surely will be delayed in Southeast Asia. Nevertheless, there is little doubt that, in time, the technology's benefits will be available worldwide. Economies of scale in manufacture of digital television sets eventually should cut costs to consumers, and it is estimated that the receivers ultimately will fall to only about USD $200 more than analog units. In theory, full conversion of television broadcasting in the United States could occur and analog transmissions cease as early as 2006, but hardly anyone believes this will happen. Japanese viewers have shown greater interest in digital broadcasting than their counterparts in the United States. In Japan, rather than converting terrestrial transmitters immediately, digital television is being introduced via satellite broadcasts. Service began with a digital television satellite placed in orbit in December 2000. At the launch of the system, there were thought to be about two hundred thousand sets or tuner/converters in use. Demand for receivers outstripped supply, however, leaving about 83,000 units on backorder at the end of the year (Nagaya, 2001). Broadcasters interviewed in the course of researching this work guessed that startup of digital transmissions in Southeast Asia would occur sometime after 2005, possibly as late as 2010 or even later.

A GLOBALIZED AUDIENCE

As the preceding discussion suggests, many features of media audiences in Southeast Asia now simply echo ones found elsewhere in the world. Audiences everywhere have become more fragmented. Even so, no longer are the primary program fault lines drawn by language or by rural-urban dichotomies. Audiences increasingly can be differentiated by lifestyle, by generation, by entertainment and information habits, and by taste. The media have tended to become more consumerist oriented, both by the popularity of private media and by greater advertising content. The new media audiences that took shape did not do so in a vacuum, rather they paralleled and reinforced social changes occurring in Southeast Asia. More people were getting stuck in traffic jams while commuting to work, eating junk food, traveling for recreation, getting better educated, buying electronic gadgets, and engaging in all the things that the rest of the world was doing.

The apparent worldwide homogeneity in behavior and attitudes is something that social observers in Asia frequently lament. They assume that globalization of popular cultures means that cultural diversity will vanish. But, the apparent similarities in cultures across Asia are misleading. They reveal only superficial aspects of societies; they do not truly express profoundly held ethos. They are the form, not the content. Beneath the surface appearance and form, program contents project the unique and authentic cultural values of their host society. The Indonesian *sinetron* is fundamentally different from soap operas elsewhere. True, soap operas from Brazil and from Japan have enjoyed a minor degree of success in Southeast Asia, but imports never do as well as comparable local programs because their cultural references remain foreign and unfamiliar. The pull of imported shows is definitely lower among the new viewers who have been added to audiences in recent years. They live in rural areas and practice something closer to traditional lifestyles than city residents. For such viewers, language may also be a factor in selecting programs; programs in English or other international languages seldom win big audiences outside major cities.

Technologies arriving in the 1990s also catered to more individual choices. The largest-common-denominator prescription that determined programming when there were only a few terrestrial channels is not the proper calculus for the current competitive environment. Just as in the rest of the world, sports fans turn to ESPN, youth chose MTV or another music channel, and for movie lovers there is an assortment of channels from which to select. What is different in Asia is a differentiation of channels built around language and cultural affinities. Whereas English, French, Arabic, and Spanish channels constitute the international offerings by satellites in other regions, in Asia, Chinese and Indian language channels present many additional choices. Although targeted principally at the Indian and Chinese diaspora of Asia, Indian musical movies and the Chinese action movies are quite popular among audiences without cultural or linguistic ties. Channels from India in Indian languages and in Chinese from Hong Kong, Beijing, Taipei, and other places are taking their share of satellite and cable audiences all across Southeast Asia.

From the early 1970s onward, policy makers fretted over the flow of foreign media and popular culture products into Asia and other parts of the developing world. Their worries were based on a concept of global media industries centered in the United States, and to a lesser extent in Western Europe. Once again, a foremost critic was Malaysian Prime Minister Dr. Mahathir. In 1996 he addressed the United Nations General Assembly in New York, where he complained about media consolidations in Hollywood and New York involving companies such as CNN.

> Freedom of the press is touted as a basic democratic principle, but control of the media by a handful of Western corporations has made nonsense of this principle. Today the Western media have taken over and all our cherished values and diverse cultures are being destroyed ("Inequities of power-sharing," 1996).

Dr. Mahathir's concern was that Eastern countries' productions would be unable to compete in their own countries against internationally successful products from the West. At the time, there was plenty of evidence to support this belief. Movie productions in most countries had exhibited a long-term decline. Dropping output of cinema studios in Southeast Asia was generally blamed on the encroachment of U.S. films, particularly the blockbuster movies that Hollywood tended to promote heavily in strong movie markets such as Jakarta, Kuala Lumpur, Bangkok, Manila, and Singapore.

The concern over restoration of movie production in countries such as Indonesia and Thailand tended to overshadow an important trend that surfaced by the end of the 1990s—the near total capture of Asian television audiences by domestic producers. So when movie output dipped, many of the film production houses and production workers moved into television where it was easier to make successful products and stay gainfully employed. The success of domestic television producers lay in the fact that new audiences appeared at the end of the 1990s. Winning audiences depended on appealing to tastes of the new viewers, something internationally distributed programs did not do. As the century drew to a close, television broadcasters shifted their emphasis from foreign to local television programming in nations all across Asia. Hong Kong presents a clear illustration. When leading broadcaster TVB went on the air in 1967, it broadcast little programming other than imported shows. By 1977, the proportion of foreign programs had dropped to about 65 percent, and by 1987 imports accounted for only 5 percent of the schedule. The timing of the programming turnaround differed from country to country. Nicholas James, managing director of Hong Kong production and distribution company Media Asia, explained that television in other Asian markets "didn't begin to develop competitively until 1990, and some not until 1993. That's why it will be well beyond the year 2000 before we see mature local television markets" (cited in Berfield, 1996).

Rapid economic growth across Southeast Asia changed media, first by changing television audiences from a middle- and upper-class phenomenon to an experience that united the whole population. Greater viewing among lower socioeconomic groups, coupled with expansion of the consumer economy, drove up demand for advertising on television. Whereas in the early 1980s the television ad sector accounted for a small portion of advertising revenues in countries such as Thailand, Indonesia, and Singapore, by the end of the 1990s, it had grown to become second only to newspapers. Flush with advertising income, broadcasting organizations could invest additional funds in local productions, making them more and more competitive against international productions. Better locally produced programs in turn drew larger audiences, strengthening local content against imported shows.

The trend of increasingly localized program production has hampered building of bridges within the region. Some years ago I noted the paucity of

Southeast Asia regional cooperation and program exchanges in the media. This lack still exists today. Logically, one might suppose that an expansion of regional ties in other domains would be reflected in radio, television, and related mass media, but this does not seem to be happening. Indonesian-produced programs rarely are seen in other countries, not even in Malaysia, Brunei, or Singapore, where language poses no barrier. Barriers do not seem to be legal or technical either. Today, when program officers import shows they tend to prefer ones from producers in Hollywood or London that are both comparatively inexpensive and have high production values. But they may not prefer to import programs at all. The number of imports is shrinking because the altered character of television audiences renders importation less advantageous. Additionally, laws imposing limits on the proportion of foreign shows have been enacted in a number of countries. There are a few exceptions to the lack of intraregional program importation; one small example: Thai movies and television serials are among the most popular television fare in Cambodia.

ASEAN—the Association of Southeast Asian Nations—is an organization that offers a platform for regional cooperation in many different spheres. Its expansion at the end of the 1990s produced a more comprehensive organization, finally encompassing all countries of Southeast Asia. In a way, however, the expansion diminished ASEAN's overall focus. Formerly, the association consisted of a grouping of countries sharing roughly similar cultural, political, and economic situations. Now, as a larger organization, it must embrace ideologies ranging from committed capitalism in Singapore to old-style communism in Laos, and political systems from military dictatorships in Myanmar to rough-and-tumble electoral democracies in the Philippines. Political and cultural matters have become difficult to address effectively through the organization. More and more, ASEAN has adopted a trade and economic orientation in recognition of the lack of coherence in other realms.

In the 1980s, ASEAN did sponsor media activities, but these initiatives gradually wound down, and the organization rarely sponsored projects after the mid-1990s. In the few that did surface, the organization seemed to have used media merely for public relations purposes. One peculiar media project, "a regional 'good-news' television channel" died before it could be implemented. The channel, to be called the ASEAN Satellite Channel (ASC), was authorized by ASEAN ministers of information in 1998. The immediate purpose of the channel was to counteract negative international news coverage of Southeast Asia on topics such as the regional financial crisis, political turmoil, and environmental issues. The channel would have carried up to eight hours daily of programming presenting more positive images of the region contributed by national broadcasting organizations of member countries. It appears that a tug-of-war over satellite usage was the project's undoing. As journalist Barry Porter (1999) reported,

ASEAN, created to promote regional harmony, has been unable to broker an amicable agreement between members with regard to whose satellite to broadcast the channel from. With the Asian satellite industry suffering from chronic oversupply due to the economic slowdown, competition has been fierce.

According to Porter, Indonesia, Thailand, and Malaysia each were eager to take advantage of the business opportunity. Vietnam and Singapore also had satellites that could have carried the channel. Estimates placed projected costs at around USD $50 million.

Although globalization is usually mentioned as a negative force for Southeast Asian cultures, it can be positive, too. The Internet and its associated technologies have made it much easier for musicians to record their performances and to distribute their recordings to a global audience. The Internet has even played a role in popularizing regional music forms. Until the 1990s, Southeast Asian musical performers had to confront two big problems in marketing their work. Major studio rental costs were so great that only the most financially well off could afford to make records. And then, even if recordings were produced, getting contracts for overseas distribution was impossible for any but the most well-established talent. But during the 1990s, the technical quality of "semi-professional" audio recording equipment became good enough to produce perfectly acceptable recordings in small "project" studios. For about the price of a rental fee for mastering an album at a major studio, one could entirely equip a decent home studio. This enabled a massive increase in the amount of music produced around the world, including Asia. Second, the emergence of MP3 as a digital storage format changed distribution patterns. This format produces computer files of music recordings small enough to be exchanged across the Internet, yet having quality comparable to CDs. Musicians are able to convert their digital recordings into MP3 files to make use of distributors based on the Net. A great deal of publicity was generated by the popularity of Napster and other types of Web music-sharing sites that employ MP3 based distribution. The complaints about such services by the recording industry were focused on the unauthorized copying and sharing of music recordings, something that amounted to pirating on the Internet. Although this is unquestionably a serious legal and policy issue, it only affects those recordings already in the traditional distribution chain. For performers and producers outside that chain—who probably constitute the majority of musicians—the Internet is proving to be a godsend.

There are several sites that allow performers to circumvent the traditional distribution mechanisms that tend to be controlled by large corporations interested only in mass markets. One of these offers a menu of Asian music, both traditional and modern, http://genres.mp3.com/music/world_folk/world_traditions/asian/. Those who visit this site can sample many hundreds of recordings. On a visit in early 2001, I counted about 960 different choices. Clicking on one of the tunes takes one to a Web site for the performer where one can listen via streamed audio or download sample cuts to audition later. Entire albums can be purchased over the Internet from these sites. Typical prices are about half of those customarily charged in retail outlets, and if one does purchase an album, a set of files is sent over the Net that can be played on one's computer until the compact disk arrives in the mail.

An additional point is that the Internet allows for greater differentiation in taste. Just as audience fragmentation in radio and television has created a panorama of niche programming to choose from, so is the range of choices expanding for music recordings on the Internet. This is enormously important to Asian musicians whose style of performance, instrumentation, and aesthetics, by definition, lie outside the global mainstream. It is an outstanding opportunity for those whose taste in music lies outside the mainstream too. For example, there are only a handful of gamelan music recordings available via retail outlets in Europe or North American, but with a little work on the Internet, an abundance of information and a number of performances can be located in minutes.

THE INTERNET IN SOUTHEAST ASIA

The Internet became the most fascinating and perplexing of all the technologies that swept across the region. While it was generally understood to be an exciting and powerful technology, one that could serve as an engine of economic development, most countries considered ways of limiting its utilization. It captured the imagination of residents through its communication power—the capacity to jump national boundaries, instantly transporting information and entertainment identical to that enjoyed by Web browsers around the globe. In a region that regards itself as a center of advanced electronic technology, the Web's allure was strong. Although slow moving at first, regional adoption increased steadily in the final years of the twentieth century. In the future, the Southeast Asian region almost certainly will build on the leadership of Singapore, Thailand, and Malaysia to emerge as a region of concentrated Internet activity.

Convergence, that overworked term describing the merger of a whole collection of electronic technologies, particularly computers, radio, and television, was brought closer to reality by the upturn in Internet popularity. This, it seemed, would generate impetus to incorporate radio, television, and all sorts of print media into a single delivery mechanism. Realization of convergence is still awaited in Southeast Asia, as it is everywhere. It likely will not be achieved until the speed of the Internet is upgraded. Internet video and audio are not very popular in Southeast Asia because they require bandwidths that exceed the capacity of international links currently available. Steven Tan, technical manager of Mcities, a multimedia Web site for music performance located in its entertainment complex off Jalan Bukit Bintang in Kuala Lumpur, admitted bandwidth problems. His Web site (www.mcities.com) broadcast highly compressed video and audio streams of live performance and music videos, but he acknowledged that with then-current bandwidth, video picture quality was suboptimal (personal communication, August, 2, 2000). In Southeast Asia, I found painfully slow access to North American Web sites in early morning hours, most likely due to heavy international traffic from business users in Japan.

In Southeast Asia, the on-line newspaper has a special attraction. Electronic newspapers overcome the distribution problems of conventional newspapers. This is especially important in the island nations of Indonesia and the Philippines. On-line editions of newspapers overseas present news that might not be available in the local press, either because reports were unavailable locally or because of censoring. In the events surrounding Suharto's resignation, many Indonesians had to turn to the Singapore *Straits Times* or to CNN Web sites to get up-to-the minute information. The increasing refinement of on-line editions of newspapers in Southeast Asia parallels their increasing significance as news sources. As demonstrated by the *Malaysiakini* Web site, it is possible to have a successful on-line newspaper even without a printed version—this might be the best example of an exclusive on-line newspaper anywhere in the world. The fact that *Malaysiakini* specializes in stories other media underreport helped build its popularity. In information-hungry, Internet-crazy Malaysia, this is a big plus. In just a few years it has become an important factor in Malaysian journalism. The good fortunes of this newspaper should not be taken as a new trend just yet. It is unlikely that on-line newspapers will be allowed to operate with significantly fewer restraints than their printed versions, even though governments may announce a hands-off policy for the Internet. Furthermore, finding the right formula for advertising and other funding streams has been a serious problem for online newspapers around the world; even electronic editions of leading newspapers such as the *New York Times* have not yet reached a breakeven point. Naturally, revenue is even more of a problem in Southeast Asia. Here advertising is not so well developed as in the major cities of Europe and North America and the reach of Internet is far less.

Asymmetrical Internet access for Myanmar—open to Burmese abroad and closed to those at home—has created a strange inequality. As one of BurmaNet's moderators Christina Fink noted, "the irony of BurmaNet is that people outside know more about Burma than people inside" (cited in Bardacke, 1996). The Burmese expatriate community is more skillful and knowledgeable in the use of technologies such as the Net as well, mainly because they have greater opportunity to use them. This is causing Burma to fall behind in the implementation of socially and economically helpful Internet applications. However, it appears the government is willing to risk sacrificing these benefits to check the political discourse that the Net and Web also bring. The government is experimenting with restricted types of access while still applying firewalls and prosecutions. Even so, the few hundred who have gotten accounts are insignificant measured against the millions in Myanmar who have no ability to tap into information via the Net. Inequality of access does provide opponents with an advantage in their struggle against the regime. As U.S.-based activist Htun Aung Gyaw explained, "we are weak. That's why we need high tech: they have an army; they have power; they have money. This is a new kind of warfare we are fighting, Internet warfare" (cited in Glaberson, 1997).

Asia itself will soon have more Internet users than any other region, largely through subscriber growth in India and China. This means that European and North American dominance of the Net could wane. Such an occurrence might diminish the importance of English on the Web and force other changes in the way the Internet works. Even in 1998, the total number of account holders in China had grown to 1 million, and the figure was expected to double every two years. Even though the proportion of Chinese who have access to the Internet is very small, the sheer size of the country's population gives it a large portion of Asia's Internet users. Ongoing development of the base of subscribers to internet service providers in Singapore, Indonesia, Philippines, Malaysia, and Thailand will only add to the giant Asian Internet community. What this means for the e-commerce firms that once fueled the so-called dot-com economy remains a question. How electronic tiger nations of Southeast Asia—in their Multimedia Super Corridors, Intelligent Islands, and CyberCities—fare against competitors elsewhere in Asia and against the rest of the world will make an engrossing story.

REFERENCES

Bardacke, T. (1996, October 5). Burmese risk stiff jail sentences for surfing the Internet. *Financial Times* (London).

Berfield, S. (1996, November 8). Asia's no pushover. *Asiaweek.*

Cable TV in Taiwan cheaper as market is unique. (1999, July 30). *Straits Times.*

Chanda, N. (1999, October 21). Goodbye to all that. *Far Eastern Economic Review.*

Cohen, M. (1998, May 14). To the barricades. *Far Eastern Economic Review.*

Elegant, S. (1996, September 19). Voice of the people. *Far Eastern Economic Review.*

Glaberson, W. (1997, April 8). A guerrilla war on the Internet; Cornell book shelver, a political exile, fights Myanmar. *New York Times.*

Hughes, B. (2000, February 3). Radio gives Philippines women long-lost voice: Simple media still one of the most powerful tools in educating public on women's issues. *The Ottawa Citizen*.

Kharel, P. (1996). Asian values: Do they exist? In M. Masterton (Ed.), *Asian Values in Journalism* (pp. 29–34) Singapore: AMIC.

Leung, W. H. (2001, April). India's long road. *Communications Technology International*.

Masterton, M. (1996). Introduction. In M. Masterson (Ed.), *Asian values in journalism* (pp. 1–5). Singapore: AMIC.

Nagaya, T. (2001, No. 15). 21st century age of digital HDTV broadcasting begins. *Broadcasting Culture and Research*.

Porter, B. (1999, November 4). Regional TV channel beset by bad news. *South China Morning Post*.

UNESCO. (1980). *Many voices, one world*. New York: Unipub.

Index

ISBN 0-8138-1907-5

9 780813 819075